03/09/2017

To Elizabeth Jensen
All the best to you and yours.
John Hanson

FAREWELL TO AN ANGEL

It All Began in Old New Orleans

John Hanson

ISBN: 978-1-60679-343-5
Library of Congress Control Number: 2015952881
Book layout: Cheery Sugabo
Cover design: Cheery Sugabo
Front cover photo: Aneese/iStock/Thinkstock

Healthy Learning
P.O. Box 1828
Monterey, CA 93942
www.healthylearning.com

DEDICATION

To the memory of my dearly departed wife and soul mate, Patty Hanson, who supported me in all my endeavors, and to the Brothers of the Christian Schools, who guided me in my formal education

ACKNOWLEDGMENTS

I had no intention of publishing my memoirs when I began to write them. I was simply inspired to leave behind for my young granddaughters the story of their Pa Pa and Grandma lest it be lost forever. It was Madeline, Lauren, Catherine, and Josey who were the inspiration behind the writings that evolved into *Farewell to an Angel*. I hope that it will be a permanent family legacy that my sweet girls can treasure when they are mature adults.

FOREWORD

John Hanson's memoirs are a thing of profound beauty, deeply authentic in an era hungry for authenticity, and putting its readers back in touch with our deepest roots and hunger for connection. This memoir provides the *Angela's Ashes* for the great and colorful New Orleans. This book is full of wonderful, unforgettable, vignettes furnishing a profound contribution to American letters. It is a joy to read and, also, contains a love story for the ages. Reading it touched, moved, and inspired me. Buy it and read it, to gladden and enrich your heart forever.

—Ralph Benko, internationally syndicated columnist

CONTENTS

INTRODUCTION

Farewell to an Angel gives the reader a personal view of the lives of a man and woman who were born, raised, worked, and found each other in the Crescent City. The man, John Hanson, was from the Carrollton neighborhood. The woman, Patty Callegan, was from the French Quarter. Their parents had only grammar school educations. They were poor, but not destitute. They always managed to shelter, clothe, and feed their families by dint of hard work.

After starting on their memoirs, John had more time to work on his as Patty was simultaneously fighting cancer. Much of his memoirs are Patty's, however, since they were inseparable from their meeting in 1966 until Patty's death in 2014. A registered nurse and ever a patient advocate, Patty wrote only briefly of her life before nursing and marriage and only as an introduction to an exhaustive guide for cancer patients.

These memoirs give the reader a unique view of 20th century America. The experiences of John and Patty are like no other. They give the ordinary person's perspective on three generations of cultural and scientific changes. Given their start in life, who could have predicted that George Halas would be John's chauffeur or Patty would serve as a private nurse to the Duke of Windsor and the King of Greece? Their paths crossed those of many "hall-of-fame" level individuals from the worlds of education, medicine, religion, business, sports, and politics. Yet, they were never enamored of the rich and famous and certainly never joined their ranks. The focus of their love was on one another and their students and patients. Their story will at times evoke both tears and laughter. Overall, it will edify.

1

NEW ORLEANS, LA: 1936–1951

SERGEANT MOM

I can't remember my birth, but my Mom spoke about it many times. I know from my birth certificate that the event occurred shortly after midnight on September 16th, 1936, at Charity Hospital in New Orleans, LA. My Mom seemed to take some pride in relating that she delivered me unassisted on a gurney in one of the drab hallways of the massive hospital. She kept trying (to no avail) to alert any nurse or staffer who passed her gurney that she needed to be brought to the delivery room.

How anyone could have ignored my Mom is beyond me. She was not the ignorable type. She would always express her mind in a loud and rather manly voice, regardless of the venue. She often told people how a phone caller would address her as "sir," whereupon she would sternly inform the caller that she was a "ma'am." As an adult, I took to referring to her as "sergeant." She was tough and demanding at home and in public. Pity the poor sales clerk who waited on her. She held all of them strictly to the belief that "the customer is always right." My sister, Ann (who was two years older than me), and I were never right in any disagreement with Mom. In fact, Mom often cautioned us that "little children should be seen but not heard." To our dismay, we remained little children in Mom's view, even after we were married and had children of our own. If we expressed disagreement with something Mom said, we were warned, "Don't you sass me!" It mattered not that we were 50 years old, and she was dead wrong.

One of the earliest pictures I have of my Mom was taken circa 1940. The winds of war were blowing, and I appear in this picture with her in military uniform. One can see from this picture that my Mom had movie-star good looks as a young woman.

My Mom, my sister, Ann, and me circa 1940

My Dad didn't spend a lot of time with me. I remember him sitting at our kitchen table pouring hot coffee from his cup into a saucer to let it cool. At home, he wore dungarees (that's what we used to call jeans) and a sleeveless undershirt. He added a short-sleeved work shirt when he left the house. He was away for many months, sailing the seven seas on Merchant ships or working on Guam. My Dad wasn't one to have his picture taken. The one picture I have of him is on his certificate of service (ordinary seaman) issued by the U.S. Department of Commerce, Bureau of Marine Inspection and Navigation.

ONE TOUGH MOMMA

Mom was "tough as nails." She related the story of her own birth, and it gives some insight into her toughness. She was one of 15 children. She was christened Ethel Patricia Fairleigh. When she and her twin brother were delivered, they were so frail that her brother died within hours. The doctor told my grandmother to hold off on his funeral, since Mom would soon die also, and she and her brother could be buried together. That was March 17th, 1912, and Mom was still celebrating St. Patrick's Day into the 21st century!

SERIAL NUMBER E457545

Z-136555

UNITED STATES DEPARTMENT OF COMMERCE
BUREAU OF MARINE INSPECTION AND NAVIGATION

CERTIFICATE OF SERVICE
(OTHER THAN ABLE SEAMAN OR QUALIFIED MEMBER OF THE ENGINE DEPARTMENT)

This certifies that John T. Hanson having taken the oath required by law is hereby qualified to serve aboard American vessels of 100 tons gross and upward in the Deck Department in a rating of Ordinary Seaman

Issued by the undersigned Board of Local Inspectors on this 16th day of March 1944

John T. Hanson

OFFICER IN CHARGE, MARINE INSPECTION
U.S. Board of Local Inspectors
Port of NEW ORLEANS, LA.

My Dad's picture on his certificate of service

Her toughness was further forged by the hard times of her childhood. My grandmother and her children were mostly left to fend for themselves by my oft-absent grandfather, who eventually ran away to Kentucky. I have no memory of him though Mom said he enjoyed the "ponies." Neither my grandmother nor any of her children had more than an elementary education. They were "put to work" early, as they were at the bottom of the economic ladder leading into the Great Depression. Mom told us that she worked as a young girl, sewing flour sacks in a factory. It may explain in part how she became a great seamstress. It enabled her to greatly stretch our clothing budget.

She was also terrific in knitting and crocheting. She had the uncanny ability to "eye" someone and, without taking any measurements, make a dress that fit them perfectly. She often dragged me with her on her visits to the small shops on Oak St. that sold yards of cloth and patterns. Mom was proof of the fact that ignorance and intelligence do co-exist. There is so much to be learned outside the halls of formal education. In fact, one can lose half their education going to college! Been there. Done that.

MURDER ON MARKET ST.

Mom tells how she witnessed a killing one summer night on Market St. in the warehouse district. She was sleeping on the second story porch of the family's cheap rental house, when she was awakened by the screeching tires of an auto below. Two men leaped from the vehicle and, illumined by the corner streetlight, gunned down a man standing on the banquette (sidewalk). They left their victim and sped away, unaware that my Mom had seen the murder go down.

When my Mom told her parents what she had seen, she was given strict orders not to let anyone know she had witnessed the crime. They feared that the murderers would silence anyone who might testify against them. Life was tough in the roaring 20s of New Orleans. A young girl could be traumatized or toughened by her environment. Mom was toughened.

NEW ORLEANS NEIGHBORHOODS OF MY CHILDHOOD

Back then, New Orleans neighborhoods were very distinct, both ethnically and geographically. You could name the streets that formed the boundaries of Carrollton, the Irish Channel, the Garden District, Lakeview, Gentilly, the 9th ward, and the French Quarter. There were several sub-neighborhoods within the expansive Carrollton section that were "colored," as they said back then. One of these was known as "Black Pearl." As time went on, population growth and integration blurred the clear cultural and geographical lines separating neighborhoods.

Back then, bars, movie theaters, groceries, drug stores, and a multitude of small businesses served the needs of clients who lived within walking distance. There were roving vendors pulling their carts or driving their wagons slowly down the unpaved streets singing out what they had for sale. "Ah got warta melon ... red to the rind."

Theaters were usually in the middle of a block. Bars often were across the street from a "movie house." Most grocery stores were called "corner groceries," because most were on the corner of an intersection. These were family-owned and operated, and the structures were divided into living quarters, grocery proper, and, very frequently, a bar. All three had exterior doors but were also connected by interior doors.

One offshoot of this set-up was that folks shopped and relaxed with neighbors ... not strangers. Folks really got to know one another more intimately, socializing as they went about their daily routines. Another offshoot ... secrets were hard to keep. The neighborhood news had many reporters.

MOM AND THE PERVERT

I remember quite vividly one example of Mom's no-nonsense toughness. It occurred one night in 1944 at the Mecca Theater in the 700 block of Adams St. in the Carrollton neighborhood, just seven blocks from our rented shotgun house at 310 Cherokee St. World War II was raging, and my Dad was off to sea with the Merchant Marines. Mom was lonesome and enjoyed dancing and playing cards with relatives and friends at the bar across the street from the Mecca. Usually, she was joined there by her mother and some of her brothers and sisters.

My sister and I were dropped off at the Mecca to enjoy a movie. My sister was 10 and I was eight. Mom would lead us right into the theater before crossing the street to the bar. We were under strict orders to remain there until she entered the theater, just before the show "let out."

On this one occasion, my sister and I were seated in about the third row, when Mom came in about 10 minutes before closing. Mom sat on my left. My sister was on my right. Just after Mom took her seat a man took the seat to my sister's right. This must have raised a red flag with Mom, as it was odd that someone would change seats so close to the end of a show. Then it happened. The stranger put his left hand on my sister's right knee. Without a word, Mom bolted past me and my sister and punched the pervert square in the jaw. Dazed, the man stumbled out of the Mecca. Ethel sat back down, and we watched the final scenes of the movie. I noted that Mom never gave the man any verbal warnings or threats, not a word! Her right cross spoke volumes, and her message was delivered loudly and clearly.

MOM AND SPORTS

My Mom and I would play pitch and catch under the oak tree in front of 310 Cherokee. We took turns playing pitcher and catcher. The catcher would call each pitch, either a strike or a ball. If you got three strikes before you got four balls, you had one out. Four balls would put a man on base. Scoring only occurred if you walked four imaginary batters before you got three outs to end a half inning.

Mom and I would walk over to the Audubon elementary school on Broadway, where she would shoot hoops with me on their dirt court. She always encouraged me. At home, I would spend hours alone, shooting an old basketball at a metal ring that I had suspended from the shed in my back yard at 310. At Mater Dolorosa, the boys would shoot at a goal in the asphalt surfaced school yard during recess.

The only way you could get a shot was to get a rebound. Once one secured a rebound, one was allowed to take an unmolested shot of one's choice. Once the shot was launched, another mad scramble ensued. I was one of the smallest kids in school, so to get a few shots during recess, I had to be more than tough. I had to learn to anticipate the direction and length of a rebound before the ball hit the basket. I think I fell in love with basketball at my first exposure to it.

Mater Dolorosa fielded a team in the Catholic Youth Organization (CYO) league, and I got to wear the team uniform and sit on the bench. I was never put into a game. One of my classmates, Louis Champagne, was very good and became a star prep player at De La Salle High School. I was at the bottom of the growth scale and behind my peers on the path to puberty.

EYE OF THE NEIGHBOR

People felt a sense of security no "neighborhood watch" program could bring. Your neighbors "had your back" and were looking out for you and your children. About half the families on a block had a set of grandparents living with them. From comfortable perches on a front porch, they observed everything that happened on their block. If I misbehaved anywhere in the neighborhood, my Mom was sure to hear about it *and* punish me. My Mom always assumed teachers and neighbors were right about my conduct, until proven otherwise. Today, more and more teachers and neighbors are reluctant to speak of a child's misconduct for fear of the doubt and wrath of their parents. Children are defended out of parental pride, instead of corrected out of parental responsibility.

DOUBLE JEOPARDY

My Mom's approach led me to be on my best behavior at school. She always said there was no excuse for not getting an A in conduct. If ever the nuns at Mater Dolorosa (my grammar school) punished me, I did everything in my power to avoid my Mom's hearing about it. I knew she would punish me for getting punished. Double jeopardy bred double caution. All of the Benedictine nuns were strict disciplinarians. My 3rd grade teacher, Sister Paula, struck such fear in me initially that I came up with the idea that I could avoid going to school if I feigned illness. When I tried it, Mom countered my ploy with Castor oil. I quickly learned that almost anything was better endured than Castor oil. It quickly became apparent that I had nothing to fear from Sister Paula as long as I behaved.

MATER DOLOROSA

Mater Dolorosa School and Church were in the same 1200 block of Carrollton Ave. The parish priest was called Monsignor Joseph. He had a Polish last name, but it was beyond most of us to pronounce it much less spell it. It sounded like "Pizza-Whiskey," as I remember. I owe my elementary Catholic education to him, because he made it possible for all the children of his parish to attend Mater Dolorosa tuition free.

Mater Dolorosa School (The church is partly visible on the right.)

Mater Dolorosa Church

1950 Mater Dolorosa graduates—I am in the front row, second from the right

I received my first Communion and Confirmation in the beautiful Mater Dolorosa Church. The church is still there, though the school has been converted to a retirement home. All I remember about my first Communion ceremony is that the boys all wore the same suits and the girls the same dresses, and each sex sat on opposite sides of the main aisle. The same occurred at our Confirmation rite, but I remember a little more as I was 11. Archbishop Rummel administered the sacrament.

Before anointing us, he quizzed us on our knowledge of our faith. He would ask a question, and we would raise our hands to be called on. I can't remember this one question, though it was concerning sex. I can't remember my answer either but I remember the reaction to it. I had never heard laughter in church before, and my response "brought down the house." I had the distinction of "cracking up" the very serious and somber Archbishop. Would that video recorders were as common in 1947 as they are today! I'd love to be able to recall that Q & A. Much later, I would teach 11 years at a high school named after Archbishop Rummel. My son would graduate from Rummel High.

THE ROMAN CANDY MAN

One memory of Mater Dolorosa was the Roman Candy Man, who regularly parked his mule-drawn wagon at the curb on Carrollton Ave. in front of the church. He did a lot of business with us during lunch hour. His mule, Patsy, pulled his colorful carriage all over New Orleans.

3015 BURDETTE ST.

When I was only about two, we lived in a shotgun double rental at the corner of Colipissa and Burdette Sts. I don't remember anything that happened during our brief stay there, but I later spent many days and nights right down the block at 3015 Burdette St. This was where my paternal grandparents raised my Dad and his two brothers (Edwin and Harold) and two sisters (Marguerite and Elnora).

My Dad's brother, Edwin, lived there with the grandparents until and after they died. His wife, Aunt Onie, bore him four boys, Raymond, Donald, Arnold, and Edwin. These four cousins would become like my brothers, as we shared childhood adventures. I would spend many weeks of summers, as well as many holidays and weekends at 3015 Burdette. At the start of my visits, only Grandma Hanson, Uncle Eddie, Aunt Onie, and the first two of their four boys lived in the four-room, single bath, shotgun house.

My paternal grandfather's picture was the first thing one saw as you came through the front door, but I never knew him, because he died before my time. His name was John Frederick Hanson. He named my Dad John Thomas Hanson, and me and my son were given the same name. His picture showed him in the uniform of a streetcar conductor. Sometimes, Aunt Marguerite stayed there too.

I didn't get to know my Aunt Elnora. She was a young woman who suffocated one cold Mardi Gras day, working at a small candy stand on Carrollton Ave. near Xavier University. The stand was not properly ventilated, and she was overcome by fumes from a space heater.

I never got to meet my Uncle Harold either. He left town as a young man and never came back. It was rumored that he was in prison.

Grandma Hanson slept in the first room, my four cousins in the second, and Uncle Eddie and Aunt Onie in the third. The fourth room was the kitchen, and no one ever slept there. My sister and I would sleep with Grandma or on a pallet on the floor. The chickens slept under the house. There was only Grandma's chamber pot and one (indoor!) toilet for all.

Strange as it may seem by today's standards, we never thought we were crowded. We seldom played in the house, preferring to "run the streets." Sometimes, we had to climb through the boys' bedroom window if we stayed out too late.

For the adults, there was the ubiquitous corner grocery-bar combo at one end of the block, and for us kids, a four-square block public playground at the other. This playground was designated "Carrollton Playground #2." The opposite corners had backstops for playing baseball and softball. There were organized sports leagues that used the ballfields, and we often watched groups of all ages play.

There was a man who parked his snowball cart at the curb and scraped blocked ice by hand. He only had about five or six flavored syrups, but he had a steady stream of customers when school was out. Later, a permanent snowball stand was set up at the northwest corner, and the cart vendor was put out of business.

One day, I saw a group of about a dozen older boys gathered in a tight circle in the middle of the playground. Curious, I approached the circle but was shoed away. Later my cousin, Raymond, explained that the older boys were taking turns mounting a girl named Jessie. I was still too young to understand the attraction or participate. Needless to say, Carrollton Playground #2 was a multiple-use facility. It is now the site of Dominican High, an all-girls Catholic school.

In 1968, Uncle Eddie committed suicide with a handgun. He had been laid off from his job as a carpenter and depression overwhelmed him. I especially remember how Uncle Eddie loved children.

Uncle Eddie

After Grandma Hanson passed away, her son, Raymond, bought the house and moved in with Aunt Onie. He brought with him his wife, and they reared two daughters at 3015. For a time, my Aunt Marguerite, between marriages and boyfriends, stayed at 3015. Another part-time resident was my great aunt, Martie. I vividly remember her rolling her own cigarettes, "*Picayunes*," on the kitchen table.

There was my great uncle, Tom. He lived in a nearby apartment above a pool hall on Carrollton Avenue. When my cousin, Raymond, was old enough to play pool there, he got into a fight and ended it by knocking out his adversary with a cue ball. It was only a short walk from 3015, and Raymond and I visited him there a few times. A part of Uncle Tom remains with me to this day. Around 1910, he built a child's rocking chair for my father. It was constructed of "tiger oak," so called because of the unique striping of the wood. It had a caned seat. Some 80 years later, my Mom passed the rocker on to me. I had it restored, and it remains in my house today.

Another memory is of Aunt Marguerite losing a ring finger from an accident at a kitchen window. In trying to free the stuck window, it suddenly slammed down on her hand when the pulley rope snapped. The finger was amputated at Charity Hospital. I was fascinated by the missing finger and asked her, "Where's your finger?" Even when I was no longer a child, I would greet her with that same question and she would smile and say, "You know." It never stopped her from helping to build the Higgins Boats that brought our troops ashore on D-Day. She worked at the Higgins manufacturing facility as a welder.

A BLOW TO THE HEAD AND A SHOT THROUGH THE LEG

Marguerite, my favorite Aunt, could be aptly described as "hell on wheels." She bummed with my Mom and took her side against my Dad when he fussed about their escapades. Once when Dad came home (310 Cherokee St. at the time) drunk, she stepped between him and my Mom and smacked him above his left eye with a small cobalt blue glass vase. Dad bled profusely. It's strange to me how vividly I remember my aunt snatching that vase from the bedroom bureau and cracking it over her brother's head, but I can't recall the moments just before and after the incident. I was only six or seven years old.

One night, Aunt Marguerite was shot while walking with one of her boyfriends near 3015 Burdette. The bullet went through a thigh. She vividly described to me how painful it was to have the wound cleansed. My child's eyes must have been as large as saucers as I listened.

Another Marguerite story has stayed with me. She told of how another lover, Jack, had slept in the woods at the site of a burned out cabin in North Louisiana. When Jack awakened at first light he found rattlesnakes sleeping on and about him. He remained still until the heat of the sun drew the snakes away. The trauma turned Jack's black hair completely white!

Marguerite was a good sport. She told us how when she was a child other children would tease her, chanting "Marguerite, go wash your feet! The Board of Health's across the street." When we would repeat that chant to her, she would just respond with a sweet smile. For years, I would greet my aunt with that directive to wash her feet and the question about her missing finger, and we would enjoy a good laugh.

I remember tripping in the back yard at 310 and suffering a deep gash on my lower left leg. It was Aunt Marguerite who swept me up in her arms and drove me in her car to Charity Hospital. It took eight stitches to repair the wound, and I still have the scar.

I remember the day I learned to swim. It was Aunt Marguerite who pulled me from the kids' pool at the Audubon Park Natatorium and put me in the "big" pool. It was a tossup as to who was more proud of my first strokes—my aunt or me. My cousins and friends spent many hours and days at the pool. I became a strong swimmer and a fearless diver. My cousin Raymond met and fell in love at first sight with his future wife there. I was with them when they met, but, at the time, had no interest in girls.

PONCHARTRAIN BEACH

Another location for summer fun was the Ponchartrain Beach Amusement Park on the south shore of Lake Ponchartrain. It was at the north end of Elysian Fields Avenue. It was segregated. Whites only. Further east, there was a place for the blacks known as Lincoln Beach. Both beaches offered swimming, but Lincoln Beach lacked the large midway, lined with the typical carnival games of skill and the thrill rides.

The Zephyr was one of the grandest roller coasters of that time. My favorite ride was the bumper cars. You could crash them into the cars of other riders. It had the same appeal for me as contact sports. Another popular attraction on the mid-way was a walk-through horror house. As you felt your way through its narrow, darkened corridors, all sorts of monsters, ghosts, and such would jump out at you.

At last, you entered a brightly illumined room that was a stage. The room was built at a slant and painted with a dizzying pattern. Rails guided you back and forth in front of an audience gathered at the foot of the stage. As you exited the stage, a relatively short passage brought you into the audience room in front of the stage. It became apparent why the audience had whistled and laughed so much, while folks stumbled across the stage. There were jets of compressed air being timely released through holes in the floor. As ladies stumbled dizzily through the maze, their dresses were blown high above their waists, revealing their underwear.

CHILDHOOD DAYS ON A FARM

Before we rented one side of the shotgun double at 310 Cherokee in 1941, we lived with a man named Mr. Clu. We were allowed room and board in exchange for my Mom doing the cooking and cleaning. Mr. Clu was something of a recluse and was a beekeeper. Living there was my first experience with "farm" life. In addition to the rows of hives, there was a large barn and a fenced pasture for a few cows and a horse. There were lots of chickens and a few pigs. A large garden provided corn, beans, okra, lettuce, tomatoes, and other staples.

One side of the property was bordered by a large drainage canal that ran from the center of New Orleans to Lake Ponchartrain. It was one of many such canals that drained the city, much of which was below sea level. A barge canal known as the Ponchartrain Basin paralleled the drainage canal. It has been filled in since, but, at the time, it ran all the way downtown.

Many of the wealthier citizens had "camps" built along the basin close to the lake. They all had boat houses. One of my Aunt Marguerite's beaus had one of these camps. I remember he kept a pet fox there. The fox would hide under a bed when guests would enter the camp.

Later, my friends and I would fish, crab, and swim in the basin near Carrollton Ave. We could reach it on our bikes. The farm was on a rare plot of high ground, surrounded by prairie land and swamp. For all our isolation, the city had installed a fire plug along the dirt road leading to the property. We would open the plug and cool off on hot summer days.

MOMMA AND MUSKRAT

We had no neighbors nearby. There was a trapper who had his shack about a mile away. Once, my Mom took me with her to visit the trapper's wife. I remember seeing muskrat hides hanging beside the shack and a Billy goat kept in a small fenced area. The goat tried to butt me, but I was able to keep him off me by grabbing his horns. I regarded this as great fun.

The trapper's wife gave my Mom some muskrat meat to take home, which led to a memorable event at the evening meal. My Mom was a great cook. She knew how to blend seasonings and spices like a professional chef. She prepared a meal around fried muskrat that evening.

Mr. Clu came out of his room to take his place at the table. We usually only saw him at meals, because when he wasn't working outside he stayed in his room. He asked Mom what she had cooked and she told him it was rabbit. She feared he might have an aversion for muskrat but was confident he would enjoy it if he tasted it without prejudice.

Mr. Clu relished the muskrat and even asked for seconds, something he had never done before. Mom couldn't restrain herself from grinning as Mr. Clu downed his second helping. Taking note of her suppressed chuckling, Mr. Clu said, "Ethel, why are you grinning?" Laughing, she revealed that she had served him muskrat, not rabbit. With an angry grunt, Mr. Clu left the table and retired to his room for several days!

THE ROOSTER AND THE BROOM

Mr. Clu's barn had a henhouse, which the chickens could access from their outside yard via an 18-inch culvert. Their nests could be accessed from inside the barn by an adult who would lift a hinged lid above them. Mom usually collected the eggs. One day, she noticed that a hole had been made on one end of several eggs and their contents emptied. This continued to happen every day, and it was thought that some animal was entering the nesting area through the culvert leading to the chicken yard.

The animal turned out to be me. One day, the rooster decided to put up a fight to protect his hens, and I took a broom to him. His loud squawking alerted Mom, and she caught me in the act of sucking the yolk and white right out of the raw eggs. She took the broom to me, and I stopped stealing eggs. I suspect the cackling rooster was laughing at me!

MOMMA THE EQUESTRIAN

We had a good laugh at Mom's expense, when at my Dad's urging, she reluctantly tried to ride the horse bareback. Stepping into my Dad's cupped hands, she swung her leg over the horse's back. She tried several times, but each time she kept right on going off the other side of the horse. We laughed hysterically, but Mom failed to see the humor and stormed off like Mr. Clu. Later, on another farm, I had my own horse and saddle, but my Mom never mounted a horse again. Speaking of horses, my mother's brother, Johnny, brought me a rocking horse while we were still staying with Mr. Clu. Written on the side of the horse was "Tom Mix and Tony." Roy Rogers and Trigger hadn't come along yet. Mom taught us to care for our things, and 12 years later, my family's children were still using Tony.

CHILDHOOD DAYS AT 310 CHEROKEE ST.

Most of my grammar school years were spent at 310 Cherokee. The Lemoine family occupied the 308 side of the double-shotgun. All of the houses were set on brick pillars and had a crawl space beneath. Each had a set of steps leading to a covered front porch.

Our house had four rooms and a bath. Mom and Dad usually slept in the first or second room and my sister and I in the third room. The fourth room was the kitchen. The bathroom was at the rear beside a small hall leading to the back yard. At the rear of the yard was a lean-to shed.

The Lemoines had identical living facilities on their side ... a six-foot wooden fence separated our back yards. The back yard was also accessible through a gate at the end of an alley that ran alongside the house. Each room had a wood frame window, the old kind with the counter weights and six rectangular glass panes. The window that took Aunt Marguerite's finger was of the same construction.

There were fireplaces in the two central rooms. We burned "stone" coal in them for heat on cold days. We had a cast-iron wood stove in the kitchen. Besides using it for cooking, Mom heated buckets of water for bathing and washing clothes. Though we had indoor plumbing, we lacked a hot water heater.

To keep food from spoiling we had an "ice box." A wide, shallow pan was kept under the ice box to catch the condensate of the ice. It had to be emptied regularly to prevent flooding the kitchen floor. Many a time, our inattention to the drip pan resulted in an unscheduled mopping of the floor. An ice man delivered blocks of ice every day or so.

Once, I sneaked onto the tailgate of the ice truck thinking to hitch a ride. The truck moved slowly at first but steadily gained speed as it headed for St. Charles Avenue, a street off limits to me. Desperate, I jumped backwards off the tailgate. Unfamiliar with the laws of inertia, I went sprawling onto the street and gained a big bump on my forehead. It could have been so much worse, if not for my guardian angel.

WASHING AND COOKING

Mom washed our clothes in a wash tub with a scrubbing board and hung them out to dry on clotheslines strung up in the back yard. Many a time, a threatening rain shower had "all hands" scurrying to get our drying laundry inside. Every Monday was "clothes washing" day, and Mom always cooked red beans. On Tuesdays, Mom did the starching and ironing. All the chores and meals were done on a weekly cycle.

Like the Army, we got the beans, but different kinds on different days. We had fried chicken and potato salad on Sundays. We sometimes had wild game, like venison, rabbit, goose, duck, shrimp, crab, crayfish, and a variety of fish, which friends or relatives would share after hunting or fishing excursions. Occasionally, Aunt Marguerite would pile us into her car and take us out to Lake Ponchartrain to catch crabs or bring us to the surrounding swamps to catch crayfish.

We never had steak but we did eat cow brains, tripe, and tongue. These were available from the "butcher shop" dirt cheap, as they were just by-products of the butchering process. Other inexpensive bovine portions were kidneys, hearts, and livers. Once in a while, we had pork chops. No matter what Mom cooked, she made it delicious. Boy, could she cook! Thanks to my Mom, I can enjoy nearly any type of food. Mom always had side dishes with her entrée. She had a hard-and-fast rule that we had to at least take a small portion of everything she put on the table, as well as clean our plate. We were reminded of "the starving children in China," if we resisted. This situation resulted in my developing a taste for many foods that I didn't like at first taste … and to this day, I eat all that I put on my plate.

Another motivating factor was that if we didn't partake of all that was prepared, we didn't partake of any of what was prepared. Once when Mom took my sister and me downtown, we had lunch at Morrison's Cafeteria. One Christmas, the three of us ate at Jim's Fried Chicken on Carrollton Ave. This event stands out in my memory, because we usually had a large family get-together meal on Thanksgiving and Christmas.

Not once did my Dad eat with us outside of our house. The truth is he didn't get many chances. It didn't bother me that we lived in a city famous for its fine restaurants and cuisine. No one told me that we were poor, and I never thought of myself that way. All of my uncles, aunts, and cousins lived the same way, and we loved, enjoyed, and supported one another. I guess we were poor, but the thought never crossed my mind.

CHILDHOOD MEMORIES OF DAD

After serving in the Merchant Marines, my Dad worked for about a year as a pipe fitter's helper in Guam but eventually returned to work for the city as a garbage man. I never saw Dad show any outward sign of affection for Mom, but I saw some of the letters he sent home while in Guam in which he tenderly expressed his loneliness and love for her.

His garbage wagon was powered by a team of mules. I remember him parking his wagon in front of 310 Cherokee, while he came in for his lunch. He named one of his large white mules "Marguerite," because she was stubborn like his sister, my Aunt Marguerite. I remember drawing a picture of that mule on a sheet of paper.

I never saw my Dad in a suit until his wake. He always wore dungarees and a work shirt or a sleeveless undershirt. He had an old Hudson automobile with running boards, and its sole use was to transport himself to work or his favorite bar. He didn't allow Mom to drive, though she longed to do so. She, my sister, and I either hoofed it or rode the streetcar or bus. The Hudson was always off with Dad during the day.

We frequently walked the three miles to 3015 Burdette or the mile to Mater Dolorosa. The public transit system would take us anywhere in the city for seven cents. The St. Charles Ave. streetcar line was only three blocks away. Transfers to other lines or buses would bring you into any section of town. Most of my uncles and aunts and their kids on my Mom's side (recall that she had 13 surviving siblings) lived in the Irish Channel, and we took the streetcar/bus to visit them. My Mom's sister, Beatrice, and her husband, Fred, lived on Pearl St., only a short three-and-a-half block walk from 310 Cherokee. Grandma Fairleigh stayed with them. Their daughter was my sister Ann's age, and they played together.

My Mom's brother, Christopher, and his wife, Agnes, lived in an apartment behind Beatrice's house. Uncle Christopher worked as a carpenter at the Army Corps of Engineers installation located only a few blocks away on the Mississippi batture. Dad never went with us on these visits.

I remember Dad had the habit of pouring his hot coffee from the cup into the saucer to cool it and then sipping it from the saucer. He always saved a little for our red chow dog, Beauty, who sat beside his chair.

One of my most vivid memories of my Dad was of the one time he disciplined me. Except for that one time, it was always the sphere of Mom to correct and punish us. On learning that I had thrown a rock at Mrs. Lemoine and knocked off her glasses, he strapped my behind with his belt. The whipping was administered in as calm and measured a demeanor as one could imagine. I richly deserved it. I guess I wasn't spoiled, because I sure wasn't spared the rod. The threat of corporal punishment was real enough and so sufficed to keep me in line.

I remember throwing another rock across Cherokee St. which bounced off the banquette and cracked the large plate glass window of Earl's Laundry. I got away clean with that one, but worried for a long time that I would be found out. I took to throwing marbles, but discovered they could crack windows too.

One day, while at recess at Mater Dolorosa, I cracked the boys' frosted glass bathroom window with an errant toss of a marble. The school yard was full of children so there was no escaping detection. My Mom had to march me over to Monsignor Joe to face the music. I remember how frightening the anticipation of that meeting was but not the judgment. I was through with throwing rocks and marbles.

ACCIDENTS HAPPEN

I remember a terrible accident that occurred in the Lemoine household. Their grandchild was horribly scalded when the child pulled a pot of boiling water from the stove. The child looked like a boiled crayfish and Mrs. Lemoine was inconsolable. She nearly faced the loss of her son, when he was shot through the shoulder in combat with the Japanese. He showed me the entry and exit scars, when he returned safely from the war. I was one fascinated little boy.

Another accident that I remember was suffered by Louis Johnson, my neighbor at 312 Cherokee, the double next door. Louis was already in his teens, when I was just six or seven. Louis and some of his friends used to dive for golf balls in the lagoons that flanked the Audubon Park golf course. One day, he was struck in the head by an errant ball and went into a coma. When he got out of the hospital, he had a long scar on his shaved head. Louis was never the same after that.

Prior to the accident, Louis had taken me aside after I called him and his friends "queers." I don't know when I first heard the word, and I had no idea then what the word meant, but it irritated the older boys, and that's what little kids do … irritate older boys. Louis took me aside and calmly explained that a queer was someone who "sucked dicks." I was terribly embarrassed. I never called anyone a queer again; though later, I was to have some run-ins with some who fit the description. I learned not to use a word, if I didn't know its meaning.

As time went on, the word evolved to "homosexual" to "gay." Just like "nigger" evolved to "negro" to "colored" to "black" to "Afro-American." I pray the day will come when all of our citizens are just called "Americans." Some words seem to develop over time an unacceptable connotation, and then, over time, their replacements grow unacceptable and are again replaced. Congressional largesse was called "pork" until it developed a bad connotation. Then, politicians thought "earmarks" would sound better. Now they are seeking to call it "congressional directed spending." A turd by any other name still smells the same.

MY FIRST JOBS

I got my first job as a small boy, while living at 310. I had been given a "Red Ryder" wagon, and I used it to deliver orders from the butcher shop on the corner. It was owned by Louis and Alice Lapuyade. They were Mister Louie and Miss Alice to me. It was unthinkable for a child to address an adult without the title "Mr." or "Miss." It was drummed into our psyche to always respect our elders. The deliveries assigned to me were within easy walking distance, and my compensation consisted of tips and the occasional coins Miss Alice would give me from the pocket on the front of her apron. I got to keep it all. Nothing was withheld for Uncle Sam.

An elderly, well-to-do lady named Miss Katie offered to pay me 50 cents if I would pick the figs from a large tree in her back yard. After working for a couple of hours, I brought her a large pail of figs. When I asked her for my pay, she changed our agreement. I would have to peddle the figs to residents along St. Charles Avenue. I never questioned my elders, so I spent hours knocking on doors to sell the figs. My Mom never had a problem with questioning anyone, and when she found out what Miss Katie had done, she gave her a "piece of her mind." Some of the most well-to-do folks in this world can be the stingiest.

NEIGHBORHOOD COMMERCE

The intersection of Cherokee St. and Benjamin St. was only about 100 feet from 310. Lapuyade's butcher shop, Earl's laundry, and the Fandel grocery store occupied three of its four corners. Just around the corner on Benjamin St. was Sarge's Candy Store. Sarge lived behind the candy store and most everything in it cost between a penny and a nickel.

I remember a large sign high on the wall behind the counter that advertised Coca-Cola. It pictured a bowlegged cowboy standing with his back to us beside his stallion. Without revealing any privates, it clearly showed the two to be urinating. In large letters, the sign read, "Coca-Cola, the Pause That Refreshes." That ad would be *so* politically incorrect today. It's funny how certain things strike you when you are a young child, and they stick in your memory for so long.

Mahalia Jackson, who became a famous singer, lived in a shotgun-double between Sarge's Candy Shop and Earl's Laundry. I remember black adult men gambling in front of her house. They had dug a hole in the dirt strip between the banquette and the street. From a common distance away, they would see who could putt a golf ball into the hole with the fewest strokes. Sometimes, they would simply toss coins to see who could land their coin closest to a line in the dirt or on the banquette. Strangely enough (by today's customs) they called one another "nigger" with affection and without offense taken. However, a slight change in tone in the use of this appellation could result in a deadly fight.

I often observed black men walking past my house on Cherokee. I found it amusing when two of them were approaching one another from opposite directions. They would start an enthusiastic conversation long before they reached the point of passing one another and, without stopping, continue their conversation until they were again out of earshot.

The Fandel Grocery relied on trucks to deliver their stock, but Mr. Lapuyade made early morning trips daily to the French Market to obtain his meats and fresh produce. Fandel's grocery had a bread box on the banquette on the Benjamin St. side of their building. Fresh bread was delivered by truck every morning before the store opened. Early morning customers simply lifted the lid of the box and took the bread they needed. They would return later to pay for it. Now that was an honor system! I don't think it would work in today's world.

Bundles of *Times-Picayune* newspapers were dropped beside Fandel's grocery as well for distribution by "paper boys." Later, I would become one of those paper boys. Beans were stored in large bins under the front counter. We would scoop them into a paper bag, and the Fandels would weigh the bag to determine the price. Soft drinks were sold in glass bottles. Their price included a deposit, which was refunded when the empty bottle was returned.

It was common for merchants to give their customers a little something extra to thank them for their business. It might be a piece of hard candy or licorice or a similar treat. They called it "lagniappe."

One block down Benjamin St. from Fandel's Grocery was another grocery at the corner of Benjamin and Hillary Sts. It was owned and operated by the Trahant family, who lived in a house connected to their store. One could go one block up Hillary St. from the Trahant establishment, take a left on Dominican St., and walk one block to the intersection of Dominican and Adams Sts. Bill's grocery and bar, along with his house, were there. My Grandma Fairleigh frequented the bar with her son, Christopher, and daughter, Beatrice. Three and a half blocks up Adams St. was the aforementioned Mecca Theater. At the corner of St. Charles Ave. and Hillary St. was a Rexall Drug Store. It had a soda fountain, with bar stools (no booths) along the counter. There was a streetcar stop on this corner, which was only three and a half blocks from 310.

St. Charles Avenue is one of the most beautiful thoroughfares in the country. The median contains two sets of tracks for the streetcars. Riding the St. Charles streetcar is a bargain basement way for tourists to leisurely view several of the most famous districts of New Orleans. St. Charles Avenue is lined with beautiful old oak trees, churches, and mansions. The route also passes through the Carollton and Central Business districts.

OTHER CLOSE CALLS

My first childhood ride was a tricycle. I took to pedaling it down to Fandel's Grocery and back. Once, I took a right at the corner and ventured half a block up Benjamin St. On the return trip I began pedaling full speed. Not being familiar with the laws of inertia, when I attempted to turn left at the corner I veered off the sidewalk into a fireplug, jamming a handlebar into my side. It hurt like the dickens, but I completely forgot about it until I found myself barreling down that same sidewalk the next day.

The two sides of the Fandel's Grocery building ran right along the Benjamin and Cherokee sidewalks creating a blind corner. Only recalling the crash into the fireplug when it was too late to slow down, I decided to continue straight across Cherokee St. I didn't see the dump truck coming down Cherokee. Fortunately, the truck driver must have had great peripheral vision and jammed on his brakes. When I got my tricycle stopped, I was right in front of the truck. The truck's massive bumper rested just above my left shoulder and barely short of the left side of my head. I've been keeping my guardian angel busy ever since.

As a 7th grader at Mater Dolorosa, I was playing touch football with my friends during the lunch hour. The school had barricaded each end of Plum St. alongside the church to provide more play space. We used the curbs alongside the paved street as sidelines. On this one occasion, tree limbs torn away by a recent hurricane (no names were assigned back then) were piled along one curb.

Running full speed, I was knocked off my feet and plowed head first through the branches. It took a while to extract me as one of the sharp ends of a branch had ripped through my pants leg and traveled out the bottom and past my foot. After I was assisted to back off the branch, I returned to the huddle. Only then did I feel the blood gushing down and out of my trousers. That branch or another in the pile could just as easily have gone into my neck or stomach if the orientation of my plunge had varied by an inch or two.

My guardian angel was still on the job and would be with me through many narrow escapes to follow. This time, I was stitched up at the Nix Clinic only two blocks away. My right leg now had seven stitches to go with the eight in my left leg. I still have the scars. The best part was I got out of school the rest of the day. The nuns had an older boy give me a ride home on his bicycle.

MISCHIEF MAKERS

About the time I turned 10, my Mom purchased a used bicycle for me from a bicycle shop in the 8300 block of Oak St. This acquisition greatly expanded the area I could explore for my age at the time. Working my way through grammar school, I learned where a number of my classmates lived and began to visit their houses and hang with them. Our neighborhood was tucked into the long sweeping curve of the Mississippi

River called the nine-mile point, which was about three miles downstream from the Huey P. Long Bridge. My closest friend, Mike Aymami, lived on Dominican St., between Bill's grocery/bar and the river. Mike and I and three other neighborhood kids planned many of our adventures from Mike's house. Mike delivered groceries for Mr. Bill, and one day, Mr. Bill gave him some rotten eggs to throw away. Mike decided to enlist our help, and we decided to wait until after dark and throw them through an open second-floor window of a plant on Dublin St. that manufactured ice.

After unloading three or four eggs apiece, in rapid succession, we ran across the street and mingled with the kids playing at the Dublin St. playground. The two men who rushed out of the ice house reeked with the odor of the rotten eggs and were in a very foul mood. Their curses filled the air, but there was no way they could cull us out from the playground crowd. Later, we pretended we were the workers in the ice house and acted out what we imagined had been their reaction as the eggs splashed down on and around them. There's a comedian in every bunch and our rendition had us in stitches.

Once, Mike and I and our friends Merrill and Ronnie were sitting in an empty grain silo that stood beside the river road, which followed every curve of the Mississippi levee. In that section, the road was named Leake Avenue. We had just begun to experiment with cigarettes. We did so at the peril of discovery by our parents, who universally disapproved of children smoking.

Ironically, society was more addicted to nicotine at that time than today. Rare was the adult man or woman who did not smoke. The cigarette was the ubiquitous prop in the movies. No wonder. The health hazards of smoking were unknown, and cigarettes were advertised without warnings or restrictions. Later, it would be a New Orleans physician, Dr. Alton Oschner, who would point to the health hazards of smoking and begin the anti-smoking movement.

There were only four common brands, but they were undiluted of tars and nicotine and non-filtered. For 25 cents, you could buy Camels, Lucky Strikes, Chesterfield, and Phillip Morris in packs of 20. They were so heavily advertised on the radio and billboards that I remember some still. "I'd walk a mile for a Camel." "Lucky Strike means fine tobacco." The radio ad that began with, "Call for Phillip Morris."

Well, after lighting up, Mike and I glanced over at Merrill, our resident comedian. He had placed five cigarettes between his lips and was puffing away. We all began to choke and laugh at the same time. I wonder if someone passing by thought the silo had been converted into a smokestack. I never took to the habit, but Mike became a chain smoker, and no one was laughing when lung cancer took him before he turned 40.

Another activity our small group engaged in we called "roofing." We always engaged in "roofing" after dark to lower our chances of detection. It consisted of climbing up onto a garage or house roof and seeing how far we could travel without touching the ground. We crossed over St. Charles Avenue, when we went roofing. Too many folks might recognize us on the river side of the Avenue.

We allowed ourselves to use fence tops, but most of the houses were close enough to one another to tempt jumping the gaps between roofs (this sense of bravado must have kept our guardian angels quite busy). We occasionally drew the ire of residents but were always gone before the police responded. What else were we to do on summer nights? There was no TV, no video games, and no malls. And, fortunately for us, no 911. We found scaring people to be fun and not just on Halloween.

One ruse we particularly enjoyed. We would stuff an old black sock and tie it shut with black thread. After dark we would hide in the shrubbery on one side of the banquette and toss the sock into the grass between the curb and the banquette. We would wait along Adams Street for patrons leaving the Mecca to come walking by. When some older ladies approached our hiding spot, we would pull the sock across their path. We chose older ladies, because they would always scream in terror and pull back from the "rat." We also chose them because they couldn't catch us when we bolted, laughing hysterically, from our place of concealment.

I never forgot that stunt, and many years later, pulled it on my wife very early one morning. She was half asleep and sitting on the commode, when the "rat" passed in front of her feet and out the door. Suffice it to say "the shit hit the fan."

We also took impish delight in ringing the bell of the black church located on the corner of Cherokee and Pearl Streets. The rope attached to the bell was in the open belfry in front of the church entrance. We would shatter the quiet of the night with the deep peals of the bell, well after the lights went out in the preacher's house next door on Pearl St. This scenario gave us plenty of time to escape to the shelter of an alley on the Cherokee St. side of the church. From there, we could hear the shouts of the preacher who had run to the church in his night clothes. We were never caught, because we were careful to ring the preacher's bell sparingly and randomly.

Another black church was located on Adams St. across from Bill's Grocery and Bar. Jazz funerals were conducted from there to the Green St. cemetery and back. We would hear the mournful music of the band as they accompanied the deceased to the grave site and would go join the curious to await the return of the procession. That was the good part.

Observers would be treated to the lively, celebratory jazz music of the band. The faithful in the procession would kick up their heels and sing lyrics like, "I'm glad you're dead, you rascal, you!" Everyone should see a New Orleans jazz funeral at least once. The lesson of the jazz funeral is to mourn the dead, but then to get over it and celebrate life.

One night, my Dad wandered into this all-black church and settled into a seat at the back to "sleep it off," after drinking too much at Mr. Bill's bar across the street. He was awakened by a warm greeting from the preacher and found his way out. This situation is the only time in my memory that my Dad entered a church and the incident remains only in the realm of hearsay. He once told me that if he entered a church, the roof would fall in on him. I've heard that God takes care of fools and drunks. I must fit into the former category, given that I've never been drunk, but God's angels have certainly taken good care of me.

We also took to exploring the New Orleans drainage system. We entered the main underground culverts via the storm drains located at every corner and the small culverts leading from them to the main culverts. We were small enough to squeeze between the bars guarding the drains. We used flashlights to light our way. It fascinated us to be able to disappear at one intersection and reappear at another. A sudden thunderstorm would have drowned us like rats, but we gave no thought to that. Our guardian angels had to be on overtime.

MOMO'S BEACH

A favorite playground for us was the land between the levee and the Mississippi. We had access to it most of the year. During the spring, the river overflowed its regular bed and rose to within a few yards of the levee top, denying us use of the river's sand beaches and willow woods interspersed between man-made structures. These structures consisted of the buildings of the U.S. Army Corps of Engineers, a ferry dock, and many camp-style houses resting on pilings and connected to the top of the levee by a gangway. There were probably 30 of these along a three-mile stretch. Their occupants were "squatters" on the federally owned batture.

There was one particularly wide stretch of beach just over the levee from the silo where we experimented with smoking. It was dubbed "Momo's Beach" after it's only resident (part-time), a black man known only as Momo. Momo had put up a small wooden hut among the tall reeds between the levee and the sand beach. It had only about 36 square feet of living space. Momo's furnishings consisted only of a couple of stools.

Like John the Baptist "crying in the wilderness," Momo preached a baptism of repentance and would baptize his converts right there in the Mississippi. Momo's Beach was integrated at a time when segregation reigned. I never saw a woman or girl on this beach, which was for the best, because I never saw a bathing suit either. Our folks strictly forbade us to swim in the river. We covered ourselves by swimming in the nude knowing that the river water would stain our drawers and be a dead give-away on wash day.

Some days, there would be about 20 boys ranging in age from 12 to 18 frolicking on the beach. Quite a few would be baptized by Momo. I suspect few of them were sincerely converted but acted on a dare.

Momo never left his hut without a makeshift cross, which doubled as a walking staff. It was completely wrapped in white cloth. Momo wrapped the top of his head in white cloth also and wore a long white robe.

The old expression "a fly in a bowl of milk" was personified to us by Momo. I don't know where Momo went when he left his beach, but some of us had spotted him boarding the St. Charles Avenue streetcar. I admired Momo. He looked out for us, always warning us to not swim out too far. He was kind to everyone, black and white alike, and never took up a collection.

From time to time, vandals would set fire to Momo's shack. On one such occasion, we saw the tell-tale smoke rising above the levee around midday. With the impulsiveness of youth, I rushed to the fire alarm on the lamp post at the corner of Dominican and Burdette Streets and set it off. When we heard the sirens of at least three fire trucks rushing to the intersection, we all hid in Mike's house, which was one house removed from the fire alarm.

Mike's mother quickly determined that we were the culprits who had turned in what would be construed as a false alarm. A false general alarm as it turned out. Momo's shack would burn to the ground again. Actually, it was located off city property and beyond the reach of fire hydrants and hoses. Mrs. Aymami told us to stay inside and hope no one would "turn us in." No one did, and I learned a valuable lesson without paying the price of being hauled into Juvenile Court or, much worse, my Mom's court.

DERBIGNY PLANTATION

We moved from 310 Cherokee in 1947. I don't recall what motivated the re-location, but my Dad was back from overseas and would remain with us until his death in 1953. We moved to the Derbigny Plantation, which was located on a long sweeping bend of the Mississippi known as the Nine Mile Point. It was on the west bank, halfway between the Huey Long Bridge and Westwego, LA. That stretch of land was sparsely populated. Most of it was woods, swamps, and pasture land.

The front of the 50-acre Derbigny property butted up against the gravel River Road there, which ran along the base of the Mississippi levee. The Collenberg family lived in a beautifully restored antebellum plantation manor. We lived in a small cottage that had housed slaves.

My parents had an arrangement with the Collenbergs similar to the one they had with Mr. Clu. My Mom worked as both a housekeeper and babysitter. My Dad drove into New Orleans to his job with the city on weekdays, but did some maintenance chores on weekends. There was a large vegetable garden (I remember picking okra) and a small stable and paddock on the property, but nothing but prairie elsewhere, except for the outhouse, which was located an appropriate distance behind our cottage. Going to the "bathroom" involved going for a walk as well.

We didn't have any utility bills, because we had no gas or electricity or city water. We burned kerosene lamps, as needed, if we stayed up after sunset. A large cistern beside the kitchen collected rain water for our use. Occasionally, my Mom babysat the Collenberg children after dark, and I got to listen to broadcasts of Tulane basketball games on the Collenberg radio, while experiencing the advantages of electric lighting.

For a short while, my sister, Ann, and I remained enrolled at Mater Dolorosa. My Dad drove us there and back on his commute to work. That put a damper on his visits to his favorite watering holes after work. Soon, we were enrolled in the public elementary school in Westwego. A school bus picked us up and dropped us off at the entrance to the Collenberg property on River Road.

The thing I remember most about my schooling in Westwego was recess. We played a game that involved scoring points by throwing, punting, place-kicking, and drop-kicking a football. I loved it, and it started me on a path that would later lead to invitations to tryouts with the Chicago Bears, Houston Oilers, and Dallas Cowboys. We moved back to the East Bank in time for me to graduate from Mater Dolorosa.

My Mom didn't take well to life on the Derbigny Plantation. She was used to having easy access to relatives and neighbors. She had never experienced anything like the isolation of the plantation or the absence of basic city utilities. My sister began to stay with the Sullivan family for whom my Mom had done domestic work. From that location, she began to attend Sophie B. Wright High School.

The Sullivans lived only one block over from 310 at 402 Hillary St. My sister became fast friends with the Sullivan's only daughter, Patsy, who was Ann's age. The Sullivans doted on her, and took her out to eat every week at nice restaurants. It moved Ann to a higher rung on the social and cultural level.

They had one of the neighborhood's first TV sets, a Stromberg-Carlson with a large cabinet and tiny screen. TV broadcasts were sporadic and only in black and white. The only one I can remember watching featured "professional" wrestling. It was a farce even back then.

Patsy had a cousin who lived next door. He and I were the same age and became friends. One early evening, the four of us were playing "detective" in the front bedroom of Patsy's house. Our parents were in the kitchen in the rear. My friend opened a drawer in the nightstand beside the bed and withdrew Mr. Sullivan's .38 revolver. I had been shown the revolver and knew it was a real gun. He thought it was a toy and pointed it at one of the girls. Instinctively, I rushed at him and thrust his gun hand straight up. The loud report brought all the adults rushing to the bedroom. I have to admit my guardian angel cut that one pretty close. My friend caught hell over that event. I wonder how long the bullet hole remained unpatched in the ceiling. Probably longer than the bruises on my friend's butt.

MRS. SULLIVAN EXPOSED

I saw a naked woman for the first time at 402 Hillary. I had gone to the front door to deliver something and when no one responded to the bell I opened the door and announced my presence. The bathroom opened onto a hallway connecting the second room to the third. Out into the hallway stepped Mrs. Sullivan. All factors considered, the first naked woman you see might as well be beautiful. I had heard folks say Mrs. Sullivan looked like Betty Grable, a popular movie star whose "pin-up" picture graced the barracks of our fighting men throughout WWII. They were right. In hindsight, I have no idea why Mrs. Sullivan unashamedly exposed herself to a 12-year old boy. Those times were not the "anything goes" times of today. Maybe, I have my guardian angel to thank for the fact that nothing came of it. I just put my package down and took off. I wasn't about to stick around for a view from the rear.

Mr. Sullivan, who had been a prep football star at St. Aloysius, delighted in bowling us over with his bullet passes. We played right in the street in front of the Sullivan house. Mr. Sullivan drove a late model car. Eventually, his lead foot earned him so many speeding tickets that he had a governor installed on the engine.

MY CHILDHOOD PARADISE

As for me, I was in something of a paradise on the Derbigny Plantation. I had my beloved Mississippi right over the levee and more wilderness than I could explore in a lifetime. Unlike the section of the East Bank of the River that bordered my old neighborhood, the batture of the West Bank was bereft of the camp-style dwellings of squatters. Upstream from the Huey Long Bridge was the sprawling Avondale Shipyard. The only man-made structure along the three-mile stretch between the Bridge and Westwego was a barge company office and dock. The rest of the batture was a mixture of willow woods, ponds, sloughs, and sand beaches.

The top of the levee was broad enough for one-way vehicular traffic, but one seldom saw a vehicle riding atop the levee. There were a few roads that led from the River Road up and over the levee to the batture. These were plied by dump trucks that would haul the rich river sand soil much desired for land fill and planting applications.

The pits left behind by the sand harvesting operations were filled by the spring flooding of the batture and became permanent ponds. These were known as "bar pits" and, over time, were stocked by nature with every aquatic species found in the river. Once, I helped the Fritz family harvest a bar pit.

The Fritz clan had a small dilapidated house about a mile downstream from Derbigny. Most of the boys were older, but one or two were close to my age, and provided playmates for me when Mom would visit with Mrs. Fritz. Mr. Fritz supported his family mainly by fishing the Mississippi.

Once a year, the family harvested the larger bar pits. The method was simple. A long seine was spread across the pit at one end. The ends were then dragged along the sides toward the other end. Soon, the net formed a large semi-circle. Starting at the other end, a line of boys and men would start splashing their way toward the net, driving the aquatic residents into the "bag."

As the line of "beaters" reached the net, one end was dragged across the pit to meet the end on the other side. The bag was pulled right into Mr. Fritz's lap as he sat in the water. He would grab one critter after another, culling out the desirable ones from the rest. One of the fish caught was a spoon-billed catfish. I had never seen one before. Another first–Mrs. Fritz cooked "garfish balls" for us. They were similar to codfish balls.

The river also hosted fresh-water shrimp. They were a smaller variety than the salt-water type that supported the large shrimp industry of South Louisiana and formed the basic ingredient in much of the seafood recipes popular locally and throughout the world. The salt-water shrimp were harvested by trawlers in Lake Ponchartrain and the Gulf of Mexico. Another method was employed by Mr. Fritz to capture the river shrimp. He would tie a bush with dark green waxen foliage to a pole and suspend it at the surface near the bank of the river. The shrimp would gather among the leaves and Mr. Fritz would simply shake them from each bush into a large scoop net. The shrimp made great bait for Mr. Fritz's trout lines, whose main yield was yellow and blue catfish.

Once, a cow got mired in a small shallow pit on the batture. In desperation, the animal's would-be rescuers tied a rope around the cow's neck and attempted to pull it free with the help of a pickup. The cow came free, but suffered a broken neck. My Mom called Mr. Lapuyade, the butcher from the old neighborhood, and he came out and butchered the cow for its meat. Cows from Mr. Shaw's dairy farm that abutted the Derbigny Plantation frequently grazed on the levee between milkings.

Once, I joined the Fritz clan to harvest hay from the levee. We gathered the hay with pitchforks and loaded it onto a wagon pulled by a team of horses. From that time on, I thought of a hayride as work, not a pleasurable excursion. Later, when I was in high school in Lafayette, LA, I would help load a truck with bales of hay and unload them into a barn loft. Oddly enough, we always came across a snake on these excursions.

MERRY CHRISTMAS

The property immediately south of Derbigny Plantation was owned by a gentleman of means named Kenny Roberts. He had a fine house and a stable for his horses there, but his main house was a mansion on St. Charles Avenue, near my old 310 address. One day, I met Mr. Roberts, and he took a liking to me. He invited me on a horseback ride, and I fell in love with horses as only a young boy could. Mr. Roberts was a scoutmaster and had his troop over for campouts in the woods near his country home. He invited me to join in the fun. I learned to safely build a fire and sleep outdoors.

Seeing my love for horses, my Dad surprised me with a special gift on Christmas, a riding mare. She came complete with a saddle for $75. I named her Merry Christmas, but just called her by her first name. I housed Merry in the unused vacant stable and paddock on the Derbigny property.

Merry was unaccustomed to young boys, and I had to teach her who was boss. Shortly after I got her, she bit me on the forearm when I approached her. It was cold and I had on several layers of clothing which protected me from getting a serious wound. All I got was a black and blue impression of Merry's teeth. Frightened and saddened, I asked Mr. Roberts for advice. He told me to watch Merry's ears. If she flattened them as I approached her, I was to punch her square in the nose. I did, and Merry never threatened me again. Her ears remained bolt upright when I approached. She did, however, kick me in the thigh, when I foolishly touched her on her left flank, when she was loose on the levee. That kick left a black and blue imprint of her left rear hoof on my right thigh. She narrowly missed my groin. Thank you, guardian angel. Taking care of Merry taught me a lot of responsibility. I had to water, feed, and groom her, as well as clean her stall. I had had a rocking horse, wagon, tricycle, and bike, but Merry was the best ride of my childhood years.

THE SHAW DAIRY FARM

The property immediately down river from Derbigny was a large dairy farm. Its front ran about 200 yards along the River Road, but it was about three-miles deep. About a 100 yards back from the road, stood the building in which the cows were milked, and the milk pre-processed. A large frame farm house stood another 100 yards behind the dairy. Its lone occupant, a Mr. Shaw, was the owner of the dairy. His son, Florian, helped run the business but lived in town. There was an outhouse and small stable behind the house. The rest of the property was all grazing land, spotted with stands of woods and swamps.

Why we moved in with Mr. Shaw I don't know, but the arrangement was similar to the ones we had with Mr. Clu and the Collenbergs. Mom cooked and cleaned. Dad came home to sleep and continued to commute to his job with the city. I rode Merry on the levee and batture and explored the vast acreage of the dairy farm. Occasionally, on horseback, I rounded up the cows from the levee and the woods. To me, that was play, not work. I was thrilled when Mr. Shaw allowed me to ride his personal mount, a black pony he called Blaze for the white marking on her forehead.

Once, Mr. Shaw sent me to Bridge City on Blaze to pick up a newspaper. It was a six-mile round trip and the most comfortable I've ever been on a horse. It was comical to see Mr. Shaw ride Blaze. He was a tall wiry man, and his feet hung just inches from the ground when he rode the diminutive Blaze. What made Blaze his favorite was her smooth, comfortable trot.

The animals on the farm had no qualms about engaging in sexual intercourse in public. One afternoon, my Mom, Dad, and I watched a large pinto stallion mount my bay mare. In due course, Merry gave birth to a pinto foal I named Beauty Ann. We were inseparable. She came when I called and followed me around like a puppy. I took to calling her simply "Boo Ann." While it was much later when I received formal instruction on the "facts of life," I got off to a good start on the farm. Later, Merry bore me a pinto colt, which I called "Stormy." Subsequently, I had to give up my horses when we moved back to the city.

Once, my Mom was talking to Florian outside the dairy. It was getting dark and my Mom expressed concern that she had nothing to cook for supper. I had been watching an opossum moving about the upper branches of a tree beside the dairy and suggested we have it for supper. Mom agreed though she had never cooked "possum" before. I felled the marsupial with one blast from my Dad's single barrel 12-gauge shotgun, and Mom turned it into a delicious meal.

The Lord will provide ... if you're not too picky and have a Mom who can cook. We also harvested crayfish, wild persimmons, and blackberries from the land. We had all the milk, albeit unpasteurized, we wished to consume.

SOCIAL SECURITY AND THE *TIMES-PICAYUNE*

In the spring of 1948, we moved back to the city, and I finished my 7th grade at Mater Dolorosa. I also got my social security card and began paying federal income taxes out of my earnings as a paper boy. Even then, the feds had their hand out for a piece of my meager earnings as a 12-year-old. I worked for the *Times-Picayune* (actually, I was an independent contractor), delivering the *States-Item* every afternoon and the *Picayune* on Sunday mornings. I'm proud to say that for the two years, three months, and four days that I operated my *Picayune* business, I never missed a delivery, rain or shine. This situation can be attributed to the fact that I never got sick, but also to the fact that our family never traveled out of town on a vacation trip. My Mom even sewed together an oil-cloth cover for the bike basket that carried my papers. It rains a lot in New Orleans. While I never received a single customer complaint, several customers sent complimentary letters to the *Picayune* concerning my service.

My route stabilized at about 125 customers, dispersed over 18 square blocks of the southwest corner of the Carrollton section. It was bordered by St. Charles Ave., Carrollton Ave., Burthe St., and Cherokee St. My clientele included some of the rich and famous, along with blue-collar families and some married students attending Tulane and Loyola Universities. Except for the mansions and upscale apartments along St. Charles, most of the houses were rentals. There were no Afro-Americans living in my delivery area, though I interacted with many when I sub-carried other routes that had no regular carriers.

I usually did a route in a predominantly black and low-income neighborhood near our old 310 Cherokee address. Some years earlier, I had delivered groceries in my red wagon in parts of that same neighborhood. In fact, the papers for that route were dropped off at Fandel's grocery for me by the man who managed all of the carriers in our district. Not only did I not have to travel to the main distribution point to pick up the papers for these extra routes, but I was paid a straight hourly wage for delivering them.

For my own route, I had to collect payment from each customer myself and pay the *Picayune* for the papers issued to me. Collecting was a drag. Not only did it take from me

Form 368

OFFICE MEMORANDUM

Date JUNE 20, 1949

To John Thomas Hansen, Route 322 Department

From A. J. Nissen, States Circulation Manager Department

The following letter was received from Mrs. F. E. Guidry,
7627 St. Charles Ave.:

"Dear Sir:

I have subscribed to the New Orleans States for many years and this year it has been my good fortune to have the nicest, most courteous business-like little paper boy I have ever had. The office tells me he is John Thomas Hansen. When he comes to collect he greets me with a smile and never fails to have his book and pencil to write down, in front of me, the amount I have paid him. I do not know him except as my paper boy but his appearance, personality and business-like manner is outstanding and I hope this note will serve to give him a boost in your estimation and with the paper.

Most sincerely,
Mrs. Ernest Guidry.,

John, I would like to take this means to congratulate you on receinving such a fine letter from one of your subscribers. KEEP UP THE GOOD WORK!

A. J. Nissen

AJN/fgo

One of the complimentary letters a customer sent
to the *Times-Picayune* concerning my service

my Saturday morning free time, but some customers gave me a hard time. You learn a lot about people when you have to collect money from them that they owe you.

I remember one lady, in particular, that I had to "train." She lived in a fancy apartment on the corner of St. Charles and Adams (a block and a half from the Mecca theater). She would greet me with "Do you have change for a 20?" After she had me carry her over for four weeks in a row, I taught her a lesson. I barely collected $20 total from my weekly customers, but on my next visit to this particular customer, I made her my final stop. I had counted out the exact change for a 20 that would be due her—all in quarters, dimes, and nickels. She gasped when I quickly grabbed the 20 she offered and handed her a pocketful of coins. She never "stiffed" me again.

Ted Andrews, the radio voice of the New Orleans Pelicans (the AA farm club of the AL Boston Red Sox) was a customer who lived in an upscale apartment on St. Charles. One afternoon, when I approached his third-floor residence, I saw some pigeons on the windowsill at the end of the hall. I sneaked up on them and grabbed one. I turned it loose before I could get a good look at this bird that was so common in the city. It was full of lice, which emerged from the bird's feathers and scurried all over my hands. I was appalled. Who would have thought that pigeons were full of lice? The birds were as ubiquitous in New Orleans as rats and squirrels.

Mike's Barber Shop was next to Mr. Andrew's apartment building. Not only did Mr. Mike cut my hair (25 cents back then), but he was a newspaper customer of mine. One day, he gave me a quarter and a list of three numbers to play for him. The illegal numbers game was widespread throughout New Orleans. One of the betting sites was in the house behind Lapuyade's Market. Sometimes, my Mom would book the bets there. The winning numbers were printed everyday on narrow strips of paper and placed in a box on a fence beside the banquette. Customers would take a strip to see if they had the winning combo. Well, I forgot to place Mr. Mike's bet and went the following day to return his quarter. He was not a happy camper. My memory lapse had cost him $50 as he had picked the winning numbers. Mr. Mike got over it, and we continued our business relationship.

Once, I got into a scuffle with a black kid who demanded an "extra" from me. He got me down almost immediately and asked, "Do you give?" Fights ended back then when one of the combatants yielded. The winner didn't continue to beat on the loser. What compelled me to yield was that my opponent was pressing the side of my face into the clam shells that surfaced the dirt street to hold down dust and mud. It was an untenable situation.

A few months later, I used the same tactic when I told another boy to stop bullying a smaller friend of mine. The bully said, "Are you going to make me?" This kid was bigger than both my friend and me. He had recently bested the top fighter at our school, who had, until then, reigned as the school champ. I was foolish to engage the big bully in a fight, but I just could not allow him to mistreat my small friend unchallenged. Thanks to my altercation with the young black kid, who demanded an "extra," I prevailed. The bully yielded when I pressed his face into the shells spread in front of the snowball stand where our fight began. All three of us had been friends and remained so. We were all classmates at Mater Dolorosa and ran paper routes out of the same distribution center.

Our distribution center was in a garage on Lowerline St., across from the Green St. Cemetery. A *Picayune* van delivered our papers there in bundles of 50 papers. Work benches lined most of the interior walls of the garage. In one corner, there was a bin for waste. There was a small desk for the manager, a prince of a guy named John Scheuermann. We counted out and folded our papers on the benches after cutting the wire that bound them and throwing it into the waste bin.

One day, one of the lengths of wire (they retained their circular shape) went off course, and one of its ends struck another carrier in the eye. The odds of this happening were infinitesimally small. It didn't appear to be a serious injury at the time, and the injured boy left to deliver papers. Fluid slowly seeped from the tiny puncture in his eye, however, and he later lost his sight in that eye. His guardian angel must have blinked.

His family operated a shoe-repair business on Monroe St. not far from Mater Dolorosa. The family of another carrier operated the same type business just down the street from 310 Cherokee and next to the black church whose preacher we tormented by ringing his church bell. Over my lifetime, shoe-repair shops have all but vanished, as most products became of the disposable variety. We had our shoes repaired if we wore a hole in them or broke off a heel. We only replaced shoes when we outgrew them, and then we passed them on to someone they fit.

MY SHORT MODELING CAREER

In the summer of 1970, while taking some graduate courses at Texas A&M, I became friends with a fellow student named Paul Niemi. We have remained friends to this day. Paul was a teacher like me but supplemented his earnings by freelance writing. His hobby was bodybuilding, and he wrote a series of articles entitled "Barbells on Campus." In these write-ups, he would describe in words and photos the weight-training facilities of different colleges.

One day, Paul noticed what he described as my "humongous" calf muscles. He inquired about how I had developed such strong calves, thinking I had some special weight-training regimen. Paul probably was disappointed to learn that I never had any interest in weight training or bodybuilding.

In time, he persuaded me to accompany him to the Texas A&M weight room, where he worked out each afternoon. He explained how the exercises were done in repetitions of specific movements called "sets." I tried to follow the workout routine that he planned for me, but I found the whole thing boring. After a few minutes, I would leave Paul to his workout, while I played pickup games of basketball in the gym across the hall.

Over the summer, Paul photographed me and others using the weight equipment and that fall, he published two articles. One was part of the "Barbells on Campus" series, and the other was on exercises popular at the turn of the century. The latter was entitled "Forgotten Exercises," and I was the model. I didn't give it much thought until the following spring, when Paul mailed me copies of the magazines, *Iron Man* and *Muscular Development.* My four poses for "Forgotten Exercises" were pictured in the February 1971 edition of *Muscular Development*.

Subsequently, I got a letter from my cousin Raymond. Raymond had always been highly interested in bodybuilding, but completely failed to engage me in it. Given my apathy for bodybuilding, he was shocked to see me in two bodybuilding rags, and insisted I explain how I got into two of his favorite magazines. The odd thing was I had been living and working away from New Orleans for years, and Raymond had never once written to me. It was the one and only letter I ever received from him.

In reality, the foundation for the development of my leg strength was laid by my bike riding during my years as a paper boy. My bike had only one gear, and, on a typical school day, I would ride it a minimum of 12 miles just to go to school, collect and deliver my papers, and return home. Part of the time, I was carrying the weight of my papers and, on occasion, the weight of a friend seated on the crossbar. Most days included the additional mileage of delivering a route as a substitute and also the mileage accumulated going about my personal business and running the streets with my friends. It was common for me to pump my pedals for 30 to 50 miles every day.

In effect, I was working out on one of the pieces of equipment common to every health club, the stationary bike. The big difference was that I was never stationary. Hard manual labor from my sophomore year in high school through my graduation from undergrad school maintained and fostered my physical conditioning. I also benefited from good nutrition, hiking, mountain climbing, and participation in sports.

DEATH OF A FRIEND

The New Orleans Recreation Department (NORD) sponsored age-level baseball leagues every summer. One of my Mater Dolorosa classmates, Cyril Ruff, organized a team consisting mostly of our class. We played our games at a field near the Audubon Park Zoo and Natatorium. We were the "Hawks."

I remember one game in which I took the mound in a later inning. The other team had pounded everyone we had inserted to pitch, and I was one of the few remaining players who had not been tried. Unremarkably, I didn't allow a single hit. I walked every batter I faced, until I was removed. Wow! A no-hitter in my first start! Over that summer, I played every position, except catcher. Oddly enough, through high school and college, the only position I played was catcher.

What has stayed with me all these years since that summer of 1948 was the circumstances of the death of our leader, Cyril Ruff. It put a lot of "what ifs" in my mind. I had delayed heading to the park for a scheduled game, because it had started to rain, and a downpour seemed imminent. When the weather cleared, I mounted my bicycle and invited a younger boy to ride on my crossbar. He wasn't a team member, but he loved to play pitch and catch with me and wanted to watch our game. His extra weight slowed me down.

As I approached the intersection of Dominican and Pine Streets, I saw Cyril zoom by on Pine St. He was riding double on a motor bike with another player. I yelled to get Cyril's attention and pedaled as hard as I could to catch him. It was fruitless.

I headed to the park, where I learned that Cyril and the other boy were going to fetch another player, as we were one short of a lineup. What if they had come to get me instead? My house was much closer. What if I had not been carrying the extra weight? I would have crossed Pine St. in view of Cyril as he approached the intersection, and we would have all headed back to the park together. I would have been the player needed to complete the lineup.

Later, we learned that Cyril and the other player were struck by a truck at the corner of Zimple and Leonidas Streets. Cyril was killed instantly, and his teammate was seriously injured. We all went to the wake, and I can remember clearly the image of Mr. Ruff's impassive face and the tears streaming from his eyes. What if? What if? It is sobering to realize that everything that comes our way in life is contingent on something that came our way earlier, whether by our choice or not.

THE NEW ORLEANS PELICANS

NORD baseball helped form many major league baseball players. I wasn't one of them. Lloyd "Poochie" Pollet was on our team, and we all knew that his older brother was Howie Pollet, who was a three-time All Star, while pitching for the Cardinals and Pirates from 1941 to 1956. Another baseball star from New Orleans whose career in the majors overlapped Pollet's was Mel Parnell of Boston Red Sox fame. Both were All-Star lefties, who retired in 1956. Parnell managed the New Orleans Pelicans in 1959 and other farm clubs, before completing a broadcasting career with the Red Sox. Many years later, I interviewed Parnell in his home in the Lakeview section of New Orleans. In 2005, that section was inundated when three levees broke during Hurricane Katrina.

In those times, I was a huge fan of the New Orleans Pelicans baseball team. I couldn't afford to attend many games, but I listened to Red Andrews' radio broadcasts. Al Flair was a star first baseman and slugger for the Pelicans who had a brief career with the Boston Red Sox in 1941. Since Al lived with his parents just down the street from Mike Aymami, I paid him a visit. He called me "squirrel" (a reference to my overbite, I'm sure) and invited me to sit behind the Pelican dugout.

I brought an autograph book with me, and Al had all the players sign it for me. I don't know what I did with that book, but at the time, it thrilled me to no end to have it. "When I was a child I thought as a child, but when I became a man I put aside the things of a child." Once I got into a Pelican's game and had a seat just behind the barrier separating the higher-priced seats from the cheap seats. I was heckling the opposition team in my child's high-pitched voice, giving my best imitation of Woody the Woodpecker. When my voice began to weaken and grow hoarse, a Pelican fan passed a snowball to me through the barrier. "Keep it up, kid!" he exhorted.

THE TULANE GREEN WAVE

Back then, Tulane was a member of the SEC, and I was a fan of their football and basketball teams. In time, Tulane had to leave the SEC, as more and more academically poor athletes couldn't make the grade in the Tulane classroom. The other academically demanding private school member of the SEC, Vanderbilt, replaced Tulane as the perennial doormat of the conference, but they gradually improved.

The Tulane football players were housed apart from the student population. A paper carrier entered their dorm at the risk of being the butt of whatever prank they dreamed up. Once, they grabbed one of our carriers by the ankles and suspended him over the stairwell. As they shook the terrified boy, all the coins shook loose from his pockets and rained down on the lower floors. Collection took on a new meaning. The players thought that was great fun. "What evil lurks in the hearts of men? The shadow knows." I guess part of life is finding out after the fact.

While a paper boy, I remember going to Tulane stadium three times for football games. Tulane played its home games there on Saturday afternoons. Twice, one of my *Picayune* customers gave me a ticket. Both times, I had to finish my route responsibilities before going to the stadium and could only get there in time to see most of the second half.

I saw Southern California beat up on Tulane the one time. The other time, I got to watch the second half of a Sugar Bowl game. It was January 2, 1950. Oklahoma dominated LSU 35–0. I distinctly remember the All-American running back, Leon Heath, running toward my seat in the north end zone. He came through a gaping hole in the right side of the LSU defense and raced untouched for an 86-yard touchdown.

Beyond that, I only remember a long pass play. The pass was thrown by Darrell Royal, who went on to a distinguished college coaching career. The third time I went to Tulane stadium, I didn't have a ticket. I was able to enter the stadium after the game ended and waited outside the Alabama locker room to get a glimpse of quarterback Harry Gilmer. I walked beside him as he departed in his street clothes. I was struck by his diminutive size and remember how he appeared to be coming from a street fight. His face bore the bruises of a fierce battle. He was not in the mood for conversation, and I can't remember the exchange of a single word between us. Harry gave me the distinct impression that I was bothering him.

EARLY EXPOSURE TO FISHING

Our *Picayune* station manager, John Schuermann, occasionally piled his carriers into his car and took us canvassing. He would stop and unload us to cover targeted addresses, whose residents were non-subscribers. When we returned, we would be taken to a new location. We would knock on doors and solicit residents to subscribe to the *Picayune*.

It was my first experience as a door-to-door salesman. It was a very intimidating, but an educational experience for a shy 13-year-old boy like me. Try canvassing complete strangers of every stripe for any purpose, and you will learn a lot about human nature and yourself.

Once Mr. Schuermann did something my Dad never did. He took me fishing with one of his nephews, who was a young adult. We motored all over the waterways crisscrossing the Lake Catherine estuary in East New Orleans. I remember how cold it was when we were underway. I huddled down in the bow to stay warm. Mr. Schuermann's poor nephew was sick to his stomach the whole time. We came home with no fish, but I had a deepened appreciation for the goodness of Mr. Schuermann.

The only fishing I had done before was from the bank of the Mississippi or one of the lagoons in Audubon Park. Just to ride in a large skiff, powered by an outboard motor, was a thrill in itself. Our little aforementioned gang of "roofers" frequently took our cane poles to fish the lagoons of Audubon Park.

Anglers were required to purchase a license that was good for one day of fishing the stocked waters. We always skipped that step and went right to the fishing. We picked spots where we could see the warden coming in time to hide until he passed. When he continued on his predictable circuit, we returned to our fishing. We caught a lot of perch and a few turtles.

My Mom made delicious turtle soup. Once, we brought home about three dozen waterfowl eggs that we had collected from nests around the lagoons. Mom made us bring them back. The unborn ducklings they contained were too far along in their gestation process. Don't count your ducks before they hatch.

The ugliest thing I ever saw in the Audubon lagoons was the body of a woman. We watched the authorities retrieve her remains from one of our favorite fishing holes. The corpse was swollen and discolored. She was the first dead human I had ever seen. I had not as yet seen any at a wake. Little did I realize that I would see many more in my life. One was the body of a large black man sprawled on his back, just across the street from Fandel's Grocery. A pool of blood from a gunshot wound to his head spewed onto the sidewalk, as a crowd of curious onlookers gathered. I left before the police arrived. No, I was not the trigger man.

CHRISTMAS SPIRIT

One Christmas season, I got the idea to try to help a poor family, who lived in an old trailer home on the batture between the Corp of Engineers and Audubon Park. I had become aware of their plight while sub-carrying a paper route that included customers who lived along the batture. I enlisted the aid of our gang of "roofers."

We gathered half a dozen bags of groceries, used clothing, and toys and sneaked up on the trailer after dark. After knocking on the door, we left our gifts and hid nearby. When the gifts were gathered up and taken inside, we returned to peek through a window. From the darkness outside, we could see them without being seen and took great delight from their happy, smiling faces. It made us happy to help some folks who were less well off than ourselves.

Like the widow praised by Jesus, we certainly did not give of our "abundance." The meaning of the old adage that it is more blessed to give than to receive was brought home to us. It sure beat the feeling we had when we disposed of Mr. Bill's rotten eggs.

GROWING INDEPENDENCE

From the time I got my paper route, I never asked my parents for money. They just lived from paycheck to paycheck and would have had none to give. I never experienced the luxury of an allowance. Because of my job, I found a way to get some nice things for my Mom. I would usually find something advertised in the *Picayune*.

I remember two things that I bought from the Krauss department store on Canal St. The first item was a Kelvinator refrigerator (ah, no more emptying of the overflow pan!). I made monthly payments on it for about a year. My Mom and my sister Ann used it for about 40 years. The other memorable gift for Mom was a really nice set of dishes and silverware.

My earnings also provided me the opportunity to pay my way to De La Salle High School. I wanted to go to DLS, because some of my buddies from Mater Dolorosa were going there. My parents made it clear that I would have to attend public school if I didn't pay my own way to private school. This situation makes me reflect on another "what if?" given that my attendance at De La Salle had a profound influence on the direction my life would take.

MORE PERVERTS

Besides the great variety of people represented by my *Picayune* customers, I interacted from time to time with non-customers, for example, the aforementioned black kid who forced an "extra" from me. On two occasions, I ran into perverts. Once, a man engaged me in a conversation, while I was delivering my own route. He seemed interested in becoming a customer at first, but soon proposed that he take me to a movie. I pretended to be delighted to be treated to a show and agreed to meet him outside the Rexall Drug Store on St. Charles later that evening. I pretended naiveté, but I knew it wasn't a movie he wanted to show me. I was just a pre-puberty 13-year-old boy, but my Mom didn't raise any stupid children.

In hindsight, I might have invited my Mom to go on this date with me, given how she dealt with the pervert who made an inappropriate advance toward my sister at the Mecca. Instead, I told my station manager, a father figure to me. Mr. Schuermann took me to the police precinct on Magazine St near Napoleon Avenue.

A police captain friend of his interviewed me, and I was told to meet the pervert and get into his car. He assured me that the car would immediately be blocked and surrounded by his officers. I would be in no danger, and I needed to enter the vehicle for the police to make their case. I agreed and nervously waited outside Rexall's for the pervert who failed to show. I never saw him again.

I did ask Mr. Schuermann what the police would have done to the pervert had they caught him. He calmly told me in a matter-of-fact manner that they would have beaten him with a rubber hose. I hadn't heard of police brutality yet, but that seemed fair to me at the time. Probably less punitive than facing my Mom.

My other encounter with a pervert occurred while I was throwing a sub-route. As I was riding my bike along the banquette tossing papers onto the porches and stoops on my left, this guy steps out of a front door and drops his pants, revealing his naked privates. He was no further than eight feet from me as I rode past. Obviously, he had observed me before and knew what time I would be passing.

He was not a customer, but I decided to give him an "extra" the next time he exposed himself to me. I had pre-folded a paper into a tight hard cylinder, and, when the pervert popped out, I threw my missile at his prideful display of his genitals. He went down in a heap. His agonized cries didn't even slow me down as I sped away. I didn't report him to the police but followed a course of action similar to that employed by my Mom at the Mecca.

The situation just confirmed for me that "Momma knows best." Never get the police to do something for you that you can do yourself. I never saw him again, and that was fine with me. I wonder though if he would have preferred the "rubber hose." I know for sure he would not have wanted any part of facing my Mom.

BACK TO THE EAST BANK

We moved from the Shaw Dairy Farm in time for me to finish grammar school at Mater Dolorosa. My Aunt Martie had met and married a man named Jules. He owned a shotgun-double, located on the batture, and we rented one side. It was just upstream from the protection levee dividing Orleans and Jefferson Parishes. It was set on pilings and connected to the levee by a gangway. The land below the house was flooded each spring as the Mississippi absorbed the melting snows up north. Since I was living on the bank of the river, I talked my Dad into buying us a used skiff for 20 bucks. I fixed it up and painted the outside forest green and the inside sky blue. We had no motor for it, but I became quite the oarsman.

Once I took my sister and a friend three miles upstream to the Huey P. Long Bridge. Going out, I shadowed the bank where the current flowed more slowly. Coming back, I went with the current in the main channel. For part of the return trip, we were closer to the west bank than the east. That was due to the large bend in the river known as the Nine Mile Point.

Once, I took my skiff downstream about a mile to Momo's Beach. One of the older black kids wanted to swim across the river and asked me if I would accompany him in my skiff in case he tired. Well, he never was in the water long enough to get tired. As soon as he felt the power of the main current, he lost his nerve and panicked. I took him into the skiff and brought him back to Momo's Beach.

From that time on, I had a desire to swim the river myself. It wasn't until I was 30 that I made the swim. I did it at a point about three miles upstream from the Avondale Shipyards. Of course, I had to swim back to collect my clothes. As a result, the day I swam the Mississippi, I swam it twice. While living in Aunt Martie's house on the batture, I often rowed my skiff across and back twice a day, checking the trout lines I had set on the west bank. My house on the east bank was nearly directly across from the Shaw Dairy. Because that side of the river was sparsely populated, there was less chance of people raiding my trout lines.

I had heard many warnings about the dangers of the river, but none deterred me from either swimming or boating in it as I pleased. One of the dangers was real enough. Large ocean-going tankers and freighters plied its waters, and a boater or swimmer had to keep well out of their way and contend with their large wakes. The same held true for the long strings of barges powered by tugs.

I never saw anyone else rowing or swimming across the river. When we were swimming, we made sure to get to the edge of the water to frolic in the waves the large vessels would push ashore. Normally, the surface was like glass, and all one had to contend with was the current. About a half mile upstream from my house on the batture was a large wharf, where ships would occasionally dock. A pipeline ran from the dock over the levee to a plant that produced creosote.

We loved the "creosote wharf," as we called it. It gave us multiple diving platforms. The height of our dives varied from about 10 feet to 30 feet, depending on the stage of the river. The multi-level dock was anchored to groups of pilings cabled together. The tops of these pilings were the highest points we could access above the water. Lee Serio and I were the only two who dared to dive from them.

What if I had struck a log drifting unseen just below the surface? I wouldn't be writing these memoirs. My guardian angel must have been paid overtime.

Eventually, my Mom found out about our swimming at the Creosote Wharf and she put an end to it. My cousin, Donald Hanson, sustained a serious gash on his ankle when he stepped on a glass shard near the shore, and we had to enlist the aid of my Mom to dress the wound. Since Mom never did discover Momo's Beach, we continued to swim there.

DE LA SALLE HIGH SCHOOL

I began attending De La Salle High School in the fall of 1950, while still living on the batture. 1950–1951 was the second year of operation of this school, owned and operated by the religious order of men known informally as the Christian Brothers. The school began small in 1949 with just two classes of freshmen. My class swelled the student body to two sophomore classes and three freshmen classes.

There were two buildings. One was a three-story brick residence, whose upper floors housed the Brothers, and whose ground floor provided space for three freshmen classrooms, a chapel, and the principal's office. The other building was a two-story wood frame structure that housed the sophomore classrooms, along with equipment, lockers, and shower facilities for our P.E. classes and budding sports teams. The north section, which fronted on the 5300 block of St. Charles Avenue, was vacant then and used as practice fields. Within a few years, a modern, two-story, four-year high school for over 1,000 boys would be built on this front acreage. The wood-frame building would be replaced with a beautiful sports complex and gym. The brick structure would be totally occupied by a swelling faculty of Brothers.

The only way I ever traveled to De La Salle (DLS) was on my bike. Usually, two friends joined me along the way, and the three of us would peddle on to school. Sometimes, we vandalized cars parked along a narrow side street by simply allowing the end of an uncovered handlebar to slide against the side of the car. This maneuver produced a high-pitched grating sound and a long horizontal scratch on a door or fender.

Today, I would want to "kill" some kid if he did that to my car. Back then, we were too immature to see the pain we inflicted on the car owners. I can't undo the damage. I can only hope people had car insurance in those days.

It was about a four-mile ride from my house on the batture to DLS. I might have ridden the streetcar, which had a stop right in front of DLS, but I needed my bike to throw my paper routes after school. I was probably the only kid at DLS who paid his own tuition. DLS was smack dab in one of the most affluent sections of New Orleans. One of my older acquaintances from Mater Dolorosa, who had to repeat a few years of school, drove his own car to DLS.

I longed to play sports, but my job as a carrier for the *Picayune* precluded that. Neither could I participate in any extracurricular activities. Of course, during my time at DLS, the school only scheduled games with the freshman or junior varsities of other high schools. All that was left for me was my classes. I liked English and Spanish all right, but algebra was a real drag. It was the only class I ever failed in my entire academic career. I always copied the algebra homework of a classmate. By test time, I couldn't do the same problems we had been assigned for homework. I didn't pay attention, because I didn't think I'd ever be able to understand algebra.

I hadn't yet learned anything in school through logical reasoning, much less abstract thought. I did well enough to keep Mom off my back through grammar school by rote memory. As long as I was making Cs and Bs, she didn't push me. The only subject she demanded an A from me was conduct. "You may not be the smartest kid in school, but you can behave yourself," she warned.

My only shining academic moment in grammar school came when I finished first in a 4th grade competition in Sister Claire's class. We were given a list of all 48 states and the capital cities of each and told to take it home and learn it. My Mom went over that list with me, until she was satisfied I had it down pat.

A little over half of our class were girls and they invariably outperformed the boys. The smartest student in our class was a girl. Sister Claire had our entire class stand along the walls of our classroom and began asking each student, in turn, to supply the capital city of each state she called out.

You stayed in the line as long as you answered correctly. An incorrect answer returned you to your desk. It took a while, but finally the smartest student and I were the last two still standing. Then Sister Claire asked the girl to name a capital, and she got it wrong and left me all alone with a chance to win. Sister Claire asked me what was the capital of Missouri, and I remember how proud I was to answer "Jefferson City." It was my first academic "first" (and my last) in grammar school.

2

LAFAYETTE, LA: 1951–1955

MY VOCATION

One day at DLS, the entire student body was brought to the cafeteria to listen to a Christian Brother named Brother Ignatius. He was a missionary who taught at the Brothers school in Bluefields, Nicaragua. At the time, there were some 20,000 Brothers operating schools all over the world.

Brother Ignatius fascinated us with stories of his work and adventures. He spent his spare time roaming the rivers and jungles of his tropical environment. I was spellbound by his storytelling. In my child's eye, Nicaragua was a paradise.

This mindset was the beginning of my deciding that I would join the Brothers and become a missionary in Nicaragua. I did become a Christian Brother, but I never became a missionary. My joining the Brothers began when I walked up to Brothers Alban's desk just before homeroom and shyly asked, "Could I be one of you guys?" The shocked look on Brother Alban's face quickly faded into one of delighted surprise.

The Brothers had a formation program for candidates to their order that, at the time, began as early as high school. The high school program was called the Juniorate. It was followed by the Postulate (three months), Novitiate (one year), and the Scholasticate (college). Brother Alban began preparing me to enter the Juniorate at the beginning of my sophomore year.

My Mom didn't object to my joining the Brothers, explaining, "It's your life to live." I can't remember any reaction on the part of my Dad. This situation reminds me of how my Mom handled a threat I made when I was about five years old. Unhappy about something she did, I told her I was leaving home and started for the door at

310 Cherokee. She said, "Wait a minute. Let me make you a peanut butter and jelly sandwich in case you get hungry." Now that gave me pause, and I decided not to leave home. My Mom had restrained me with a simple thought.

In hindsight, the reaction of my Mom and the non-reaction of my Dad to my joining a religious order of men were a bit strange. My Mom never went to Mass, except as part of first communion, confirmation, or graduation ceremonies, but she saw to it that my sister and I went to Mass every Sunday and Holy Day. With one exception, my Dad never went to church period. The one exception was the time he wandered into the Negro church across from Bill's Grocery on Adams St., and, I guess, church attendance doesn't count for much if you're drunk.

MAGNOLIA (JUNIORATE AND NOVITIATE)

My entering the formation program of the Brothers was a huge change in my life. I had never travelled more than about 30 miles from New Orleans (Covington, LA). The only times I slept outside of my own house were when I visited overnight with my cousins on Burdette St. or the one time my Mom and I visited with the family of one of her friends from the LaFitte housing project. We stayed at a camp on Lake Ponchartrain in eastern New Orleans (Little Woods). We kids slept on the wraparound, screened porch, lulled to sleep by the lapping of the waves a few feet below the camp.

Now, I would be attending a boarding school, some 150 miles west of New Orleans in Lafayette, LA. No more paper route. I would also be introduced to a new mode of transportation. I would take a train ride, my first, to Lafayette.

My Mom was provided with a checklist of items I would need. All of my clothing had to be stenciled with my name. She put it all in one of my Dad's old sea bags and saw me off from the train stop on Carrollton Ave.

Early in that trip, I crossed the Huey P. Long Bridge for the first time in a train. I had crossed it many times in my Dad's old Hudson and twice on my bicycle. Some friends and I rode our bikes over the bridge to reach Waggoner's Pond, a great fishing hole near the end of the west terminus of the train trestle.

I took pride in that I was able to make it over the bridge without dismounting my bike, while all of my companions had to get off and walk their bikes to the summit 153 feet above the river. The traffic bridge is 1.5 miles long. The train portion is nearly 4.5 miles long. I probably had as strong a pair of legs as any 12-year-old kid has ever had.

Lafayette, today, looks like a completely different town from the one that greeted me as I arrived in August of 1951. One of the Brothers met me, and we drove out to what would be my home for the next four years. Most of the rural pastureland we drove through then is now suburbs and shopping centers. Breaux Bridge road passed the impressive buildings of the Seminary for the diocese of Lafayette, and then a right turn brought us onto the long oak-lined entrance road that led to the buildings that housed the houses of formation of the New Orleans-Santa Fe District of the Christian Brothers.

After about 200 yards, the entrance road entered an oval shaped road that circled the Juniorate and Novitiate buildings. These were separate brick buildings connected by a sidewalk. There was a wooden structure outside the oval that housed the "Ancients," viz., the retired Brothers. Many of these were still active in roles supportive of those still teaching. Those who were able worked hard to provide for the needs of themselves and the 60 or so young men in formation. All prayed for the educational mission of the Brothers and for their benefactors.

The administrative office, for the district was in the Novitiate Building. From this office, Brother Richard Arnandez, who held the title of Visitor, oversaw the operation of schools in New Orleans, Covington, Franklin, New Iberia, Lafayette, and Lake Charles, LA, as well as Galveston and El Paso, TX and Santa Fe, NM and Denver, CO. The property was a working cattle and crop farm of some 50 acres. This community of young and old was almost completely self-supporting. There was much to do, and everyone pitched in according to his ability.

The Novitiate building was the largest. This beautiful brick structure had three stories. The first floor contained a commercial-sized kitchen, a scullery, and separate dining rooms (they were called refectories) for the Ancients, Novices and Postulants, and Juniors. A beautiful chapel, which was shared by all, was located on the second floor. The classroom for the Postulants and Novices, along with a few private rooms, infirmary, and offices for Brother Visitor and the Director of Novices, were on this floor. The third floor was one large dormitory for the Postulants and Novices. It was "off limits" to all others. The Novitiate was, in essence, a monastery, and there was only rare and minimal contact between its members and the rest of the community.

My new home for my three remaining high school years was a two-story brick building. The first floor had faculty offices along one side of a broad hallway and classrooms along the other side. At one end, a flight of steps led downward into a gym that ran the width of the building. At the other end of the hall was a commons room that contained desks for each Junior.

This area served as a study hall and as a place of general assembly. Our Director, Brother Daniel, regularly addressed the entire student body from a desk on a raised platform in this room. Occasionally, we were treated to a movie here. The adjacent room was used for all of the freshman classes and as a barber shop. The second floor had a dormitory for freshmen and sophomores at one end and another for juniors and seniors at the other. Our faculty was composed entirely of professed Brothers who had private rooms scattered throughout the building. Of course, all of the buildings had the usual complement of restrooms, shower rooms, and lockers.

In addition to the frame one-story building that housed the "Ancients," there were a number of small structures on the property. One housed our laundry. All of our clothes were cleaned and folded for pickup in this building. A shed in the back was used to prepare food for cooking. On a number of occasions, we had to kill and pluck live chickens and peel a lot of potatoes. We also had a print shop. The type had to be set by hand. Behind the print shop, a water tower rose high into the air. Water was pumped from our own well. A large barn was located in the pasture on the left side of the entrance road. We stored the hay we raised in the loft. There were also a few sheds used to store tractors and other farm equipment.

Our school was named De La Salle Normal. The "Normal" part was from a French word that described a school that trained teachers. The formal name of the religious order we sought to join is Brothers of the Christian Schools. In Latin, this moniker translates to "Fratres Scholarum Christianarum," which is why the Brothers added "FSC" after their name. We joked that FSC stood for food, shelter, and clothing. Of course, we raised, harvested, and cooked the food, maintained our shelter, and even sewed the habits we wore from the start of our novitiate.

While our formation was built around prayer, study, and manual labor, we also played hard. We had our own swimming pool, tennis and basketball courts, track, baseball, and football/soccer fields. When I think back on those days, I can see that the program was intended to develop a well-rounded person, an holistic product.

Most of our sports competition was intramural, but we occasionally played non-league games against other schools. Because we were not part of any athletic association, we did not compete for any titles or championships. I recall that we defeated one football district champion 30–0 and another 25–0. We had the custom of playing the "cush-cush bowl" on New Year's Day. Two teams were chosen from among those wishing to play. The teams would be named after the two teams in the Sugar Bowl and we would have at it. We played for the love of the sport. No athletic awards. We had a sports page in our award-winning monthly school paper that reported on our activities.

School track-and-field event records were kept and they provided goals to be realized. I made it my goal to break one record each year and succeeded to set school records in the high jump, pole vault, and 440-yard dash. I remember leading all swimmers and divers at one of our swim meets with 19 points. I was the catcher on our baseball team from my first year through graduation.

What I remember most is that I did not have much success throwing out players trying to steal second. What I came to realize was my greatest achievement (in my opinion) was never noted by anyone. During my senior year, I was never out of a football game for a single snap or kickoff. I played center on offense and linebacker on defense and was a member of all our special teams. I was never on the sideline, while the clock was running.

Our regular weekday schedule was rigid. We were roused from our beds by the clanging of a large hand bell and the exhortation, "Live, Jesus, in our hearts!" We responded "Forever!" That was the last thing we were allowed to say for quite some time. In our normal routine, there was no such thing as "small" talk. Silence was the rule.

On a strictly timed schedule, we gathered for morning prayer and then Mass. We went to breakfast after Mass and then went to work assignments. Someone had to take care of the dishes and sweep and dust our buildings. After work assignments, we went to our classes required by the State of Louisiana to earn a diploma. We followed a college prep curriculum to which was added instruction in Catholicism.

There were other extras thrown into our formation. Brother Daniel, our director, gave uplifting spiritual reflections to all of us in the commons room. He also gave us weekly 10-minute lessons in etiquette, constructed around passages from Emily Post. Our meals were an opportunity to practice dining etiquette. If we broke table etiquette, we were sure to hear about it.

We were also given instruction in singing. We had one of the best choirs in the state. Everyone in our school was a part of it. We learned to sing the liturgy of each Sunday and Holy Day in the beautiful Gregorian chant and added in three and four part motets by the masters. We were invited to give concerts in a variety of venues.

We had a 15-minute recess from class in mid-morning and went outside to relax (talk) and play. We had another break after lunch, before attending our afternoon classes. We practiced whatever sport was in season after our last class, before cleaning up for supper. After supper, we had study hall in the commons, said our night prayers, and went to bed. In mid-week we would go on a two- to three-hour hike in the afternoon. Pastures, woods, and swamps stretched from our back property line all the way to the Vermillion River. The only trouble we could get into was to get lost or perhaps get bitten by a water moccasin. That never happened, although Emmet Sinitiere was bitten through a hand as we captured a wild raccoon.

Our meals were very different from those I had in the DLS school cafeteria. After the blessing, we sat down in assigned groups of four for our meals. You would eat with the same three guys for a month, before new groupings were posted. We all had turns at bringing the platters of food to the tables, before sitting down to eat. At one end of the refectory, our entire faculty of five Brothers sat at one long table set on a riser, which gave them a clear view of us. Brother Director sat in the middle and directed things with a small bell. We ate in silence, using hand signals to get what we couldn't politely reach.

There was a lectern, and one of us was assigned to read a few verses from *"The Imitation of Christ"* by Thomas a Kempis or a summary of the life of the saint of the day. Another boy would then read a little about the sacraments or the liturgy. Then, we would take turns reading from a book Brother Daniel had selected for our entertainment. I can remember listening to "Kon-Tiki," "Cheaper by the Dozen," and a biography of Mickey Mantle.

Brother Daniel would ring his bell to signal a change of readers. When a few had finished eating, Brother Daniel would call on one of these to read until all had finished. This practice of reading during meals did more than just introduce new information to us. It helped us learn to read aloud to an audience. As teachers, this attribute would be a part of our stock in trade. Believe me, it was, initially, a very intimidating experience for shy little me to stand and read to the entire student body and faculty.

I'll never forget a reading (one of my first) I did entitled "The Holy Oils." When I read the title, Brother Daniel interrupted, "The Holy What?" I said in my New Orleans accent, "The Holy *Earls*." He corrected me, "No, Johnny, that's *Oils*." I replied, "That's what I said, *Earls*." This Abbott and Costello routine was repeated several times, before I was replaced. I had no idea what everyone was laughing about. Later, Donald Mouton, who was a class ahead of me, took me aside, and taught me how to properly pronounce the word, *oil*. My accent at the time was ninth-ward New Orleans, sort of like Brooklyn with a drawl. The Juniors from New Mexico had Spanish accents. Most were from towns in Cajun country, and they added the distinct Cajun accent to the mix.

Brother Daniel, our director, is one of the finest persons I have ever known. He was totally devoted to our spiritual, intellectual, and physical development. He was a strict disciplinarian, but always evenhanded and fair. He set a good example with his piety and work ethic. He led the way in keeping the grounds of "Magnolia," as our property was referred to, groomed and beautiful.

The area within the oval that contained the two main buildings was beautifully landscaped, with neatly manicured lawns and plantings. There were several shrines spaced along the outside of the oval. There was an oak-lined lane that ran tangent to the oval on the far side of the novitiate building. It led to the cemetery, where most of the district's deceased Brothers were interred. This plot was enclosed by a page fence and set among pine trees. There were groves of pecan trees and rows of persimmon trees, whose nuts and fruits complemented our diet.

Brother Daniel organized us into the various work crews required to manage an operation such as ours. The older, more experienced boys led the younger ones. The crews were reformed every month so that, over time, everyone would learn to do everything necessary to support our community. Brother John ran the large-scale farming operation. From time to time, he would call upon our labor pool, especially when hay was harvested.

His major responsibility was the herd of Charolais beef cattle, a very unique breed that originated in France, the country of origin of the Christian Brothers. Our Magnolia herd was one of the first to be brought (smuggled via Mexico) into the states. We had one 2200-lb bull that knocked a 2800-lb bull through a metal fence.

Once we were all engaged to build a large concrete slab that provided the surface for both tennis and basketball courts. Until then, these courts were dirt. To get the job done, each class was released, in turn, to work a shift. A progress report was posted, which showed which class had laid the most concrete. This practice introduced the element of competition between freshmen, sophomores, juniors, and seniors and led to class pride, which served to grease the wheels of production.

My sophomore class came out first. Our physics teacher directed the operation. We had three trucks next to the construction site that held loose gravel, sand, and bags of concrete powder. Some shoveled gravel, and some sand. Some toted the bags of concrete. All three ingredients (plus water) were mixed in a set ratio in a portable concrete mixer. From the mixer, the wet concrete was conveyed by wheelbarrow to the forms. Every portion of this process involved heavy lifting, and everyone literally had to "carry his weight." We missed some formal classes, while on release to work on the courts, but we learned some valuable life lessons that were just as important. The whole project was done in just a couple of weeks.

On Saturdays, we did some deep cleaning. All of the wood floors were swept and oil mopped. The furniture in the refectories was moved out, and the tiled floors swept, mopped, waxed, and polished. The long-tiled corridors got the same treatment. The chapel was made ready for our Sunday High Mass. We practiced to perfection the chants and hymns that we would sing.

We gathered in the commons, where Brother Daniel publicly announced our academic grades for the past week. For each class, he started with the worst student and worked his way up to the best. I led my class all three years and graduated as its top student.

We all followed the exact same schedule, which put me in the situation where I had to take Algebra II without ever having passed Algebra I. I managed that with no problem, thanks to my new environment, which provided me with the structure and motivation I had never previously known. We normally enjoyed a game or a hike on Saturday afternoons, but sometimes, we would borrow a school bus from Cathedral High (a Brothers school in town) and visit the campuses of one of the four Brothers schools from Franklin, LA to Lake Charles, LA.

We usually prayed the Rosary on the way out and back, but that left us plenty of time to talk, joke around, and sing. Typically, the Brothers, who operated the host school, feted us and arranged for some fun entertainment. Sometimes, the school faculty or one of their school teams would play basketball or baseball against our varsity. On an outing to Hanson Memorial in Franklin, LA, a large group of the Brothers' students put on a minstrel show for us—black faces and all.

Sundays were days of rest highlighted by our High Mass. Everything from the vestments, flowers, and singing was first class. We had some significant blocks of free time. Most of us read, played a musical instrument, or engaged in a hobby.

I usually had some wild animal "pets" that I kept in an outbuilding. My Mom and my Aunt Billie shipped me a large cage they built themselves. Over the years, I had dormice, flying squirrels, raccoons, and an opossum.

Once, I trapped a cardinal (a red bird) in one of my traps and threw him in with my possum who immediately ate him. At vespers, we chanted the verse "Brethren, be sober and watch because your adversary, the Devil, goeth about seeking whom he may devour." From that day on, one of our juniors would chant his own version of the verse when we checked on the possum. "Red bird, be sober and watch because your adversary, the possum, goeth about seeking whom he may devour." The kid had a weird but clever sense of humor.

I also killed a number of water moccasins on my hikes in the woods. Once, I paused the group I was leading through the boonies to take their picture. Without looking, I took some steps backwards to frame the photo. After snapping the picture, I turned and spotted an angry moccasin coiled to strike me with my next step. I owe so much to my guardian angel. I took to mailing the fangs of moccasins to a friend in the Scholasticate, who traded them for rattlesnake fangs. This young Brother from New Iberia, LA was nicknamed "T-Boy," a pretty common moniker for Cajun boys. I can't remember his religious name, but we both loved the wilderness.

There was one thing that Brother Daniel insisted we do every Sunday. We had to write home. This practice not only kept us close with family, but it also developed our letter-writing skills. My Mom and I traded letters for years.

Brother Daniel had the infirmarian measure and record our heights and weights every month. There were doctors and dentists in Lafayette who would treat us pro bono. They were former students who appreciated the education they received at a Brothers school.

We had no TV, video games, or computers. Our family was allowed a limited number of Sundays on which they could come to Magnolia and spend the day with us. We were only allowed to go home for a few weeks in August. I am convinced that the separation from my family only made our hearts grow fonder. Sometimes, we don't appreciate something until it's taken from us.

From time to time, we gathered in the commons after supper and had some special entertainment. This situation usually occurred on a special feast day. Brother Daniel would rent a movie, which would be projected on a pull-down screen at the head of the room. There was always the intermission necessitated by changing the reels. Sometimes, we had a talent show. Jo-Jo Bertrand, a Cajun from St. Martinsville, could crack us up just reading the phone book. We had one guy who came out and did a great imitation of Liberace. I staggered out pretending to be drunk and sang in a slurred voice, "I got drunk last night, dear Mother! I got drunk the night before. But if you say so, dear Mother, I'll never get drunk anymore!" I then slurred through a lame joke about a woman who came to a party wearing gownless evening straps. At that point, Brother Daniel gave me the hook. Next act.

SUMMER VACATION TIME

Following every academic year but our senior one, we would take enhancement courses during June and July, before going home to spend August with our families. We also spent a week at the campus of St. Paul's High School in Covington, LA. It had all the recreational facilities of our own Magnolia home in Lafayette, and we were allowed much more time to recreate ourselves. Because the regular student body of St. Paul's was gone for the summer, the facilities provided for their boarding students were ours to use.

When I returned home in August, my Mom had moved into the small house she purchased at 140 Berkeley Ave. in Harahan. My Mom's brother, Uncle Chris, built an extra room onto the shotgun house, giving it an L shape. I learned a bit about hanging, floating, finishing, and painting sheetrock, as I gave my uncle a hand. Over the years, I painted that house several times. I also removed two large trees.

Another of my Mom's brothers, Uncle William, worked for an oil company out of Venice, and one weekend, he arranged for me to go out into the Gulf of Mexico on a shrimp boat. There was a boy about my age who also went along for the trip. We left in the afternoon and trawled until dark. My friend and I separated out the shrimp from the crabs, catfish, and stingrays.

After dark, the captain anchored the boat under a large flare near a rig. The surface under the ring of light emitted by the flare was alive with speckled and white trout, feeding on the bait fish and insects attracted by the light. The other boy and I used cane poles to haul in trout after trout until we finally retired about 2 a.m.

At daybreak, we were back to work trawling for shrimp. Uncle William picked me up at the dock late that afternoon. I brought home 55 trout and a hamper of crabs. One memory that stands out from my trip to Venice was seeing a man with a paper bag full of alligator skins exchanging them for $12 a foot.

DEVELOPING WRITING SKILLS

In my first year, my English teacher, Brother Leo, required our class to write an essay that would be submitted into a competition open to every high school student enrolled in all of the Brothers schools in the New Orleans-Santa Fe District. The essay had to make an argument that St. Joseph was the greatest saint. I built my essay around the fact that God had entrusted the greatest responsibility to St. Joseph by entrusting His Son and Mother to his care.

A month or so after our essays were submitted, I learned that I had won first place. One of our seniors placed second. I learned of my triumph as we were having dinner in the refectory. Brother Daniel rang his bell and called me up to the head table to tell our assembly of the honor I had brought to our school. He presented me with a small statue of St. Joseph. I was one proud, but still shy, little kid. At least, by then, I could pronounce "oil" with the best of them.

Our teachers had a knack for connecting classroom instruction to real-life situations. While I was one of his sophomore English students, for example, Brother Leo recruited me to proofread a book he was authoring on the life of St. John Baptist De La Salle, the founder of the Christian Brothers. This assignment was an indirect way of improving my spelling, vocabulary, and grammar, as well as developing my knowledge and appreciation for our order and its founder.

Brother Leo also had me write articles for our school newspaper. Seeing these published boosted my confidence in my developing writing skills. One thing then led to another. In my junior and senior years, I became the feature editor for our award-winning school paper. The "Junior," as it was titled, received the top rating given (superior) by the state every year it was published. My duties included selecting articles and writers, proofreading and blocking out the feature page, and keeping the moderator and writers happy.

One of the most important things I learned was how to work under pressure and meet a deadline. Once, our faculty moderator rejected an article I had written just 30 minutes before he was to take the proofs to the printer. Needless to say, I was quite upset, but I channeled my anger into writing an article to fit the space planned for the rejected article. It went out on time. I had written about my experience of having a last-minute rejection of an article. The moderator liked it. He thought of a title for the article on the way to the printer.

DEBATE AND SPEECH

In my junior year, I partnered with Donald Mouton, a senior, on our debate team. Debating helped us develop our poise and speaking skills, but, perhaps most importantly, it also taught us to think on our feet. Rote memory of data was not enough to refute the arguments thrown at us by our opponents. For one thing, you never knew beforehand what challenges they would propose.

Debating was only one activity of our speech team. We also competed in extemporaneous speaking and discussion competitions. In extemporaneous speaking, you would be given a random topic and required to prepare a short timed speech in, you got it, a short time. In discussion competition, you would be assigned to a group composed of students from other schools and given a series of topics to discuss. Each student would take a turn at chairing the group.

Once, we were driven to Northwestern University in Nagotoches, LA for one competition, but all I remember was we left early in the morning, and the fog was like pea soup, making for a scary ride. We experienced another scary ride one rainy night on a trip to New Iberia for a practice debate with St. Peter's High School. On the way, our driver, Brother Raphael, slid our car off the road and, after doing a 360 in the wet grass, got us safely stopped. After getting back on the road, an embarrassed Brother Raphael swore us to silence regarding the side trip.

St. Peter's was a Christian Brothers school and one of their faculty, Brother Edward, moderated our debate. The topic for that year was "Should NATO Form a Federal Union?" Donald and I had the affirmative side.

The debate was so uncompetitive that Brother Edward kept dozing off. The story was told that Brother Edward once went to a doctor and complained of his insomnia, "Doctor, I sleep alright at night and in the morning, but in the afternoon, I just toss and turn." One of our opponents had a very thick Cajun accent. I remember two expressions he employed that had us in stitches afterwards. It would have been uncharitable to laugh while an opponent had the floor. He actually used these two phrases: "You don hafta be a mathamechanical genus..." and "...da *pheasants* in Russia would revolt."

We faced off against the best high school debate teams in the State at the State Debate Tournament that was held in February of 1953 in Lafayette. A Brothers School, Cathedral High, hosted the day-long event. Starting early on a Saturday morning, Donald and I won our way to the finals that evening and defeated the DLS team from New Orleans for the championship.

My triumph was sweetened for me by the fact that Lawrence Trahant from my old neighborhood was a member of that DLS team. Lawrence was a scholarly nerd who saw himself as superior to other kids, especially anyone who would stoop to engage in playing sports.

It was a proud moment that I didn't get to savor. As soon as the debate ended, one of the Brothers took me aside to inform me that my Dad had passed away. It was arranged that I ride back to New Orleans with the DLS team.

The funeral remains a blur in my mind, but I remember one thing clearly. Riding in the funeral procession, I told my Mom that I would leave the Juniorate and return home to help her. I was only 16-years-old, but I was determined to do whatever was necessary to support my Mom. My Mom looked me in the eye and calmly said, "No. If I have to mop floors, you will stay where you are." She knew that I was in a better place than I had ever been. Aside from our Lord and Savior, only my future wife would show me greater love than this.

Subsequently, my Mom got a job in the food services department at Oschner Hospital. She saved every penny she could and bought herself a house in Harahan about five miles from Oschner. She caught the Jefferson Highway bus, just a block from her house, and it brought her right to the hospital.

"DOWN TO EARTH" INSTRUCTION

In my senior year, Brother Luke was our trigonometry instructor. He had us survey all 50 acres of Magnolia and map all of its boundaries and structures to scale. He manned the surveying tripod and transit, and we handled the measuring tapes and surveying poles. We went over every foot of the property and recorded each measurement on a notepad. Many of the distances had to be derived from measured lengths and angles by using trig formulas we had learned in class.

Each of us was partnered with another classmate, and each pair had to present our final plat or survey plan for grading. I was partnered with a senior from Santa Fe. The scale we employed was such that we had to carefully scotch-tape many sheets of blank paper together in order to accommodate our survey. The plat we submitted was about five feet by five feet when we unrolled it. Now, how "down to earth" can classroom instruction get?

Another project was completed about a year after I went to Magnolia. In the field beyond the Novitiate building, a wide circular trench was dredged to form a fishing pond, with a small island in its center. It covered about two acres. The state stocked it with perch and largemouth bass. One day, we had a fishing rodeo for the entire student body. I took first place in the "most fish caught" category by landing over 50 perch. I had gained a lot of experience catching perch in the lagoons of Audubon Park.

I took my first plane ride while in the Juniorate. It was a reward offered by Brother Visitor for some academic achievement I can't even remember. The plane was a small one, in the single-engine genre of a Piper Cub. We took off from the small Lafayette Airport and flew around a few minutes. What I mostly remember was the noise of the engine. It drowned out any verbal communication with the pilot.

THE ANCIENTS

Some of the Ancients seemed to be just that. The majority of them had been exiled from France when the government became anti-religious and especially anti-Catholic. They then set up schools in Mexico, until that government too began to persecute Catholics. Some priests and religious were executed for their faith. So, early in the 20th century, these Brothers were uprooted again and developed the New Orleans-Santa Fe province in the United States.

These Brothers were up in years, and many were in ill health, and some quite senile. While French was their native tongue, their years in Mexico and the United States had made them proficient in Spanish and English as well. Brother Adolph demonstrated this linguistic background when he would call Punch, a boxer dog who was the Magnolia mascot, with the tri-lingual command, "Come ici, Perro!" When he crossed paths with one of us, he would chuckle, wag his finger, and say, "You think you are wise, but you are otherwise!"

Another Ancient, Brother Theophile, was the community tailor. He made all the habits for the Brothers of the province. He had a beautiful voice and, from time to time, sang solo and a cappella a beautiful hymn honoring St. La Salle. The opening lyrics were "Honor a toi, glorieux De La Salle, apotre des enfants et guardian de la foi." French was the official language of the Institute and a unifying influence to its members worldwide. It was the language we all studied at Magnolia.

THE NOVITIATE

Candidates for the Novitiate arrived on two tracks. Young men seeking admission directly from the outside world served six months as postulants, before they would begin the one year Novitiate. Young men coming from the Juniorate only served three months as postulants. We had a head start in the practice of prayer, study, labor, and discipline that defined life in the Novitiate.

When my class graduated De La Salle Normal in mid-May of 1954, we crossed over to the Novitiate building, where we remained in residence until mid-August of 1955. We knew the Novices who had graduated from the Juniorate in 1953. These men would be leaving in mid-August to enter the Scholasticate located in Santa Fe, NM. On August 15th, we would receive the habit and start our year of novitiate.

The departing novices would attend St. Michael's College, while continuing their religious formation. The men who had entered the novitiate without any Juniorate training were new to us. These two or three novices would be with us until they left for Santa Fe in December. They exercised a sort of seniority over us, as they had already received the habit and assumed their religious names.

One of these individuals had entered after going to high school in Santa Fe, NM. This newly minted Brother had what I took to be a rather haughty attitude and took it upon himself to correct any little deviation from the rules on my part. One of the customs that we practiced, while dining in the refectory, involved standing up from the table, facing the crucifix, and saying a short silent prayer, if one caused a distraction. Now, I quickly observed, that it was left to the individual to decide if the disturbance warranted this act of repentance.

My nemesis, however, took it upon himself to make this decision for me. At meals, he sat directly across from me and the head table was only an arm's length away. At this table, sat Brother Gabriel, the Director of the Novitiate and Brother Edward, the Sub-Director. Brother Gabriel observed everything, and he was well aware of how I was being treated. For one thing, when a platter of food was placed beside me, this novice would (silently, of course) demand I pass the food to him before I took any. If I made the slightest sound manipulating my fork, spoon, cup, or whatever, he would sternly signal me to rise and say the customary prayer.

This scenario went on for about a week, until one morning at breakfast, I did something on the spur of the moment. One of the servers, wearing an oven mitt, started to place a platter of scrambled eggs beside me. Not realizing the platter was hot, I took it in my left hand.

Brother Julian was already gesturing with both hands for me to pass him the eggs. Showing no reaction to the blistering pain, I did so. Brother Julian dropped the platter onto his place setting, causing a great clamor. The table in front of Brother Julian was strewn with broken dishes, spilled coffee, and scrambled eggs.

All eyes turned toward the noise. After he stewed a few seconds in the deafening silence, I calmly signaled him to stand up and say the customary prayer. He did so, his face red as a beet. Out of the corner of my eye, I observed Brother Gabriel, an embodiment of gravity, struggling to keep a straight face. The corners of his mouth quivered, as he struggled to suppress a smile. That was the only time I ever gave the signal to stand to anyone, and the totally humiliated novice never gave it to me again or demanded that I pass food to him first. Brother Gabriel never said a word to me about the incident. His silence was his tacit approval.

I struggled mightily to adapt to the Novitiate life and would have quit after a few weeks, but Brother Gabriel was able to persuade me to continue. For one thing, I have always found it hard to refuse anyone. For another, Brother Gabriel excused me from some of the more difficult sessions and assigned me to a special job. I was given a .22 caliber rifle and told to shoot blue jays.

The squawking of these birds disturbed the Brothers (especially Brother Sub-Director), as they strolled along the oak-canopied lanes on the grounds in meditation, prayer, and study. I had no idea what was done after I moved on, but this welcome distraction helped ease me into the routine of religious life. Soon, I was following the program to the max, and the blue jays were happy again. Not so much Brother Sub.

A PERFECT SCORE

In the novitiate, we studied five different subjects, and we were graded on a scale of 1 to 10 for each. Scoring a 10 in any of the five was rare, akin to scoring a 10 in Olympic gymnastics. Most of the tests, which were written, required essay responses. One was performance-based, as we had to sing a liturgical piece solo in Gregorian chant. We were accustomed to singing the liturgy together, but it was intimidating to sing solo. Any little slip-up stood out like a sore thumb.

We received some college credits in dogma, church history, and French. After we had studied for months, Brother Visitor himself came to our commons room to announce the grades we scored on our final exam. After all the scores had been announced, except mine, Brother Visitor paused. His face revealed both his surprise and pleasure. I had scored a perfect 10 on all five of my tests, a result never before achieved in novitiate annals.

I had achieved a perfect score on a standardized physics test as a senior in high school, but this accomplishment was a much more difficult achievement. I don't know if anyone ever repeated it, but I was proud to have been the first. It was this same visitor, Brother Richard, who arranged for an "angel" to contribute $50 a month toward the cost of my formation. My angel was a prominent architect in New Orleans and a former Christian Brother, who remained anonymous to me for years.

AN UNINVITED VISITOR

Brother Visitor came to our commons room in the novitiate from time to time to give us a conference, a sort of extended reflection on some spiritual topic. We all knelt for a short prayer, after Brother Visitor mounted the riser at the head of the room. As one of the novices rose, he observed that there was a snake curled up under his desk and raised his hand. "What is it, Brother?" Brother Visitor inquired. "There's a snake under my desk." Brother Visitor's eyes grew large as saucers, and his mouth gaped wide.

I said "I'll get it," and raced to collect the intruder. Scooping up the snake, I said, "It's only a king snake." Brother Visitor put his hand over his breast and let out this great sigh of relief and said "Thank God it wasn't a rattler." In that moment, Brother Visitor showed me his effeminate side. I released the snake outside and returned to my desk.

Brother Visitor gave his conference, and we continued with our next exercise. Talk about unintended consequences. I had put that snake in one of the drawers of my former tormentor's desk, looking forward to hearing him scream out loud in his beautiful tenor voice. Somehow, it got out, and my plan went for naught. No one ever asked how the snake got into the room, and I wasn't telling.

BROTHER CLARENCE AND THE DEAD CHICKEN

Once, a group of four of us were cleaning chickens in the shed behind the laundry. I was teamed with Brother Clarence. He would take a live chicken from its cage and, holding its feet with one hand and pinning its wings with the other, place it on its side on the wooden table (chopping block). I would stroke the bird soothingly with my left hand to calm it down. When the chicken relaxed, I would quickly behead it with a hatchet. It was Brother Clarence's job to immediately swing the chicken into a barrel behind him. There, the bird would flop around for a few seconds and bleed out. Well, I chopped, and Brother Clarence flung the chicken toward the barrel. The headless fowl hit the side of the barrel, fell to the concrete floor, and began to run aimlessly about, with Brother Clarence in hot pursuit. We forever after teased him that he couldn't catch a dead chicken.

HABITS AND NEW NAMES

During the first three months in the novitiate, we wore our regular clothes, but looked forward to August 15th, the Feast of the Assumption of Our Blessed Mother into Heaven. This occasion was the day when those who were accepted would receive and begin to wear the habit of the Christian Brothers. We would also be given a new name. We had some choice in the selection of our religious name.

The habit of the Christian Brothers

At the time, two names followed the title "Brother." The first name had to begin with either A, B, or C, while the second name could be that of any saint. The combination had to be unused, or unique. When I took the habit, I became Brother Christopher Patrick, F.S.C. From then on, I was Brother Patrick to my confreres. Some years later, all of the Brothers began to use their secular names to simplify dealing with civic authorities. Had I remained with the order, I would now be Brother John Hanson.

NOVITIATE SPORTS

We novices played sports games among ourselves but had no regular team. These pickup games were judiciously allowed to give us a break from the rigid discipline of a monastic-style schedule. We did play one football game against a group of non-novices. It was the custom to play the novices against the Juniorate team around All Saints Day.

Most of us novices had played with our former classmates who formed the Juniorate team, so we didn't really think of them as an "outside" group. Of course, they practiced daily under their coach, Brother Richard, who used to coach us, and they played a schedule against true "outside" groups. The year that our novices played the juniors, we were heavy underdogs. The talk was that they were the best team that the juniors ever fielded.

Our Director, Brother Gabriel, appeared detached, but he really wanted us to win. I could tell because he put aside some time for us to practice. My teammates selected me as captain, and Brother Gabriel left it to me to coach our team. This situation put me in a position to prove something to Brother Richard, my former coach. Under him, I played center and linebacker. I begged him to give me a crack at playing offense, as a passer, runner, and/or receiver, since I thought I would be more valuable to our team in that role. He wouldn't even give me a tryout so that he could judge for himself if I was right or wrong.

Well, now I was the coach, so I put myself in the position of quarterback playing out of the shotgun, which allowed me to both pass and run the ball. I designed some plays for us that we had never run under Brother Richard. To keep these plays secret from Brother Richard, Brother Gabriel bused us to St. Martinville State Park for me to install and practice them with our Novice team.

At one of our practices, my former nemesis challenged me on the blocking technique I was teaching. I said nothing, but huddled the offense and ran a play at him (he was playing defensive end). I handed the ball off and ran interference for the ballcarrier. The end stepped in to make the stop, and I knocked him on his derriere … a pancake block. It was the first time I had to straighten him out, since I handed him the hot platter in the refectory. Similar to before, I did so without saying a word to him. Again, he turned red as a beet, but kept his mouth shut.

As a leader, actions speak louder than words. In our big game, I ran for one touchdown and threw two touchdown passes to account for all of our scoring. We won 19 to 13. I grinned with satisfaction, as I shook Brother Richard's hand. He stonily said, "Good game, Johnny." I thought to myself, "I told you so." Brother Gabriel was so pleased that he let us attend the movie shown that night at the Juniorate.

ANOTHER NOVITIATE FIRST

I experienced another first as a Novice. Two novices acted as cantors when we went to the chapel to chant the Divine Office prayers. They would chant the opening Latin line together, and then the entire assembly would join in to sing a number of lines. Then, the cantors would sing the introductory line to the next section, whereupon the assembly would join in again to complete the next section. This process was repeated until all sections of prayers were completed. We sang a cappella in Gregorian chant.

I remained a cantor for the whole year, with Brother Gabriel assigning a new cantor to lead the office with me every month. It had been Brother Gabriel's practice to change both cantors every month. I was the first to hold down that job for the entire 12 months of the Novitiate. I can only speculate that Brother Gabriel kept me on that job so long because I never fell asleep and missed a cue. It definitely had nothing to do with the quality of my voice. More with my attention to detail, I suspect.

3

SANTA FE, NM AND DENVER, CO: 1955–1959

ST. MICHAEL'S COLLEGE (SCHOLASTICATE)

When our year of Novitiate was completed, we took temporary vows (one year). They were the standard religious vows of poverty, chastity, and obedience that members of the Institute had taken since 1719. A special ceremony was held for the vow, which occurred in the chapel at Magnolia.

The following morning, we packed and boarded the St. Michael's College bus for Santa Fe,NM. There, we would join a community of Brothers, called the Scholasticate, and continue our religious formation, while obtaining college degrees and the necessary credits to obtain teaching certificates from the various states in our district, as well as most States of the Union. Those of us who had never seen a formation higher than Monkey Hill in Audubon Park were awestruck when we saw mountains, as the sun rose the following morning.

We could feel the bus laboring to climb steep grade after steep grade. In just 24 hours, we traveled from a location 28 feet above sea level to an elevation of 7,000 feet. Not only did we have to get acclimated to the altitude but also the low humidity. Santa Fe was in the high desert country, just south of the base of the Sangre de Cristo Mountains.

Off to the west, rose the Jemez Mountains (site of the secluded and limited access Los Alamos government complex that worked on the atomic bomb). About 70 miles to the south, Sandia Mountain loomed above Albuquerque. The daily sunsets behind the Jemez Mountains were spectacular. God painted a new masterpiece for us every day.

The Brothers had been educating boys in New Mexico since 1859, when they started St. Michael's College as a prep school in an adobe hut. In 1874, it became the first chartered college in New Mexico, but it wasn't until 1947, that the college operated as such. The prep school had become St. Michael's High School and is still going strong. The college was only beginning its seventh year when our gang arrived. Twelve years later, the college changed its name to the College of Santa Fe and enrolled its first female students.

In the late 1980s, the college greatly expanded, with the Greer Garson Theatre, Communications Center and Studios, the Driscoll Fitness Center, the Visual Arts Center, and on-campus student apartments. It also began offering many new degrees. For lack of funds, it is currently seeking various merger options.

We nicknamed St. Michael's the "College of Knowledge and Corridors." It was still housed in the barracks of what had been a World War II army hospital. Oschsner Hospital in New Orleans began by using a similar former army hospital (Camp Plauche) at the foot of the Huey P. Long Bridge. Each unit was a spur off of a single long corridor, and all could be reached without ever stepping outside.

We had our own separate living space for our Scholasticate community. These modified barracks contained our chapel, dormitory, refectory, commons area, and rec room. It was all off limits to the secular student body. We mixed in with the general student population when we attended classes.

There was a large chapel, gym, and library for all the students. The Brothers who served as administrators and faculty members had their own private living area. On Sundays and feast days, we would all gather together for Mass in the main chapel. Our religious exercises were somewhat truncated, compared with what they had been in the Novitiate. We were allowed the free time necessary to pursue our course work. After the Scholasticate, our religious exercises were further truncated when we were employed to teach in one of our district schools.

For the first time since the Juniorate, our group broke up to attend the different classes required to earn the degree of our choice. We did attend the same classes in religion, philosophy, and education. For the most part, it was just us young Brothers in these classes, though we were mixed in with the general student body, as we took the usual mix of college courses required of various majors and minors.

One of the major differences between us and the general student population was that our course load was planned to earn our degrees in six regular semesters and two summer sessions. We had received a kick start toward that end by earning 21 credits during our year of Novitiate. However, these credits counted little toward our secular education. They were part of our religious education and meant little toward teaching certification by State Departments of Education.

After I had finished my studies at St. Michael's, I was certified to teach Spanish, English, math, general science, chemistry, physics, Latin, and French in high school. The average college student graduates with 120 credits or so. I earned 181 undergraduate credits. I also completed the stringent courses in theology required by the Institute, which included in-depth study in dogma, morals, worship, and Thomistic philosophy.

At Ole Miss, I earned a master's degree in combined sciences (physics and math). My wife has been calling me an encyclopedia for a long time. It all goes back to my very broad formal education with the Christian Brothers and the informal, but invaluable, know-how garnered from my varied work experience. One valuable thing I learned was to never stop learning after you graduate.

THE STUDY OF BEING

The most satisfying course I took at St. Michael's was metaphysics. If you want to challenge your mind, try making an argument to justify studying metaphysics, the study of being. St. Michael's was fortunate to be able to acquire the services of Father Michael Faraon, a Dominican priest, to teach this course. Father Faraon was considered to be among the best philosophers of metaphysics in the world.

Because our class, which had been together through the Juniorate and Novitiate, was the first to take his metaphysics course, we had no idea what he would be like. We expected him to be tough though, and approached the first lecture with some trepidation. Father Faraon was an engaging and "down-to-earth" teacher.

The first thing that was different about his course was that there was no textbook required. We simply took notes, if we wished. All we did was go to class and think ... or not. There were no assignments or tests ... just the mid-term and final exams required by the school. The second thing was that memorization of facts was more of a liability than an asset in mastering the subject. I loved the course because everything a person needed to grasp the concepts was already in that individual's head. One just had to think.

Father Faraon typically conducted each class by posing questions, which we would volunteer to answer. One of my classmates attempted to answer an initial question by quoting Emmanuel Kant. Father Faraon demanded that he define one of the words in his quotation. The thoroughly embarrassed Brother was unable to do so.

Right off the bat, Father Faraon made it clear that we had better think for ourselves, if we were to succeed in his class. If you made a statement in Father Faraon's class, you had better know the meaning of each word in that statement, regardless of its source.

In the last class before we reported for our mid-term exam, Father Faraon wrote on the blackboard the questions that would be asked on the exam. He numbered each question and said that certain questions had to be answered. We could choose to answer a certain number of the others. It was strictly an essay exam. After the exam, we waited anxiously for the results, as our whole grade depended on them alone.

When Father Faraon returned our papers the following week, he did so by calling each student to the front of the class, announcing his grade, and handing him his test. He began with the lowest graded paper, a C. That one went to our devotee of Kant. He gradually handed out the remaining papers, with the grades making it to a few Bs.

When my test was the only one left to return, in mock anger, Father Faraon slammed it on his desk, exclaiming, "I don't believe in adding a plus to a grade, so I added an asterisk. I had to do something special and I'll tell you why. A colleague visited me over the weekend, and I tried to answer to his satisfaction one of the questions that was on your test. I could not. Then, I remembered reading Brother Patrick's essay answer. I retrieved it and gave it to my colleague to read. After reading it, he said he now understood the point under discussion. So, I've given a grade of A asterisk to this paper."

I collected my exam and returned to my desk with the only A given by Father Faraon. I was never more proud of any of my academic achievements. I had earned my A because I, arguably, had answered a metaphysics question better than my teacher. For the remainder of the course, I was consulted by my classmates, especially Brother "Kant."

A philosophy course I found especially useful was logic. We studied syllogisms of every construction and learned to discern from the principles of logic, to ascertain if their conclusions were valid or invalid. Many years later, it struck me when Bill O'Reilly revealed during a debate with a guest that he, a Harvard graduate, didn't know what a syllogism was. If Bill did it "tongue in cheek," he certainly did a great job of faking it. It's amazing how so many politicians violate the principles of logic, as they spin the truth to support their position. Everyone who registers to vote should be required to learn logic ... but then, voters aren't even required to learn to read and write. But, I digress.

SATURDAY OUTINGS

Nearly every Saturday, our director (I had Brother Ferdinand, Brother Luke, and Brother Francis as directors in my time) would load us all on the school bus and take us to a nearby place of interest. A place of interest for our directors meant a scenic location, like a state park or wilderness campground. Food and drinks were brought along, and we were free to explore or hang around the bus. Some loved to play instruments, sing, and just swap stories. Others, like myself, would lead a group on as long of a hike as we could make and still get back in time for supper.

The trailhead to Lake Peak, elevation 12,405 feet, was just about nine miles from Santa Fe. Other trailheads were within 60 miles of Santa Fe. During my years in Santa Fe, in addition to Lake Peak, I climbed to the summits of Santa Fe Baldy (12,621 ft.), Pecos Baldy (12,500 ft.), Truchas Peak (13,104 ft.), and Wheeler Peak (13,159 ft.).

At each summit, there was always a cairn that held a notebook inside of a metal cylinder. It was the custom to record the date of your climb with your name. I wonder if my name is still in those notebooks. I recorded it more than once on most of those mountains.

These climbs were physically challenging. The hike to the base of these mountains was usually about nine miles. At the base, the ridge of the mountain formed a semi-circular rim around a crystal-clear lake. The ascent from the lake to the top of the mountain was up a grassy, boulder-strewn slope of about 45 degrees. No wonder most of our community stayed near the bus.

I loved the physical challenge of these climbs and the tacit competition to see who would sign the book first. No one ever beat me to a summit, although this one Brother was always close behind. Once we were headed for the summit of Truchas Peak, when we passed a group of outsiders who had stopped to rest their horses. They were planning to get to the lake below the peak, camp overnight there, and ascend the peak on foot the next morning. They were amazed that we were making the trip up and back on foot on the same day. Well, we only had one day.

CAMP LASALLE

The Brothers in Santa Fe had a large camp house with a number of smaller cabins along the Pecos River upstream from Pecos, NM. It was named Camp LaSalle, and the Brothers conducted a summer camp for kids there. Most of the kids came from schools throughout the New Orleans-Santa Fe District. We would always spend a week or two relaxing there when the camp sessions were over. We had a chaplain who said Mass for us in a little, old adobe chapel across the road from the camp. It had walls about three feet thick. The camp had a stable, so we could go horseback riding.

There were numerous deeper holes in the river for swimming, though most of the river was about knee deep. It was strewn with boulders, and the current could easily knock your feet out from under you in spots. Brother Ferdinand liked to fly fish in the river, but a couple of us just reached under the rocks and managed to grab the slippery rainbow trout with our hands.

A FOREST FIRE PREVENTED

There were a number of lesser streams that flowed through smaller canyons into the Pecos valley. I explored most of them, always curious to see what was around the next bend. Once, a confrere and I found a large pool beneath a beautiful waterfall. We skinny-dipped in it, since we hadn't brought along any swimsuits. I hadn't swum in the nude since my days at Momo's Beach and the Creosote Wharf.

Once, we started up the canyon behind the chapel and spotted smoke coming from the top of the ridge to our left. It had to be a wild fire, so we quickly returned to the camp to call the ranger station and then headed for the fire, equipped with axes and shovels. We struggled up the overgrown and very steep slope to the fire and began to encircle it with a firebreak. In a couple of hours, a ranger reached the site. He thanked us for preventing a forest fire and recorded our names and the time that we had spent fighting the blaze. He indicated that the forest service paid volunteers for their work fighting fires. I don't recall ever seeing a dime, but, then, we all had a vow of poverty and any income received would have been turned over to Brother Director.

HIGH COUNTRY FOSSILS AND GRUMPY DRIVERS

One time, we were bused from the camp upriver to the trailhead of Pecos Baldy. It was, for me, my first climb of that mountain. The lake at the base was full of trout that were less wary of grabbing a lure than most, as few fishermen visited their isolated home. We happened to see a couple of strangers reeling in trout with every cast, and I planned to bring along a rod and reel on my next trip. On this trip, I planned it to be an overnighter, so we could get in an afternoon and morning of fishing.

When you're at the summit of a mountain like Pecos Baldy, the view is a magnificent 360 degree panorama. The nickname of New Mexico, "the land of enchantment," takes on new meaning. You forget the grind of the climb, as you relax and enjoy God's beautiful creation spread out below you as far as the eye can see.

One thing I observed was that a long ridge stretched north to Truchas Peak. This view gave me the idea for another overnight trip that would include scaling Truchas Peak. Such a feat had never been done by any of our scholastics from Camp La Salle. We would have to blaze our own trail for much of the trek.

On subsequent trips, I led groups of four or five confreres on both the fishing trip and the climb of Truchas Peak. Both trips were made in the month of August, while we vacationed at Camp La Salle. One memory of the fishing trip was waking up to find the temperature was 25-degrees Fahrenheit.

On the Truchas trip, I remember that on the return trip, one Brother found a large fossil and decided to carry it back. Since I was responsible for the group, he asked me if we could do so. I told him that it was all right, but he would have to bear the extra burden alone. Everyone had been assigned equal shares of equipment to carry. This Brother doggedly carried that 30-pound rock for a couple of miles, before abandoning it on the high ridge on which he had found it. I wasn't about to put the entire group between the rock and a hard place. This trip challenged the physical endurance of every man and we had to get back to the trailhead to meet our bus as scheduled.

Our bus driver was a Brother, who was in the class one year ahead of me. This Brother never went on any long hike himself. He was a dour, serious man.

The dirt road that wound along the Pecos valley was tortuous and rife with pot holes. After unavoidably hitting a number of them, we teasingly yelled to our driver, "Hey, you missed one!" Without a word, our driver stopped the bus and backed it up about 50 yards. We all bounced around, as he drove the bus across a number of the potholes that he had missed on his first run. We never joked about his driving again.

GROUSE AND ELK

On my hikes through the high country, I sometimes came upon some interesting wildlife. What made these encounters fascinating was these birds and animals were not afraid of me. They had never encountered a human before, and since I was neither known predator nor prey, they demonstrated no fear or interest. Twice, I brought back mountain grouse for our dining pleasure. Both times, I knocked them down by hurling a rock. Once, I was walking through chest high grass in a large stand of Aspen, when a herd of some 30 elk raced by me just 15 yards away. The elk and I were 11,500 feet above New Orleans. That was a real thrill.

ROLLING DOWN THE VALLEY

In my second year at St. Michael's, the college bought a used Greyhound bus and painted it in the school colors of red and gold. It was so much more comfortable than the regular school bus we had used before. Instead of benches, we had individual seats with padding, headrests, and footrests. Luggage racks ran the length of both sides.

On our first trip, we headed for Camp La Salle. Like most mountain roads, the road that climbed up the valley of the Pecos River was dirt-surfaced and narrow, with many curves that mirrored the twists of the Pecos. There were broad flat areas in the valley, but they were few and far between.

On one such spot, the movie actress, Greer Garson, had constructed a vacation home. Ms. Garson loved Santa Fe and was a patron of St. Michael's. The college's theater, communications center, and studios were named after her. About halfway between Ms. Garson's house and Camp La Salle, the bus nearly slowed to a stop, as it moved over to the right edge of the road to allow a vehicle to squeeze past.

I was sitting on the right side of the bus and saw that we were in danger, because to the right, the land sloped nearly vertically downward about 15 feet before it leveled out. As I felt the right side of the edge of the road collapsing under the weight of the bus, I knew we were going to roll down the embankment. I grabbed both luggage racks and placed my right foot against the right side of the bus below the window (fortunately, my row of seats was empty). The bus thudded against the slope and rolled unto its roof, before a boulder ended its roll. As the bus made the second 90 degrees of roll unto its roof, I continued to grip the luggage racks, but first placed my left foot and then my right foot between the luggage racks.

As the bus stopped its rollover, I found myself standing on its ceiling between the racks. I had remained upright by "walking" across one side of the bus and halfway across its ceiling. The rest of the passengers were piled together from front to back among seat cushions and luggage. Smelling gasoline, I quickly ushered my dazed and frightened Brothers out of the rear emergency door. No one suffered any more than some bad bruises. The passengers on the left side had fallen on the right-side passengers on the first roll, and they all became further entangled on the second. Even in the religious life, I continued to need my guardian angel. He sure placed the boulder that stopped our roll in the right place.

BANDELIER DEER AND RATTLESNAKES

Another place we went to picnic and hike was the park of the Bandelier National Monument. The picnic area was at the head of Frijoles Canyon in the foothills of the Jemez Mountains. The canyon wall above was pocked-marked with the ancient dwellings of the Pueblo Indians. The ladders used by the Indians still were useful to visitors to ascend to the different levels of caves.

I quickly exhausted my interest in these archeological ruins and headed down the canyon to the Rio Grande River. A trail about three feet wide had been carved into the side of the narrow, deep canyon. One side of the trail was too steep to descend and the other too steep to ascend.

On one occasion, I was jogging down the trail into a sharp bend. A mother deer and her fawn just happened to be trotting around the bend from the opposite direction. As we nearly collided, the deer stopped, whirled around, and sprinted back down the trail, with her fawn and me in hot pursuit. Maintaining my full momentum and accelerating to my full speed, I closed the gap between myself and the fawn and laid my right hand on the rump of the wild deer for a couple of strides before the deer and fawn pulled away. It was a once in a lifetime experience … to touch such a beautiful wild animal in its own natural environment.

We had been advised to be careful of rattlesnakes in the rocks along the Rio Grande. Of course, to me that was an invitation to seek them out. One of our Brothers was a biology major. Too corpulent to go hiking down to the river, he asked me to bring him back a live rattler if I could. I fetched one back in a gunny sack. Brother Director would not allow the snake inside our bus, so our budding herpetologist tied the sack to the front bumper to transport its deadly occupant back to the college. Our biology major kept the rattler in a large glass aquarium and milked it periodically for samples of its venom.

There was another prominent mesa on the Rio Grande, known as Red Mesa. Brother Director took us there once, so we could make the short climb to the top and take in the view. He thought the rattlers would still be denned up in hibernation. He was wrong. My co-skinny dipper and I killed two. The second one, a Western Diamondback, was 63 inches long and about six inches in diameter at its midsection. I'm sure our guardian angels were all busy that afternoon. In similar terrain, we once came upon and, very carefully, checked out a very large porcupine, an animal I never encountered in Louisiana. Other species unfamiliar to us were the ubiquitous jack rabbits and horned toads.

PRIVACY UPGRADE

Our dormitory at St. Michael's offered us an upgrade in privacy from what we had so far experienced. You could no longer see the beds of your Brothers from your own. Panels about seven feet tall formed an eight-foot square for your cell. There was no door, simply an opaque cloth curtain hung in the entrance opening. Separated by a central corridor, these cells lined both sides of the barracks. Down the hall, there were rooms containing an appropriate number of toilets, wash basins, and showers. The very end of the hallway emptied into that great long hallway that connected all the barracks of the complex.

HALLOWEEN INITIATIONS

It was the custom every Halloween for the senior class to initiate the new Scholastics. This rite was nothing like the hazing practiced in many colleges back then, but the anticipation of the unknown sufficed to make the newcomers nervous. When I was in my second year, I got the idea that I would have some fun at the expense of the seniors and played a few practical jokes on them that would naturally be attributed to the newcomers.

We only had a half hour from when the alarm bell was rung in the morning to the start of morning prayer in the chapel. One of our seniors had such a heavy beard that he would get a five-o'clock shadow around one in the afternoon. He also was one of those people who took a while to fully awaken.

I went into the cabinet in the common washroom, where he kept his toiletries and lined the edges of his double-edged razor blades with scotch tape. He had a cup of shaving soap and a brush that he used to lather up. After his first sleepy shave, which only removed the lather, he enjoyed two more sleepy, but smooth, shaves, before he washed off the lather and hurried to the chapel. He arrived late, unshaved, and red-faced with embarrassment. At the initiation, he tried his hardest to determine which of the initiates had sabotaged his morning shave. None of them had a clue as to what he was talking about. I was no help.

THE BEETHOVEN EVENT

One night, one of our scholastics played a trick on our Kant devotee. Now, I wasn't in on this action but found myself involved in the reaction. There was a room adjoining our commons room that had typewriters for our use. Brother "Kant" was typing away in front of a half-opened window. It was pitch dark outside.

Our prankster took the album cover of an LP record of selections by Beethoven and, from the outside, placed it upright in the window in front of Brother "Kant." When he eventually raised his eyes from the typewriter, he was staring into the image of Beethoven's madman face.

The prank had some unintended consequences. Brother's ear-piercing scream scared everyone in the building. I looked up from my desk to see him bolt out of the typing room and race screaming at the top of his lungs toward the main corridor. I caught up to the hysterical Brother halfway to the barracks that served as our chapel.

Fortunately, other Brothers were right behind me, and, together, we were able to hold him down. He had been swinging his fists wildly as he bounced off the walls of the corridor and left impressions of his knuckles in the sheetrock. It's amazing how strong a hysterically frightened person can be. It's also amazing how easily such a state might be induced.

THE SCHOLASTIC PUBLICATION

While at St. Michael's, I was one of the founding editors of the *Scholastic*, a monthly magazine on topics of interest to my confreres, not only in the Scholasticate but also throughout the district and, as it turned out, throughout the world. I had researched the history of our Scholasticate from its origins to my time. The Brothers had established this phase of the formation of new members with a tiny community in Las Vegas, NM. The community withstood many hard times and survived, and grew into its current state and location in Santa Fe.

I entitled my history of our Scholasticate, "A House Built on Rock." Shortly after it was published, I received a personal letter from Brother Nicet-Joseph, the superior general who ran the Institute from the mother house in Rome, Italy. Imagine my surprise and delight. The superior general answered to no one but the Pope. He was like the CEO of a 20,000-man worldwide enterprise. I was a lowly trainee. I'm sure he was busy, so it meant a lot that he sent me a personal letter of congratulations and appreciation regarding my article. It is one of the things I'll always remember about my days in the Scholasticate.

PEN STATE (YES, NOT PENN STATE)

We visited the New Mexico State Penitentiary on two occasions. The first time, we went there to play a baseball game against the prison team. Just driving from the entrance gate to the ball field was strange. The bus had to pass through a number of gates, which kept closing behind it. Just before we parked at the field, we passed a large exercise yard. There, some of the largest, meanest looking men you can imagine were lifting weights and pummeling punching bags. Their shirtless muscular upper bodies were festooned with tattoos.

There were some aluminum bleachers behind the dugouts and behind the backstop. They only contained about six rows, which a few dozen curious convicts occupied. The two parallel stretches of wire fencing surrounding the prison and our field were topped with razor wire. The path between the fences was about 20 feet wide and patrolled by guard dogs. The outer fence was electrified. There was not a blade of grass on this field, carved into the high desert a few miles south of Santa Fe.

When a ball was hit over both outfield fences, I remember one con yelling, "I'll go get it!" Of course, he did not. The cons didn't lack a sense of humor, at least. At one point in the game, one of our Brothers drew a walk and proceeded to steal second, third, and then home. With the theft of second, some of the cons began to stomp on the bleachers and yell "thief!" Like a crescendo in a classic piece of music, their cries of "thief" and their stomping grew louder and louder with each succeeding advance of our baserunner. They continued to scream "thief, thief, thief," even after he returned to the dugout. Ironically, many of the convicts were serving time for their own thievery.

In another moment of the game, the cons were at bat, when the batter took issue with the umps calls. I was catching, which placed me between the batter and the ump, a barrel-chested brute of a man. The angry, bat-toting con turned and let out a string of vulgarities. The ump reached right over me (I was in my catcher's crouch), grabbed the con by the throat, and commanded, "Shut up! Do you want to give this place a bad reputation?" The con shut up and added no more to my vocabulary.

When we talked about that game, we told folks that we had played Pen State. Understandably, the convict team only played home games. It was a real change of pace for the cons to have an outside group visit the pen to entertain them, so they were on their best behavior to assure that the warden would continue allowing such visits.

On another occasion, our choir returned and presented our Christmas concert. Brother "Kant" sang a solo that drew catcalls and whistles, which were quickly squelched by guards. We figured they had the "hots" for him. It was hard for Brother "Kant" to live that and his Beethoven scare down. About 22 years after I finished at St. Michael's, the inmates at the New Mexico State Penitentiary rioted and took control of the prison for two days. Between February 2nd and 3rd of 1980, 33 prisoners were murdered, and another 200 seriously injured.

Except for games with Pen State and the Seminarians of the Santa Fe Diocese, all of our games were intramural. We would simply choose up sides and go at it. We played football and baseball on fields marked off on the grassless open spaces. We were often joined by tumbleweeds, erratically blown through our playing area.

Spring winds would occasionally stir up a dust storm while we were playing baseball. Visibility was reduced to only a few feet, which forced a suspension of play. Once, when the dust cleared, a runner who had been on first base was found to be on second base. I had the opportunity to catch a professional class pitcher in a Brother who had abandoned a contract with the Detroit Tigers to join the Institute.

We had a nice indoor basketball court, and we played there when available. We played a lot more basketball than the other sports, as fewer players were required, and foul weather was not a hindrance. I would often shoot hoops by myself, if I couldn't scare up anyone to join me. I had gained over two inches in height and 20 pounds in weight since the Novitiate, and I had close to zero body fat. I was catching up to my peers in my physical maturity.

INDIAN JOE AND THE RESERVATION

There was an interesting character we dubbed "Indian Joe," who did odd jobs around the college. One Brother and I made friends with Joe, as we were working in a common area. We had both hunted waterfowl back in Louisiana, and when the topic came up, we asked Joe if he knew how to make a duck blind. Joe replied, "Sure, Brother, you poke his eyes out." We laughed about that incident many times.

Indian Joe lived on a reservation in Bernalillo County near Albuquerque. He agreed to get the two of us and our mothers, who were visiting, onto his reservation. He would direct us on a driving tour only, since we were not allowed to leave the vehicle. We took pictures from inside our car, as Joe described the dwellings and customs of the tribesmen.

One structure was called a *Kiva*. It looked like the top of a silo poking out of the ground. There was a square hole cut into the center of the top for access. A primitive ladder led down to the floor about 15 feet below. Joe explained that secret, sacred rituals were conducted by the tribe's medicine man in the Kiva.

THE LAW OF COSINES

Brother Ignatius used to tell a tale about three squaws from Indian Joe's reservation who were sterile. All three sought the help of the medicine man. He advised that they kneel on the pelt of an animal and pray three times a day in order to get pregnant. He advised that the rarer the animal pelt used, the better the result would be. One squaw was able to secure the hide of a black bear. Another outdid her by obtaining the hide of a cougar. The third came up with the rarest of the three. When one of the Albuquerque Zoo's hippos was put down after a fight, the zoo donated the animal to the tribe for meat. The third squaw got the hide of the hippo, an animal much rarer than a bear or cougar.

In time, the first squaw and the second squaw each delivered a baby boy. The third squaw had twin boys. Brother Ignatius concluded that this proved "that the squaw on the hippopotamus was equal to the sum of the squaws on the other two hides." Many of us told this tale to all of our geometry classes when we covered the Pythagorean theorem.

ASSIGNMENT TO DENVER

In early January of 1958, my graduation from St. Michael's scheduled in May had to be postponed. One of the Brothers teaching at J.K. Mullen High School in Denver, CO was unable to continue his teaching duties there. My director, Brother Francis, informed me that Brother Visitor was assigning me to replace the missing faculty member.

This assignment would kill two birds with one stone. Besides keeping the faculty at Mullen at full strength, it would earn me my credits in practice teaching. It meant also that I would not be ready in the fall for a teaching assignment in one of our district schools for the 1958–1959 school year. My classmates who had entered the Scholasticate with me would be joining faculties throughout the district in August, and I would be returning to the Scholasticate to finish work on my degree. This situation resulted in my earning a full extra semester of credits in the spring of 1959.

All of our school curriculums fulfilled the requirements for our students to earn a diploma granted by their state of residence. In addition (and irrelevant to the state requirements), our Catholic students were required to study Catholicism. Based on our college credits, we were licensed by the states to teach certain subjects. We were all prepared and commissioned by the order to teach Catholicism.

When I arrived at Mullen High School, I was certified to teach all but one of the subjects assigned to me, which was typing, and a waiver allowed me to teach that. In addition to typing, I taught religion and English courses to freshmen and Spanish and English courses to sophomores. So, for my practice teaching, I taught a full schedule, not the usual single course. My efforts at Mullen earned me two credits in Education 303, Observation of Secondary Teaching, and four credits in Education 304, Supervised Teaching. The only two grades of C on my transcript were given to me for these two courses.

Strangely enough, I never once observed any of the Mullen faculty teaching, and no one ever entered my classroom to observe my teaching. We were all occupied with our own classes, from the beginning to the end of each school day. I trust those two C grades were "educated" guesses. For all my other graded courses, I received 37 As and 17 Bs. So, those two Cs really stand out. My undergrad transcript shows a GPA of 3.651, and my diploma was issued to me magna cum laude.

J.K. MULLEN HIGH SCHOOL (FT. LOGAN, CO)

I arrived in Denver by Greyhound bus in the dead of winter. Brother Director picked me up at the bus terminal and immediately took me to Sears to buy me a parka and some winter overshoes. The Mullen campus was covered with snow. The front range of the Rockies glistened in the west under a deep blanket of snow. The Brothers' residence was a wood-frame building. It contained a commons room, where we each prepared our lessons at our personal desks. It also had a chapel, recreation room, and private rooms for each Brother.

For the first time in my life, I could close the door to the room in which I slept. There was another wood-frame building that housed the orphans for whom the Brothers had cared since 1932. These young men attended classes with the regular tuition-paying prep students, who made up the bulk of the student body. A third wood-frame building housed classrooms on the second floor and a metal-working shop on the first floor. The grounds occupied what had been an operating dairy farm of nearly 500 acres.

Bear Creek ran through the Mullen acreage near the north property line. Just over the creek sat the Mullen Mustang football field. Just south of the creek, there was a large pond. Fields of shoulder-high grasses flanked the creek to the west. I loved exploring these feral grounds. I saw lots of pheasants in the field and ducks in the creek, as spring unfolded. A bird dog usually followed me on my nature walks.

Once, I saw a pheasant land in the high grass along the creek and sent the dog to flush it out. I crouched down in the high grass and hoped the pheasant would rise up and fly my way. It did, and as it approached my position, I poised to leap up and grasp the bird's legs. I timed my leap just a split second too soon and the bird managed to gain just enough altitude to avoid my grasp. I missed touching it by only an inch or two.

A few students stand out in my memory of my semester at Mullen. One was a young miscreant, who chose corporal punishment over being confined to campus for the weekend. In accordance with school policy, the student bent over and grasped his ankles, while I doled out 10 lashes to his butt with a leather belt. There were no hard feelings, as the boy greatly preferred the spanking to being grounded. I firmly believe it hurt me more than it did him.

Another orphan student who remains in my memory was an orphan boy who was mildly retarded and, as is frequently the case, a very sweet and innocent person. He took a special liking to me and followed me about as much as he could after school hours. One night, he and I walked the perimeter of the pond gigging for bull frogs. I probably should say we "giggled" for bull frogs, given that this adventure greatly amused my companion and that amusement was infectious.

Another boy who took a liking to me was a budding athlete. I can't remember his name, but I remember visiting him in the hospital after he broke his neck while practicing the high jump. He lay in his hospital bed in traction, with a weight applying tension to his skull through a plate and pulley. He was paralyzed from the neck down.

I felt such compassion for this happy-go-lucky, sports-loving kid, who would probably be a paraplegic for the rest of his life. He smiled and talked cheerfully to me and another brother who had driven me to the hospital. I attempted to console the boy, saying to him, "God must love you a great deal." He looked at me quizzically. "Look at the cross He has asked you to bear. He loves Mary, His Mother, above all, and look at the cross she was asked to bear. He must love you a great deal to trust you to bear such a great cross. God gives us crosses out of love, and out of His mercy, He gives us the strength to bear them."

The boy then told me that he deserved whatever God sent him because of his sins. He mentioned some of them. The worst was probably disturbing his classes. I was humbled by the sense of the holiness of God possessed by this child. It was in view of this holiness that he judged himself. I had been through the Juniorate, Novitiate, and Scholasticate and still had a long way to go to catch up to the spiritual development of this child. "Out of the mouths of infants and sucklings, Thou hast perfected praise." We prayed the rosary, and my confrere drove us home. On the way back, my driver managed to do a 360, as he skidded down an icy hill to a safe stop. My guardian angel was still on the job.

TEMPTATION AT GRAND LAKE

Near the end of my stay with the Mullen community of Brothers, we took a weekend vacation to Grand Lake, CO. We drove the section of the Trail Ridge Road between Estes Park and Grand Lake. Trail Ridge is the highest continuous road in the U.S., reaching an altitude of over 12,000 ft. We stayed at a swank and isolated cabin right on the lake. A couple of us took a horseback ride deep into the adjacent Rocky Mountain National Forest.

At a rest stop deep into the forest, our horses got loose and hightailed it back to their stables. It didn't bother me one bit, as horses only slowed me down when I traveled mountain trails. Our cabin was provided by a Mullen benefactor, and one of his beautiful daughters made me feel uncomfortable as she unabashedly hit on me. I hadn't experienced anything like that since 8th grade at Mater Dolorosa, when one of our girls maneuvered me into going to a school dance with her. Nothing came of the benefactor's daughter's flirtations. Thank you, guardian angel. I'm sure my rejection did nothing to her confidence in her feminine wiles. Something did come of my going to the Mater Dolorosa hop with a date though. I won the door prize.

4

OPELOUSAS, LA AND OXFORD, MS: 1959–1964

ASSIGNMENT TO AIC IN OPELOUSAS

After completing my baccalaureate degree work during the 1958–1959 school year, I was assigned to our community in Opelousas, LA, deep in Cajun country. Our Brothers had been invited by Monsignor Broussard to operate the 7th through 12th grades of the boys' side of the Academy of the Immaculate Conception (AIC). There was a girls' component separated from the boys' school by the gymnasium complex. The 1st through 6th grades were sexually integrated, and their classrooms were on the girls' side.

Boys and girls shared the gym, band room, and lobby, and ate in the cafeteria in the girls' building. This arrangement allowed for daily social contact between AIC's 7th through 12th grade boys and girls. It took advantage of the sexual mixture to the benefit of many clubs and extracurricular activities. The production of the school newspaper, school plays, and band and choral concerts are prime examples of activities that are greatly enhanced by a ready mix of the sexes.

At the time, AIC was the only Brothers school in the New Orleans-Santa Fe District with this arrangement. The others were all affiliated with a local girls' Catholic high school. These "sister schools" had their own completely separate campuses. Their girls could only meet our boys for formal activities after school hours.

I firmly believe the AIC arrangement was better than associating with a "sister" school. I also believe that both arrangements were superior to having a coed school, where the boys and girls took classes together and had to struggle to overcome the significant distraction that their mixture engendered, not to mention contending with the very different male and female psyches and pace of physical maturation. AIC also provided the opportunity for informal social interaction in the cafeteria and gym lobby during the daily lunch hour.

OUR AIC FACULTY

When I joined the AIC community, our Brother director, Brother Anthony Archuleta, served as principal, and there were four Brothers and four lay teachers on the faculty. Mrs. Bernard and Mr. Olivier taught the 7th and 8th graders, and Joe Tuminello and Jimmy Fontenot coached our athletic teams and taught P.E. Mrs. Joyce Ortego was our school receptionist/secretary. Brother Bertrand ("T-Bob") had the senior homeroom, Brother Richard (from my Juniorate days) had the juniors, Brother Godwin (a year ahead of me in formation) had the sophomores, and I had the freshmen. Over the five years that I worked at AIC, I mainly taught freshmen classes, but I also taught a few courses to 8th graders, sophs, juniors, and seniors. AIC was the only school at which I taught Latin. We had a fairly frequent turnover of faculty during my tenure, as some of our Brothers were reassigned or left the order.

Brother Anthony ran a tight ship and encouraged faculty and students alike to succeed in and out of the classroom. He served as moderator for our paper and yearbook. He was an excellent photographer and developed his own pictures, teaching interested students his skills. The school paper and yearbook never wanted for pictures.

Our school fielded football, basketball, baseball, and track teams, and Brother Anthony saw to it that we all supported our student-athletes by attending their games and meets. We also selected our top students to compete in the district and state rallies in all the academic subjects. In addition to the regular curriculum required by the state, we taught four years of religion courses. The parents of our boys were willing to pay tuition for this holistic approach though public schooling was available for free. Opelousas and St. Landry Parish were very Cajun and Catholic.

There was one academic activity, initiated by Brother Anthony, in which all the students from 7th grade through 12th competed. Every English teacher was given a list of some 100 words, and they were to teach the meaning and correct spelling of each. Every six weeks, Brother Anthony would call out 25 or so of these words over the P.A. system, and the students would write them on a test paper. The papers were collected and graded, and the results posted. The top students received an award. The lists were varied every six weeks. This really helped our students to develop their vocabulary and spelling skills. The fact that a 7th grader could beat a senior motivated the upper classmen to avoid that embarrassment.

OUR DAILY ROUTINE

Following homeroom business, we all gave a reflection, followed by an hour of religion class. This schedule was followed for me by one-hour lessons in French, general science, algebra, and English. I had the same 35 students in each of these courses, which meant five different lesson preparations, as well as a lot of quizzes, assignments, and tests to grade. Given our religious affiliation, we had no wives or families to distract us, so we were able to carry that load. Total and single dedication can accomplish a lot.

I remained at AIC for five years. During that time, I gained some additional certifications and taught Latin and physics. By the time I left AIC to join the DLS faculty in New Orleans for the 1964–1965 school year, I had earned my master's degree by attending three summer sessions at the University of Mississippi on a National Science Foundation scholarship. My Louisiana teaching certificate certified me in Latin, Spanish, French, English, general science, chemistry, math, and physics. I've taught all of these over the years, as well as Louisiana history, typing, and civics (for which the certification was waived).

AIC FOOTBALL

Football was big in Cajun country, and AIC took it seriously. Our Wildcats played in class A, one level up from the class B level that our enrollment justified. They were so good that they could compete with the larger schools and draw bigger crowds. There weren't nearly enough class B schools fielding football teams in our area. There were plenty of them playing basketball and baseball, so AIC competed in class B in those sports.

Our home football games were played Friday nights under the lights at the stadium used by Opelousas High School. The girls and boys of AIC formed a marching band, pep squad, and cheerleading team. Brother Anthony was up and down the sidelines, taking pictures, and I sat high up in the stands, filming the game for our football coaches, so they could later critique and grade the players.

For out-of-town games, Monsignor Broussard usually rode with the Brothers, and I usually did the driving. Sometimes, I drove the pep squad and cheerleaders in our big blue and white school bus. We were a close-knit community, and the parents were generous in support of our school.

SATURDAY NIGHT SCHOOL

Our students were held to a set standard of discipline and behavior, with the full support of the principal and their parents. We were able to be innovative in our teaching approach because of this backing and cooperation. This mindset was lost in education over the years as the parents began to give ear to the complaints of their children, providing them the benefit of the doubt over their teachers. The teacher became wrong until proven right, rather than right until proven wrong.

I once instituted a practice at AIC that had a profound beneficial effect for the students involved. I had the full cooperation and gratitude of their parents. Twenty years later, I met resistance from the parents to the same practice. In another 20 years, I was forbidden by the school administration to employ it. In just two generations, parents had come to prefer failure to the success accompanying discipline where their spoiled children were concerned.

At AIC, I gave my algebra students a quiz and homework every day and a comprehensive exam every Friday. Upon grading my first weekly exam, I found that seven of my 35 pupils had failed it. I got on the phone and called the parents of each of them. I told them that their son had failed to learn the week's concepts, and that he would be unable to keep up when we built on those concepts the following week.

In effect, their son would dig himself a deeper and deeper hole and fail the course. He would have to attend summer school to earn the math credit required to earn a diploma. I asked them to bring their boy to school at 7 p.m. Saturday night, and I would see that he learned what he missed. All seven parents assured me their boy would be there and thanked me for helping him. Enthusiastic cooperation. No resistance.

I met my first Saturday night class, equipped with multiple versions of the test my failing students had taken the day before. I spread them out to forestall any cheating and told them to bring their test to me when they finished. If it was perfect, no errors, they could go home. If not, they had to go back to their seat, wait until all the first versions were completed, and then take the next version. Same rule. Between versions, I would lecture on the concepts they were failing to get. Their attention became rapt. Each subsequent test showed improved results until around 10:30 p.m., all had turned in perfect tests.

As students turned in perfect tests and walked out of the room, the eyes of the remaining students followed them with envy. Five of the original seven never failed another regular test. Only two of them repeated the experience of Saturday night school. These two both returned about three weeks after their first Saturday night remedial session.

When they slipped up the third time, they came prepared. They studied the material carefully, and they knew the drill. They were confident they would quickly ace the test and be released. When these two entered the classroom, I noticed they were well dressed but had no idea what they had planned. Well, they failed the first round of tests, just narrowly, making a few careless mistakes. I could see that they were anxious and were pressing, as they failed many more rounds, before finally handing in perfect tests around 10:30 p.m.

One of these boys had repeated the 8th grade, before becoming one of my freshmen, and faculty members had warned me that he would be trouble, viz., unable to perform academically (ironically, his dog, which followed him to and from school every day, was named "Trouble"). My thinking was that Jimmy was smart, because anyone who could get into and out of trouble as fast as he could had to be smart. I only had to get Jimmy to apply his smarts to his schoolwork.

Saturday night school supplied the motivation. It was an offer they could not refuse. Their choice was to do their schoolwork during the week, when they had to be in class anyway, or they could do it on Saturday night. I picked Saturday night, knowing that our students flocked to the dances at the Opelousas Teenage Center on that night.

It took Jimmy a while to make the connection, but after his third and final Saturday night class, he observed, "This is the same stuff you were teaching all week! I'm never coming back again." And he never did. Neither did anyone else.

Jimmy was having trouble with English, barely passing. I had to resort to something other than Saturday night school. I noticed that Jimmy loved sports and joined all the teams. So, I had him write an article about one of the games AIC played. I helped him with corrections and suggestions after his first draft. After the article had been polished, I submitted it to Brother Anthony, and it was published under Jimmy's name in the school newspaper. Jimmy was filled with pride. I had whetted an appetite that became insatiable. Jimmy had a reason to learn English grammar and composition. He eventually became editor of the sports page.

There's more to Jimmy's story. By the end of the semester, he made the honor roll and remained on it for the rest of his high school years. He also played on our varsity sports teams for his last three years. He became a leader of our student council. Subsequently, Jimmy went to college in Lafayette at what is now the University of Louisiana Lafayette (ULL), where he was elected president of their student council.

Jimmy visited me a few times after he went off to college. Once, with a shocked expression, he told me, "Brother, you know they have boys in my math class who don't even know the quadratic formula?" Well, I was unaware of that, but I well remembered when Jimmy was unable to solve the simplest linear equations. On another visit, Jimmy asked me if I remembered that final Saturday night class, when he and his sidekick had reported all dressed up. I replied that I remembered it well. Jimmy said, "Well, we knew that we could get in and out quickly by acing the first test. Confident that we would do just that, we planned a double-date. We left our girlfriends in the car next to the gym and told them we would be right back. Of course, as you will recall, we didn't leave class until 10:30. By then, our dates had called their parents to come and get them." I had no idea that I had ruined their Saturday night fun, but I know Jimmy appreciated what I had done. We could now laugh about it. Later, Jimmy became a superintendent with the St. Landry Parish school system.

A generation later, I held a Saturday night class again at Rummel High School in Metairie, LA. This situation involved a very different set of circumstances than those surrounding my freshman algebra students at AIC. At Rummel, I taught physics to seniors. They were proven good students, taking physics as an elective. None of them were in danger of failing, as long as they made the effort. Anyway, it would have been a disservice to them to force their effort, as they were all college bound. If they hadn't learned to motivate themselves by their senior year in high school, they would be ill-prepared for college success.

Only one of my physics students in my 11 years at Rummel failed my course. Had he tried, I probably would have passed him with a "D," but not only did he not try, he made the mistake of "bad-mouthing" America. He was an Iranian, and his Ayatollah was still holding 52 American citizens hostage. I made no effort to motivate this ingrate to pass and gave him the "F" he earned.

What led me to have a Saturday night class at Rummel resulted from the administration having me teach a course dubbed "senior math." The only thing senior about the course was that it was set up for a group of underachieving seniors who had performed poorly in their first three years of high school and needed one more math credit to graduate. The materiel could have been mastered by well-motivated freshmen.

Rummel could justify this academic concession, since these 30 students, out of an enrollment of 1200, were not college bound. I felt obligated to ensure that they earn this math credit and graduate with their class. Accordingly, when five failed their weekly test on Friday, I started to call their parents and have them see that their wayward sons come to school on Saturday night and be brought up to speed.

The reaction I got from these parents, one generation removed from those at AIC, was quite different. On one of my calls, a mother informed me that her son could not attend the remedial class. When I asked why he would be unable to come, she explained that her family was going to the LSU-Ole Miss football game in Baton Rouge. After a lengthy pause for dramatic effect, I whispered into the phone, "a football game?" After another pause, I raised my voice to normal volume, "a football game?" One more pause, and I shouted, "A football game? You're going to allow your son to fail this course and not graduate with his class over a football game!"

I had placed her in the position of vying for the title of "worst mother of the year" if she answered yes. So, she said she couldn't leave her son alone while they went to the game. I reminded her that her son was 18 years old and was perfectly able to take care of himself. She then tried one last excuse, "But we'll have the car, and he won't have a way to get to school." "I'll pick him up," I replied. Well, I did, and he and the others never failed another weekly test, and they all earned their math credit.

About 10 years later, I met two of those individuals who attended that Saturday night class, while making a business call. They were both working as ITs at the company I was calling on. One told me with great appreciation that Saturday night school had turned his life around, giving him confidence that he could learn math, and leading him to pursue his college degree.

To complete my story of Saturday night school, I have to fast-forward another half generation to my stint as a faculty member at Brother Martin High School in New Orleans. It was a school run by the Sacred Heart Brothers. When I ran into the usual mix of unmotivated, lazy students, I was prepared to give them the Saturday night option. This time, I didn't even get to offer it to the parents. The administration forbade its implementation on the grounds that it was "too punitive." The times they were "a changing" and not for the better.

For the first time (other than in the case of the Iranian boy), I had to fight with the students and their parents all year only to end up having some of them fail. I believe, based on experience, that Saturday night school would have nipped the problem in the bud. I had never heard so much failure blamed on ADHD in my first 30 years of teaching. I had never seen so many students taking Ritalin. So, from 1959 to 1999, my Saturday night motivational tool went from enthusiastic acceptance and grateful appreciation on the part of parents to resistance and complete rejection. Ritalin was an abject substitute for Saturday night school.

INFORMAL BASKETBALL COACHING

During my first semester at AIC, I looked forward to the start of our basketball season. I was an avid fan of the sport and played it at every opportunity. Brother Bertrand cautioned me that our boys' basketball team would be as bad as our football team was good. I'd have to take consolation from the success of the AIC girls' basketball team, which was very good. We played larger, class A schools in football, but in basketball, we played smaller, class B schools, that for the most part, never fielded football teams.

Because of our small enrollment of around 125 boys, our pool of basketball players came from the same pool of football players. The sophomore class of my first year at AIC was loaded with talented athletes, who formed the nucleus of very successful football teams for my first three years at AIC. They also were the nucleus of a very unsuccessful basketball team during my first year. As good a coach as they had in football in Joe Tuminello, they only had Jimmy Fontenot, Joe's football assistant, to coach basketball.

Jimmy's ineptitude was not the only factor in AIC's poor performance in basketball. Our boys began playing their schedule only a few days after their football season ended against teams that had been practicing and playing games all the while. Basketball was king at these schools that had no football. AIC didn't win a single game my first year at the school.

With the end of the season, I began to mull over in my mind what I might do to improve boys basketball at AIC. During spring football practice, I implemented my plan. I began by asking my freshmen if they would like to form a freshmen basketball team. Among those interested was Benny Richard, a gym rat like myself who frequently shot hoops and played pickup games with me. From among the volunteers, I selected those I knew from experience were the smartest and most cooperative. I would build these into a team around Benny.

We began practicing after school on a dirt court outside the gym, going over and over a few plays designed by Adolph Rupp, the legendary coach of the University of Kentucky. One afternoon, Donald Dean strolled by and teased us, saying that our stupid plays would never work. Now, Donald was one of those top athletes from the sophomore class who played on that year's failed varsity basketball team and, with his buddies, was expected to play again next fall as a junior. I told Donald, "If you'll get four more loudmouths like yours, we'll see how our plays work."

Donald rounded up the varsity players, and we arranged to play a regulation game in the gym. I had made friends with Jim Latiolais, the AIC girls' coach, and he agreed to officiate the game. This arrangement would assure that the varsity could only use their superior size and bulk within the rules.

When the game was over, Donald and his teammates sat disconsolately on the floor unable to discern what had hit them. Our lowly freshmen had defeated them 66–34. I approached them to explain why they had lost. "Every one of you could beat my boys one-on-one, with the exception of Benny. But, basketball is five-on-five. Our five were playing together as a team and you guys were each playing independently of your teammates."

Although I had only coached one unofficial game, the seed of a new attitude had been planted and next year, under the coaching of Coach Latiolais, who replaced Coach Fontenot, the basketball team won 10 games, and in subsequent years, made the playoffs. Two of the players I started out as freshmen made All-State as seniors. Benny Richard received a full scholarship and starred at Northwestern State in college. The expectations for boys' basketball at AIC were completely changed.

SEMI-PRO BASKETBALL

On weekends, I often used my free time to play basketball. The gym was a stone's throw from the Brothers residence, and quite a few good players would gather to compete. One Saturday, Remi Prudhomme, an All-American defensive tackle at LSU, was barreling toward the goal, when I stepped into his path to take the charge. I was shoved back several yards and landed on my back, with Remi on top of me. A deathly silence ensued. The players expected what normally happens when a 6'4", 250-lb guy pancakes a 5'10", 165-lb guy. Quickly discerning that no one was injured, an AIC footballer ran to us and asked Prudhomme, "Remi, are you OK?" His indirect tribute to my toughness had all of us roaring with laughter, as we resumed playing. My guardian angel was still on the job.

Coach Latiolais had been on the basketball scene in Louisiana and in the Army. His high school team from Lawtell, LA had gone undefeated until playing in their class state championship game. He had been a star in armed services competitions. He had played forward at 6'5". He still played in semi-pro tournaments on a team representing Lawtell.

On several occasions, Jim invited me to play with him and his buddies in pickup games at the AIC gym. Impressed with my play, he invited me to play with his team in weekend semi-pro tournaments. Twice, Brother Anthony gave me the go-ahead. In the first tournament, we played in the Opelousas High School gym. Jim put me in the starting lineup. Never having played with the group before, I was lost on offense and didn't score much. Later, I asked Jim why he even played me. He said, "Brother, you are the best defensive player I have ever seen."

Our first opponent had a player, Jimmy Morrow, fresh out of ULL (then USL), who was an All-American. Like most All-Americans, he was selected for his offensive prowess. I was assigned to guard him and held him to zero baskets, except for the one he scored unmolested, when I was on a fast break going the opposite way, and his team reversed the break with a steal.

I played my second and final semi-pro tournament in nearby Port Barre, LA. I scored 25 points and shut down an All-State opposing player just out of Washington High School. I was selected to the All-Tournament team and received a trophy for my efforts. Brother Anthony never allowed me to play in any more tournaments.

As a fundraiser, our AIC faculty played a basketball game against the Opelousas High faculty. The gym was packed, as the natural rivalry between the only two high schools in our small town drew fans from each school. We had some good players among the Brothers who made up most of our faculty, and we had the services of Coach Tuminello, as well as Coach Mills. We wore the uniforms of our AIC team, and our opponents wore those of Opelousas High. Judging by the volume of post-game comments on the subject, I suspect that many spectators came to see legs that they had never seen before (basketball shorts were really short back then). I don't remember the score, but we smoked them.

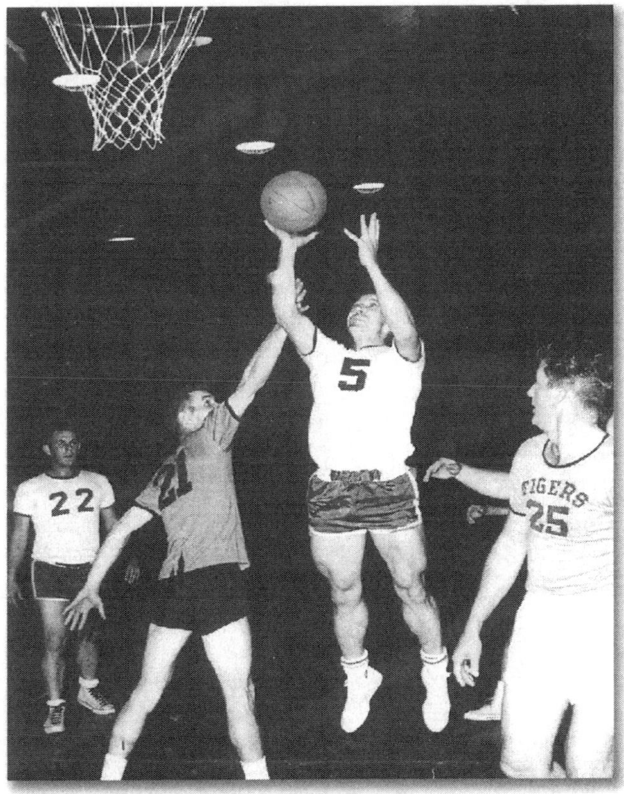

I'm on my way to the rim to lay in a finger roll in our fundraiser against the OHS faculty. Mickey Mills (22) is visible on the left.

FUNDRAISING

Speaking of fundraising, it was during my stay at AIC that I realized that I had a special aptitude for it. All I needed was a good cause. All of our classes competed against each other to see which could raise the most money. An ongoing cause was the Catholic Missions. I kept a bar graph of each freshman's donation amount posted on our bulletin board. This step injected an element of pride and competition, which was very motivating. Our class always led the school. There was also an annual fundraising drive among all the Brothers schools in the New Orleans-Santa Fe district. It was known as the St. La Salle Auxiliary.

I got the idea to expand the base from the students to their parents. Mr. Abdalla, the father of one of my students, owned clothing stores in Opelousas and Lafayette. When he was approached to support the St. La Salle Auxiliary drive, he summoned a gathering of some of the wealthier business men and professionals in town. At this gathering, they all agreed to donate at least $100, as well as to solicit more. It was explained that the funds collected were to support the retired Brothers, our "Ancients" at Magnolia. Our freshman class raised more money for the drive than any school in the New Orleans-Santa Fe district, some of which had 10 times the students at AIC.

DONKEY BASKETBALL

Another fundraiser was held once a year at AIC. The school would sell tickets to a donkey basketball game. A husband and wife team out of Memphis, TN would book dates with schools throughout the South, and the schools would choose the players and provide the gym. The most common matchup was between faculty members and students. I participated in the AIC games all five years that I was there, as well as in the ones held at De La Salle and Rummel in my years there.

The donkeys were outfitted with padded hoof covers to protect gym floors. The players rode bareback and only had reins attached to a halter (no bit) to control their mount. The rules were simple. A player had to have his donkey's reins in hand to possess the basketball and had to be on the donkey's back to pass or take a shot at the basket. The crowd was mainly composed of the student body, but many parents and locals swelled the take.

Efforts to possess the ball could best be described as a "free for all." Getting aboard a donkey with ball in hand did not assure a player of a shot. Every opposing player who could stay aboard their ride would attempt to wrest the ball away and/or push the ballcarrier off his mount and the donkeys would attempt to buck the ballcarrier off their back.

A favorite ploy of the donkeys was to gallop down the court and suddenly lower their head and come to a sudden stop. This endeavor would usually dislodge the rider and send the ball rolling away. It was all spills and thrills, as the referee would control the general movement of the herd with the threat of a cattle prod. It was a laugh fest for the crowd.

The games were understandably low scoring. I always led everyone in scoring. I just loved the rough and tumble of the game and had a knack for controlling my donkey.

Once at a game at DLS, two senior football players sandwiched me between their donkeys and tried to push me off my donkey. If they had known their physics, they would have realized that their opposite forces would offset one another with little effect on me. Grasping the ball between my knees, I shoved outward with both arms (in opposite directions) and knocked both 200 pounders off their donkeys.

When asked about my prowess in donkey basketball, I told my students (tongue in cheek) that I was used to dealing with jackasses. I must have impressed the owner of the business because years later I chanced to see him as I was going to Sunday Mass in Memphis, and he instantly remembered me from among thousands of players he had seen in games in hundreds of schools.

THE EDUCATED TOE

A group of Brothers from AIC and our Cathedral High School in Lafayette put together a touch football team to play against the Juniorate team at Magnolia. We all played both ways. I handled the kickoffs and extra points. On kickoffs, I kicked from a tee, serving up only touchbacks to give our defense good field position. On extra points, I confused the Juniors since I took a direct snap. They didn't know whether I would run or pass the ball. When I drop-kicked the first extra point, they had a third option to defend. I drop-kicked four PATs that afternoon, and Brother Ignatius nicknamed me the "educated toe." The same Brother Richard who had coached the Juniors against my Novitiate team was now playing with me. We had become teachers on the same faculty. After drop-kicking several extra points, I surprised the Juniors by passing to Brother Richard for a PAT.

A BICYCLE NAMED TCHAIKOVSKY

The Brother Ignatius who dubbed me the "educated toe" was the same missionary Brother who had enthralled me with his stories about his adventures in Nicaragua, when I was a freshman at DLS in New Orleans. "Iggy" was a great storyteller who could invent a story on the spot that would be applicable to whatever the prevailing circumstances might be.

He once gave a nickname to a bicycle that he rode from our school in Galveston, TX to our school in Lake Charles, LA, a distance of 119 miles. "Iggy" told us he named the bike "Tchaikovsky," because the seat broke about halfway through his trek. When asked to make the connection, "Iggy" queried us, "Isn't he the one who wrote the 'Nutcracker's Suite?"

Iggy hated it when our Visitor called him back to the states from his mission in Nicaragua. He once remarked, "We all have to be careful, or we can go to hell. Anyone can go to hell. Brother Visitor can go to hell."

LOUISIANA, SPORTSMAN'S PARADISE

Many of the well-to-do parents of our AIC students owned fishing and/or hunting camps, and we were invited to enjoy their facilities over a weekend or more. Some of the dads accompanied us and served up the finest Cajun cuisine this side of Heaven, along with all the appropriate libations. I've never been in a community where the parents showed so much appreciation for what the Brothers did for their sons. There was a swampy wilderness area, just west of the Atchafalaya River, which stretched over many square miles, from just north of Krotz Springs all the way to Palmetto. It was laced with a spider web of waterways called "Second Lake" that afforded miles of some of the best freshwater fishing in Louisiana. Each of us relaxed in our own way. Brother Anthony liked to nap and read. "T-Bob" and I liked to fly fish. "Iggy" and I liked to hunt and swim. We all liked to eat.

One winter, a couple of us accepted an invitation to hunt waterfowl from a hunting camp in the marsh south of Lake Charles, LA. Landry High, a Christian Brothers school, was located there, and one of their faculty members was a man whose novitiate training overlapped mine. He was from New Iberia and loved to hunt. We wound up on several trips into the marsh as hunting buddies.

One morning hunt was particularly memorable. On the afternoon before, he and I had observed thousands of geese feeding in the open marsh. When we walked toward them, the geese took flight, with the sound of their wings making a terrific din. The following day, we lay on a small rise under a camo tarp as the dawn broke. We could hear the swish of their wings, as bird after bird flew just over our heads and settled in the water surrounding our position. Every few minutes, we peeped out carefully at the sky until there were no more geese coming in.

The marsh grass was just high enough to conceal us in our prone position. As we looked over the top of the vegetation, we could not see the geese. As we had planned, we aimed our 12 gauges just over the grass and whistled loudly. The heads and necks of thousands of startled geese popped up in front of us. We fired, he to the left and I to the right. We fired our second and third shells at birds in flight as the first blasts got them all airborne.

The body of a goose will absorb all of the shot from a single shell, but when one fires through a forest of goose necks, one shell can kill several geese. We collected 12 geese when the firing was over. It was kind of comical getting the geese to raise their heads up out of the grass with a whistle and then blowing their heads off. Collecting the downed geese and hauling them back to camp through the marsh was quite physically challenging … and then we had to dress them for the freezer.

The next day as I walked into the marsh, a lone goose flew over me, and I knocked him down. As I went to retrieve it, a mallard duck flew over from my left to my right, and I downed him. Before I took two steps, a fast flying teal crossed from my right to my left, and my third and last shell took it down. I had shot three different species of waterfowl, before I could collect the first.

On the way back to camp, I met a confrere who had shot a goose that had flown deep into a section of deep marsh covered with thick vegetation. There was no way for a man to get to the downed bird. As we discussed his dilemma, a man came along with a retriever dog. When he was told where the goose went down, he pointed in that direction and commanded his dog to fetch the goose. The dog plunged into the water and began fighting his way through the water and thick vegetation. Gradually, the sound of the dog's splashing grew fainter and fainter, until we could no longer hear it. After we waited for about 45 minutes, the dog returned with the goose. Man's best friend never ceases to amaze me.

On the way back to camp, we killed several marsh rabbits that peered out at us from large thorn patches along the path. These rabbits are about three times the size of regular cottontails. I had occasion to kill two nutria while hunting in the marsh.

The first one was in an open stretch of prairie. This nutria took it in his head to block the trail and threaten me with his yellow teeth. I had a 12 gauge but I didn't want to fire it and scare off some ducks I was stalking. So, I struck the nutria on the left side of its head with my gun barrel. I was surprised that the blow killed it instantly.

The other nutria I killed to protect a dog that chased the nutria into the water. The depth of the water forced the dog to swim. As the dog closed on the nutria, I shot the rodent. The dog's owner knew the nutria would have the advantage over his dog in the deep water and was beside himself as I fired. He was fearful that I might hit the dog in my attempt to save him.

ESCAPE FROM ANGOLA

Once, a prisoner escaped from the State prison in Angola, LA and hid in the swamps of the Second Lake area. The sheriff of St. Landry Parish was an interesting Cajun, named "Cat" Doucet. After winning one election by a large margin, he had boasted in his thick Cajun accent that he had won by a "landscape." Try as he might, "Cat" could not flush the convict out of the swamp. He even brought in dogs from Angola to track the escapee. That didn't work well, as the prisoner had trained those very hounds while at Angola. Fortunately for "Cat," the man tired of living on the land and surrendered himself after "Cat" had given up.

WALKING ON WATER

On one occasion, T-Bob, Iggy, and I hiked over the west levee of the Atchafalaya River and explored the bar pits for something to shoot. We had one .22 caliber rifle between us and decided to take turns shooting at the large carp that slowly cruised just a foot below the surface. T-Bob shot first, and the carp wasn't in the least disturbed by the bullet. Iggy then took a shot with the same result. This situation set my mind to seeking an explanation because Iggy was a crack shot, and he could decapitate a water moccasin 30 feet away. How could he have missed? The huge target presented by the carp lay within 10 feet. Then, I remembered that light refracts or bends into a new path when it changes medium (like from water to air). This phenomenon was making the fish appear to be higher in the water. Not sharing my thought with T-Bob and Iggy, I aimed below the image of the fish. What occurred next I had only seen in animated cartoons. The carp exploded straight up out of the water frantically swishing its tail. It appeared to be walking across the surface as it did all in its power not to sink back into the water. It traveled some 10 feet across the surface of the pond, once recovering from "tripping" over a log before disappearing into the depths. T-Bob and I stood stunned, our mouths agape. We had just seen a fish walking on its tail! Iggy calmly said, "I think you hit him." Apparently I must have creased the belly of the carp. Sensing that something had attacked it from below, the carp had done its level best to head for the sky. Later, Iggy and I made our way to the river bank and swam across the mighty Atchafalaya. After sunning and relaxing a while, we swam back. T-Bob had returned to our camp, not having any desire to swim in the Atchafalaya.

FLY FISHING WITH T-BOB

T-Bob treated me to my first exposure to fly fishing at Second Lake. We used a small aluminum skiff, powered by a light outboard motor to move us from one site to another. When we neared a likely spot, we would cut the engine and silently approach, one of us controlling the skiff with a paddle, while the other worked a little top-water popper over the beds near the shore. We were usually casting from about 25 feet from the bank. Motivated by hunger, as well as their instinct to protect their nests, the perch would literally explode into the lure and then fight gamely against our light tackle.

Once, T-Bob pointed out a large water moccasin resting on the surface. When I failed to see it in its camouflaged position, T-Bob made a cast over the snake and drew the lure over it. Oops! The lure hooked into the skin on the snake's back. Trying to shake the snake free of the hook when I grasped the leader, the writhing serpent landed in our skiff in a foul mood indeed. We were wearing only flip-flops and bathing suits. Before the snake was able to deliver a successful strike, I was able to dispatch it with a paddle and flip it overboard. Thank God my guardian angel enjoyed fishing.

GOLFING IN OPELOUSAS

One of our parents arranged for the Brothers to be guests at a nice nine-hole golf course a few blocks from AIC. Brother Richard introduced me to this sport. He persuaded me to accompany him and T-Bob for a round from time to time. We tried to play when few golfers were on the course.

My clothing was hardly that worn by the typical golfer. I played in a tee shirt, Bermuda shorts, and tennis shoes, using borrowed clubs. We did not use caddies. I only used four clubs—a 2-iron, a 5-iron, a 9-iron, and a putter. They were the only ones with which I felt a modicum of control. Accustomed to doing well in the common man's sports, it was embarrassing to me to struggle with this rich man's sport. Well, at the time, I had never known any poor men or black men who played golf or tennis.

One morning, I had a great moment on the course. The ninth hole had a fairway that dog-legged left. I told my ball this, but it had a mind of its own and crossed the boundary between the 9th and 1st fairways, ending up about 30 yards in front of the first tee.

I saw a foursome preparing to tee off, and hoping they didn't see me or my ball (I stood behind a large shrub), I waited for them to tee off. But, they saw both me and my ball, and signaled me to play my next shot before they teed off. Embarrassed by my clothing and the lie of my ball, I hurried to play my next shot and get out of the foursome's way. As I approached my ball, I pictured in my mind how the ball would have to be struck to land on the 9th green and hole out. The green was elevated some 10 feet above my lie and sloped away from me. It was about 30 yards away. I couldn't see the surface of the green and only about the top third of the flag stick. Crime and punishment. I was not supposed to be approaching the 9th green from the 1st fairway! I knew that I would have to loft the ball high up with a trajectory that would just clear the lip of the green. Any shorter and the ball would roll down the steep slope of the green and come back to me. Any longer and the ball would roll across the green.

Without even a practice swing, I immediately addressed the ball and struck it with my 9-iron. After following the path I had pictured in my mind, the ball disappeared over the lip of the green. The cheering of the patient foursome and my companions told me that I had holed the shot. I strode over to the green like I knew what I was doing, like I did this every day. I never ever came close to making a shot like that again, though with all the errant shots I took I had plenty of opportunities! Talk about beginner's luck.

LITERARY RALLIES

Having 35 students meant that the pace of my instruction was too slow for my brightest students. To maintain their interest, I permitted the top five to go ahead and work through the text on their own, coming to me privately if they ran into problems. They had to answer every question and do every problem in every chapter. They still had to pass the six-weeks tests, as scheduled by the administration.

These students would finish the entire course by late spring in time to review it. These boys would be the ones I entered in the district literary rally. The top finishers at district earned the right to compete at the state literary rally, held at LSU in Baton Rouge. The competitors at State included students from both public and private schools throughout Louisiana. Every spring, we sent a busload of AIC students to State to compete for honors in every subject in the curriculum (except religion). We took home a lot of first place through fifth place awards.

NEAR ACCIDENTS

Once, when I was driving a full bus of AIC State rally participants to Baton Rouge, we narrowly avoided a collision with a large truck, loaded with just harvested sugar cane. At the time, the main highway connecting Opelousas to Baton Rouge was U.S. 190, a four-lane divided highway. While tooling along at 65 mph in the right lane through the cane fields east of Krotz Springs, I spotted a fully loaded trailer of sugar cane parked on the right shoulder.

Hidden from my view by this trailer was a second one parked in front of it. The driver of the second trailer suddenly pulled out into the right lane. My best option to avoid rear-ending the trailer was to turn into the left lane. I checked my side-view mirror, only to find that the left lane was occupied by an oncoming vehicle. I slowly braked to allow the left lane to clear before switching into it.

In the interim, the front bumper of our bus drew within about six feet of the rear of the cane trailer, before the vehicle in the left lane passed us, giving me the room needed to turn smoothly into the left lane. It must have appeared to my young passengers that we were about to be inundated in sugar cane. The bus, filled with the happy sounds of teenagers on holiday, suddenly became silent as a tomb. A few seconds after we had safely skirted the trailer, the dead silence was broken by raucous cheers and applause. There were a lot of guardian angels on the job.

On the return trip, I passed a truck at the peak of the Huey P. Long Bridge over the Mississippi. I probably only had a clearance of one foot on either side. As I squeezed through the gap, the passengers fell silent again. This time, however, there was no applause or clapping when we got in the clear. I was young, foolish, and overconfident, and I'm sure my guardian angel must have been sorely tired (along with the angels of my young passengers).

DIVIDING 5 INTO 3

The AIC boys' building was a single-story structure, with a central hallway that ran its length. On the left, one passed in succession the office of our secretary, Mrs. Ortego, the office of Brother Anthony, our principal, and the senior, junior, sophomore, and freshman classrooms. On the right, one passed, in order, the library, and the 7th and 8th grade classrooms. In addition to the classroom entry/exit doors to the hallway, there was an additional entry/exit door to the outside, which greatly simplified fire drills.

One day, Coach Fontenot substituted for Mrs. Bernard's 7th grade math class. The door to the 7th grade classroom was open to the hall, as was that of the junior classroom. The juniors were quietly working on an assignment, when they clearly heard Coach Fontenot bellow, "How in the hell can you divide 5 into 3?" The roar of laughter from the juniors brought Brother Anthony all the way from his office to investigate. Math was no more of a forte for Coach Fontenot than coaching basketball.

ANOTHER PLANE RIDE

There was a Dr. LaFleur, who had a son in my class. His boy was one of the brightest students I ever taught and excelled in the literary rallies. Dr. LaFleur took me for my second plane ride in his private plane, one similar to the one I rode in while in the Juniorate. The noise was the same, and the aerial view of St. Landry Parish mostly indistinguishable from that of Lafayette Parish.

TEACHING SUMMER SCHOOL IN LAFAYETTE

We didn't hold summer school at AIC, but Cathedral High School in Lafayette did. I taught a civics class there one summer. The director of the community was Brother Frederick Dillinger, who was a near relative of public enemy number one, John Dillinger. Brother Frederick, tall, lean, and somber, took pride in how he could freeze a mischief-maker with a stare. Cathedral drew students needing summer remedial work from public, as well as private, schools.

During a recess, Brother Frederick observed a young Cajun boy about 11 years old, sitting on a bench smoking a cigarette. Brother Frederick decided to put an end to this violation of school rules with his renowned stare. He stood beside the bench with arms folded and glared down at the boy. The boy looked up at Brother Frederick for a moment, took a puff from his cigarette, and looked away. Brother Frederick took a pace or two and continued to just stare menacingly at him. After looking up at Brother several more times and taking several more puffs, the young Cajun said in a calm, measured manner, "Anyhow, ya see me, I don give a damn." Obviously, Brother Frederick needed some more work on his stare.

DRINKING NOTHING

Brother Daniel, my director in my Juniorate days, was part of the Cathedral summer-school community. We had become peers. It was during that summer that I realized how much Brother Daniel enjoyed a good stiff drink. He would organize cookouts and always provide abundant libations. He had one special drink he mixed that he named "nothing." It contained equal parts of sloe gin, blackberry brandy, and Cuban rum, poured over a glass full of small ice cubes. It went down smoothly, like a sweet punch, without a noticeable buzz. On the other hand, if you had a few, the delayed kick would knock you for a loop. The delayed buzz was very noticeable. When asked why he called his concoction "nothing," Brother Daniel explained, "If your director asks you what you have been drinking, you can tell him, 'nothing.'"

SUMMERS AT OLE MISS

I spent the summers of 1962–1964 as an Oxford scholar. Well, isn't the University of Mississippi located in Oxford, MS? I had received scholarship offers from the University of Vermont, as well as Ole Miss, from the National Science Foundation. Several other Brothers from our District had attended Ole Miss and earned their masters degrees there, so I followed their lead. The degree programs offered were in science and math. The primary focus of the NSF program was to improve science and math education in American schools, particularly after Russia beat us into space with the successful launch of Sputnik. Brother Charles Kline and Brother Virgil Fenerty started in the program a year or two before I participated, so they were there to support me with their experience. Brother Luke Swatloski, who had been my physics teacher in the Juniorate, and Brother Ignatius ("Iggy"), who was on the AIC faculty with me, and Brother Gerald Dotson, who was a year behind me in formation, were all in attendance at Ole Miss for some of my summers there.

PASSING JAMES MEREDITH

In my summer session in 1963, I passed James Meredith as we were walking in opposite directions on one of the campus sidewalks. He had been admitted to Ole Miss in October of 1962, amid a flurry of rioting and political opposition. Mr. Meredith was alone, as, by this time, it was no longer necessary to protect him with federal marshals. I recognized him immediately from his widely disseminated pictures and the fact that he was the only black student on campus.

He avoided eye contact, and ignored me with an expressionless face when I offered him a friendly "good morning." I can understand his attitude after the atrocious treatment tendered him before and after his admission to the University. He had a legitimate ax to grind, and I applaud his courage at putting it to the woodpile of segregation ... successfully. Meredith demanded his rights as an American, not as a member of some race or civil rights group. He was a brilliant scholar and a republican.

DR. BARNES

There was a professor of mathematics at Ole Miss whose classes several of our Brothers attended. I was not one of them, but I learned that Dr. Barnes was something of a recluse who lived with his elderly mother. Once, in a complete departure from his normal serious demeanor, he asked his class, "Where was Moses when the lights went out?"

He appeared more amused than his befuddled students, when he gave the answer, "In the dark!" I filed this story in my mind, as I've always been an aficionado of corn. Then, one day, I saw Dr. Barnes coming down a hallway, and I asked him (we had never previously met), "Dr. Barnes, where was Moses when the lights went out?" This act on my part turned out to be a real icebreaker.

Later, when I passed Dr. Barnes near the natatorium, he remembered me, and we got into a conversation. I discovered that he was locked into the world of caring for his mother and mathematics. Except for taking vigorous walks by himself, he engaged in no hobbies or recreation. He had no friends, only professional associates. I asked him if he ever went swimming in the nearby pool, and he seemed ashamed to admit he didn't know how to swim. I told him I could quickly teach him how to swim and coaxed him to meet me at the pool one afternoon. He did, and I had him swimming after an hour. This new found skill thrilled Dr. Barnes no end, and we became friends. We continued as pen pals after the summer.

Dr. Barnes, curious about my profession as a religious, engaged me in questions about the Catholic faith. He was an agnostic. However, he was not only very intelligent but was intellectually honest. I answered his probing questions as best I could. About two years later, Dr. Barnes wrote to tell me he was being baptized as a Catholic. His mother had died, and he had purchased the former home of William Faulkner. He invited me to stay at his new house, if ever I was in the Ole Miss area. The Faulkner estate was quite grand, and my Mom and I stayed there one night on a journey from New Orleans to Prestonsburg, KY. Dr. Barnes lived alone, and we were swallowed up in the spaciousness of the Faulkner house. My grandkids will be able to say "My Paw-Paw slept in William Faulkner's house," when they study American literature.

COMMANDER HORTON, USN

My academic advisor and physics teacher at Ole Miss was Mr. George Horton, a retired navy commander of a destroyer deployed in World War II. He was a brilliant teacher and as down to earth as they come. I took to taking rough notes every day in class and refining them later in the evening. We were off every weekend, and I tried to avoid all studying and relax. On Sunday evening, I would review the notes of the previous week. This approach enabled me to avoid all cramming before tests and exams.

On the Friday before one semester final scheduled for the following week, I asked Mr. Horton if I could take my final at a different time than scheduled because of some conflict with my community responsibilities. He smiled and said, "How about right now?" I agreed and took the exam right then and there. My high score validated the approach I had taken of thoroughly digesting course material every day.

TRUSTING YOUR OWN JUDGMENT

In an optics course, we did considerable lab work to back up theory. There was one particular formula that I learned to verify in the lab. By doing so, I could use the applicable data to calculate such variables as wavelengths and frequencies. On one test, we were given as one of several problems one that involved this formula. We were directed to the test problems by their text page and number. At the back of the book, answers to the even numbered problems were listed. Since we had to show the steps used to solve the problems anyway, it was permissible to check some of our answers against those given in the book. Naturally, everyone did.

It turned out that on this one problem the solution given in the back of the book was incorrect. When I checked my answer and found it to be different than the printed solution, I concluded that the book had made a mistake and let my solution stand. When I handed in my paper, I suggested to Mr. Horton that he check the book-provided answer himself. The answer provided in the text was off by a factor of 10. Every student in our class except me and my lab partner, Roy Ellzey, had thrown in a multiple of 10 to make their correct answer agree with the incorrect one in the text. When Mr. Horton returned our tests, he was not pleased with the action of the majority of our class in not trusting their own knowledge. On the other hand, he was tickled with Roy and me. We received the only two A grades. Mr. Horton and I remained friends over the years.

In 1964, I arranged to have him give a special presentation he had perfected for high school students at Rummel High School. His presentation was entitled "The Utility of the Useless." It demonstrated the principles of physics behind many of the things used in everyday life. I paid his honorarium out of my physics budget and surrendered my apartment to him and his wife, while they were in town. In 1968, Mr. Horton, now a professor emeritus at Ole Miss, helped me get my first college teaching job with the University of Kentucky.

During World War II, Mr. Horton was a commander of a navy destroyer. Once, he and his staff were speculating on the critical mass of the fission material in an atomic bomb. Mr. Horton offered that it would be about five pounds. He was too close to the top secret amount and was soon under investigation as to how he came by his knowledge. Mr. Horton was one of the finest men I have ever known.

AN ACCIDENT IN OXFORD

The AIC community enjoyed the use of a new Ford four-door sedan, provided by the local dealership that was owned by the family of one of our students. I would drive it to Oxford, and our summer school community would use it to get around. Once, Brother Gerald and I took it to a popular reservoir out in the countryside. I was driving with Gerald in the front-passenger seat, when we rounded a sharp blind curve to the left on the narrow dirt road. When we were out of the blind spot, I saw a speeding sedan heading right for us. The sedan braked violently, but it continued to skid toward us. I stopped my car and turned it slightly to the right, in order to have my left front bumper and tire absorb most of the energy of the impending collision.

No one was hurt beyond a bruise or two, but both vehicles were seriously damaged. The skid marks left by the other driver bore out to the police that the other driver was at fault. As with the bus accident in the Pecos River valley, I remained calm and reacted defensively.

This ability to assess an imminent danger and instantaneously formulate a defensive plan of action stayed with me through later wrecks. The plans were always based on my knowledge of the physics laws of motion which instantly came to mind. It amazes me that the human brain can go through a complicated process in a split second.

Of course, there is always my guardian angel to thank. He most certainly must have been with me on another road trip I made with Brother Anthony, my director at AIC. I was his chauffeur, since he did not drive. We had spent a few days in Memphis with the Christian Brothers College community before leaving for Opelousas early on a Sunday morning.

Brother Anthony urged me to make it to Natchez, 261 miles south, in time for Sunday mass. Ignoring speed limits, I drove as fast as I could along the narrow twisting roads of north Mississippi. I calculated from my watch and odometer reading that I had averaged 74 miles per hour. That was probably a trip on which I should have had an accident and certainly should have received a speeding ticket. Brother Anthony was delighted that we made Mass on time, and we continued home to Opelousas at a leisurely, legal pace.

THE BEAUTIFUL COEDS OF OLE MISS

There must be something in the water at Ole Miss. Its campus is populated by an extraordinary number of beautiful coeds. It's not that other campuses are bereft of beautiful women; it's just that they are so commonplace in Oxford. One of the sororities provided consecutive Miss Americas—Mary Ann Mobley in 1959 and Lynda Lee Mead in 1960. There is always an Ole Miss coed finishing high in the Miss America pageant.

One afternoon, I was at the pool practicing different basic dives from the springboard, along with other Rebels. One of these was a beautiful blond wearing (what else?) a polka dot bikini. Out of the blue, she walked up to me and cooed, "Do you want to teach me how to dive?" She stressed the word "me" and made the word "dive" sound like it contained the letter "I" five times.

I had observed that she dived quite well and, not wanting to get into an explanation of my vow of chastity, I blurted out, "You already know how to dive." She turned away, obviously shocked and surprised at the rejection, and soon got another guy to take the bait. There is only so much temptation a man can resist. Thanks again, guardian angel.

My lab partner in my optics class, Roy Ellzey, was one of a number of secular students enrolled in graduate school with the assistance of a NSF grant like mine. Roy played the leading role (Joe Hardy) in the drama department's summer production of the musical comedy, "Damn Yankees." I attended one showing and chanced to meet backstage before the performance a coed playing one of the female roles. She was a gorgeous green-eyed, redhead. There was no need to reject her, as she did not come on to me, but I did tell her in the show-biz tradition to "break a leg." It's a good thing I didn't say that to the beautiful blond at the pool (even though she was certainly putting on an act). I would have needed my guardian angel's protection big time. What is it they say? "Hell hath no fury like a woman scorned."

5

NEW ORLEANS, METAIRIE, HOUSTON, AND CHICAGO: 1964–1966

ASSIGNMENT TO DE LA SALLE IN NEW ORLEANS

I learned that Roy Ellzey was looking for a math teaching job for the 1964–1965 school year. I had been assigned to teach physics at DLS that year (ending five years at AIC). I contacted Brother Amedy, the DLS principal, who subsequently offered Roy a math teaching position at DLS. In addition to becoming colleagues, we fostered our friendship. A few years later, Roy and his wife assisted my new wife and me by hiding our car at their house so we could take off for our honeymoon, with our car free of trailing junk and "just married" graffiti. I visited Roy's wife, Susan, at Touro Infirmary on the occasion of the birth of their first child and represented the DLS faculty at the funeral of Roy's dad in a small town in Mississippi about 100 miles from New Orleans.

I had another "golf experience" during my one year at DLS. I was playing with Jerry Dotson. Jerry was about 5'11" and a stocky 220 pounds. One of the fairways at City Park paralleled the four-lane Wisner Blvd. Jerry, a right-hander, drove a screaming hook that went out of bounds left and struck a car travelling in the rightmost lane. The car didn't stop. Neither did Jerry. He calmly teed up another and gave it a whack. I'm thinking "Oh, no!" His second shot hooked even more and struck a car across the median, traveling in the other direction. The driver didn't stop, but yelled out some choice words for Jerry. You just have to believe in guardian angels!

At DLS, I taught only seniors. I had one religion class and four physics classes. John Arthurs was one of my physics students. I tutored him to insure that he maintain his eligibility to play basketball and baseball. He was one of the best athletes in the storied history of DLS athletics and one of the highest-scoring forwards in Tulane basketball annals. He played for the Milwaukee Bucks of the NBA, before entering the banking business. When I had John as a student, I didn't realize that I would one day have his sister as a student at Chapelle and his brother, Billy Arthurs, as a colleague on the Rummel faculty.

The 1964–1965 DLS basketball team made it to the state finals in Shreveport. I drove a busload of students to that competition. I left in the morning from the DLS campus, drove the 342 miles to Shreveport, watched the game with our student fans, and drove back to campus. There were some sleepy students on my bus, when we pulled into DLS the following morning. I had been up for over 24 hours. There would be times when I regretted getting my chauffeur's license when I worked in Opelousas.

I often played basketball in the state-of-the-art DLS gym with the varsity players. On occasion, Coach John Altobello, a legend in Louisiana coaching annals, allowed me to scrimmage with his players at a regular practice. Most of my playing was done on weekends in pickup games with our regular gym rats. Three varsity players joined me to have some excellent two-on-two games–John Arthurs, Lee Bourgeois, and Ned Konkne. John Arthurs was later to star at Tulane and play in the NBA.

There was a young boy who was not in high school yet, who couldn't get enough of basketball. I frequently opened the gym so he could practice. Later, he starred for DLS and the University of New Orleans and became an excellent college coach. His name was Duane Rebaul. As fate would have it, Duane would become close friends with one of Mike Aymami's younger sisters, and, years later, I would see him again at Mike's wake.

Mary Lynn, the oldest Aymami girl, first dated me and then tried to hook me up with another girl. On her second attempt, she introduced me to the girl I would marry. Like me, Mary Lynn had been a member of a religious order and, like my wife, had become a registered nurse.

After a stint with the Marines, Mike had also joined a religious order (Trappists). After leaving the monastery, Mike just went from odd job to odd job and was driven to excessive drinking by depression. Eventually, his chain smoking led to lung cancer, and he died within a month of the discovery of the tumor that formed in his lungs.

Another Aymami son died within a few months of Mike. He was one of several New Orleans firemen who were killed when a burning building in the French Quarter collapsed on them. In his addiction to nicotine, Mike emulated his parents who were both chain-smokers. His father died of emphysema.

The Aymamis were a close, loving family and enriched the lives of those who had the good fortune to know them. My wife and I gradually lost contact with them after Mike died and Mary Lynn married and moved away. For years after my childhood escapades with Mike and our little gang of miscreants, I had communicated with Mike and Mary Lynn by mail when I was out of state.

RETURN TO THE LAY LIFE

After I left the Christian Brothers, following the 1964–1965 school year, I moved back into Mike's neighborhood and stopped by the Aymami house nearly every day for coffee and conversation. Mike had this small fluffy dog, which he named (what else?)

"Fluffy." Fluffy would beg me to take him for a walk by scratching at the cabinet drawer, where his leash was kept, and I would invariably comply. Later, my wife, Patty, would join me on my visits to the Aymamis and on walks with Fluffy.

When I left the Christian Brothers, I at first stayed with my Mom and Louis Lapuyade. Mom had married Louis at Mater Dolorosa, while I was in Opelousas. I needed a place to stay, until I could land a job and find a place of my own. Mom and Louie lived in a small house on Benjamin St., behind Lapuyade's meat market. It was across the street from Mahalia Jackson's house and Sarge's sweets shop. It was just around the corner from my childhood home at 310 Cherokee.

For a couple of weeks, I stayed with Donald Armand's mom and dad in the Jefferson suburb. Mrs. Armand had come to Santa Fe with my Mom to visit Don and me when we were in the Scholasticate. The Armands came to be close friends with my Mom and Louie. On occasion, these two couples would spend weekends at the camp the Armands owned on the Chef Menteur. They relaxed, enjoyed some great meals, played cards, and went fishing.

THE BEAST IN ME

Behind the Armand camp, there was a boat house. Mr. Armand housed a large skiff, powered by an outboard motor, in this structure. An L-shaped boardwalk ran along one side and end of it. After Hurricane Betsy virtually destroyed this boat house, I helped Mr. Armand and his partner, a Mr. Broussard, rebuild it. These men owned and operated a vehicle repair shop in River Ridge. They were both large, powerful men who had done hard physical work all their lives.

One day, while we were in the rebuilding process, I was outside working on salvaging some corrugated roofing, when Armand and Broussard walked out of the nearly completed boat house, exhausted and swearing. They said they had tried with no success to pull up a piling that was obstructing the docking space. They said they were going to rest awhile and then try to rig up a block and tackle to extract the piling. When they went into the camp, I went into the boat house to see if I could do anything to help.

As it turned out, the piling was located in the corner of the L-shaped boardwalk. This placement allowed me to do a deep knee bend, while bracing my feet on each leg of the boardwalk. Using my leg muscles from this position, I was able to free the piling, which I shouldered and carried out of the boat house. On the way to the landing, I met the returning Armand and Broussard. Their mouths dropped open, and they shook their heads in amazement. Armand said, "John, you're an animal."

SUMMER WORK AND HURRICANE BETSY

After a month of crashing at the Armands and Lapuyades I was able to rent half of a shotgun double at 406 Hillary St. It was next to the double in which the Sullivans had lived during my childhood. The young man to whom I gave a bicycle ride to a NORD baseball game on the day that Cyril Ruff was killed had lived with his family in the other half at 404. The young man who shot a hole in the Sullivan bedroom ceiling had lived at 406. Because the house had a parlor, two bedrooms, a kitchen, and a bath, I had plenty of room.

I had taken a job for the summer, doing books and payroll for National Lumber & Demolishing Co. Since it was located beside the Huey P. Long train bridge on Jefferson Highway, I could reach the office via the St. Charles streetcar and Jefferson bus. The job supported my rent and living expenses, while I put in some applications for a teaching job.

After a couple of months, it also enabled me to buy my first car, a new 1965 Volkswagen Beetle. It was the only model VW made back then. It got great gas mileage and was very dependable. I drove it everywhere, including trips to Shreveport and Lafayette.

I made the trip to Lafayette during Hurricane Betsy. I had taken a teaching job at Ecole Classique, and the approach of the storm had closed the schools. I looked upon the closure as an opportunity to visit a friend in Lafayette and paid no heed to any possible danger posed by the threatening tempest. Strong gales and rain buffeted my VW all the way to Lafayette, but I arrived safely at my friend's house.

Before retiring for the night, my friend suggested I move my VW from under a large oak beside his driveway to a spot on the lawn in front of his house. Although eastern New Orleans received severe damage and much loss of life due to flooding, the eye of the storm passed over Lafayette. The large oak tree beside my friend's house fell on the spot where I had at first parked my VW. My guardian angel was still on the job.

THE KNIGHTS OF COLUMBUS

Seeking to obtain some life insurance, I joined the Knights of Columbus Council 3411 in uptown New Orleans. The Knights offer some of the best insurance that money can buy to their members. The insurance agent from our council was Francis Roccaforte, who sponsored the council's basketball team. Francis recruited me to play, and I became a starter and played in our league until I left New Orleans in 1968. Most of our players had played in high school and a few in college. I became close friends with a number of the players and other council members.

Our council had as a member the father of one of our players. His name was Jimmy Seghers, and he was well known throughout all the councils in Louisiana. He had occupied all of the major offices and, at the time, was the State Deputy for Vocations. He thought that I, as a former Christian Brother, could provide a unique perspective on the religious life, as we visited various councils and made presentations on vocations. I agreed and made many presentations with Jimmy, traveling as far as Shreveport.

Knights of Columbus Council 3411 basketball team—I am in the front row, far left; Francis Roccaforte is in the back row, third from the left

Jimmy's eldest son was a priest in Chicago. His next son, Art, was a photographer and would one day shoot my wedding. His last son, Miles, played on our council basketball team. Miles claims I taught him to develop a taste for scotch, given that it didn't leave him with a hangover. Personally, I've never truly tested that theory. Jimmy had one daughter, Gayle, who was my age and had been a nun. We dated a few times and later were colleagues with her brother, Miles, on the Rummel High faculty.

THE HOUSTON OILERS, DALLAS COWBOYS, AND CHICAGO BEARS

One day, while Father Seghers was visiting from Chicago, he, Miles, I, and some other friends went over to DLS to play basketball in their new gym. It was during the Christmas holidays, so we had to wait for one of the Christian Brothers to bring us a key. While we were waiting, I started to kill time by kicking field goals on the DLS practice field. Father Seghers was very impressed and commented that I was better than the guy kicking for the Bears in Chicago.

Unbeknownst to me, upon his return to Chicago, Father Seghers contacted George Halas, "Papa Bear," the owner and coach of the Bears. Early in January of 1966, I received a phone call at my rental, 406 Hillary St. To my great surprise, it was George

Halas, the founder of the National Football League. Father Seghers must have done a great selling job, because Mr. Halas wanted me to come to Chicago and work out with the team. I informed him that I would be willing to do that, but only with the understanding that I would not sign a contract for the upcoming season. After that I would be available.

I explained that I had already made a verbal commitment to teach physics at Rummel High for the 1966–1967 academic year. The Rummel principal, Brother Ephrem, had searched high and low to find a physics teacher, and I had given him my word. My word was my bind. Mr. Halas said he understood and respected my position, but he still wanted me to come. In a few days, I received a letter from Mr. Halas, detailing my itinerary. Enclosed was a check to purchase my plane ticket. I checked with Delta and found that the check would only cover a one-way trip. I wrote back to Mr. Halas. Subsequently, along with an apology, his secretary, Frances Osborne, sent me the funds to cover a roundtrip ticket.

At the time, I was in my first teaching position since leaving the Brothers. It was with Ecole Classique, a private school owned and operated by Sal Federico and his wife. Devout Catholics, their faith permeated the spirit of their school, although no students were pressured toward Catholicism. They taught a curriculum that would lead to a diploma that was recognized by the state of Louisiana. More on my time at Ecole, after I relate my flirtation with pro football.

I had never worn properly cleated football shoes to kick, just tennis shoes. The owner of a sporting goods store, just down the street from Mater Dolorosa, gave me a pair of football shoes to use in my Chicago tryout. Hap Glaudi, perhaps one of the best known sportscasters in New Orleans history, interviewed me and filmed one of my workouts. It was shown on his WWL-TV segment of the 5 and 10 o'clock news. Many of my relatives and friends viewed, it but I never did see it, as I was on a plane to Chicago when it aired.

Allan Trosclair, a former Christian Brother, assisted me as a holder during the filming, which was done at the Metairie Playground football field. Allan was a great punter and all-around athlete. We played basketball together in city leagues.

After my return from Chicago, Richie Pettibon, an All-Pro safety for the Bears, got together with Allan and me for a look at Allan, whom I had recommended to Mr. Halas. Richie observed his punting and his passing and receiving skills and reported back to Mr. Halas, who had given me Richie's number. That workout also took place at Metairie playground.

When I arrived in Chicago, I reported to the desk at the LaSalle Hotel for my room assignment. All of the unmarried players were housed two to a room in this hotel, which was directly across the street from the Chicago Bears offices at 173 Madison Ave. I had the room to myself as it turned out.

LaSalle Hotel in 1966

The next morning, I reported to the Bears receptionist, as directed, only to find that Mr. Halas was called out of town for a funeral. She gave me a per diem check, which she cashed for me. I was to report back the following day to meet Mr. Halas and go to my workout.

I met one of the defensive tackles, John Johnson from Purdue, and he invited me to go to a Cubs game with him after practice. This situation was a Godsend, as he drove me to his condo, treated me to lunch, took me to Wrigley Field for a Cubs game, and dropped me off at O'Hare for my return flight. I learned that John had started a business that sold model shipbuilding kits. It was hard to imagine John, who was 6'6", weighed 275 lbs, and had huge hands, assembling these model sailing ships from all the tiny component parts. John gave me a kit for a three-masted ship, and I assembled it when I returned to New Orleans. I kept it for quite a few years afterward.

My trip to Wrigley Field was memorable. I had never attended a major league game before. At the time, the Bears played their home games at Wrigley and were admitted to the Cubs games gratis. We had prime seating right behind the Cubs dugout along the third-base line. The Cubs were playing Casey Stengel's hapless New York Mets. The joke was that if a young high school player dropped easy fly balls, the Mets "had their eye on him."

On one occasion, Ernie Banks launched a very high fly ball to short right-center field. The center fielder, right fielder, and second baseman for the Mets all sped to its landing spot on a three-man collision course. Just before the merger, the three players shouted one after the other, "I got it!" followed immediately by three shouts of "Take it!"—all in rapid succession. All three stopped just short of crashing together, and the ball hit the ground surrounded by three red-faced Mets. Ernie Banks stood safely on second base.

Another incident in that game showed me that Chicago fans could be very demanding of their players. Ron Santo, the Cubs All-Star third baseman, booted a ground ball and was roundly booed throughout the rest of the inning and game. Santo had been on a consecutive game hitting streak that was featured in the sports news. Not having got a hit so far in this game, he approached his last at-bat with his streak in jeopardy. When Santo lined a clean single into left field, the fans booed him anew. Now, that's what I call tough fans! Late in the game, the Cubs inserted Bill Hand as a relief pitcher. John was delighted, as Bill was a friend and neighbor.

MY FAMOUS CHAUFFEUR

I checked in with Mr. Halas at his office after his return from the funeral, and he personally drove me in his big black Lincoln to Soldier Field. He gruffly pushed me aside, when I attempted to hold the driver's door open for him. I didn't mean to offend him. He was then 71 years old, and I presumed he would not mind a little help. A charter member of the Pro Football Hall of Fame since 1963, he had 63 years as an owner, 40 as a coach, 324 wins, and eight NFL titles as a coach or owner. And, for a short while, he would serve as John Hanson's chauffeur!

At Soldier Field, I was led to the locker room and dressed for practice. Nearly the entire team was there—dressed in tees, shorts, and cleats. The locker room was as Spartan as could be ... concrete floors, small metal lockers, and long wooden benches. I joined in the calisthenics and stretching exercises led by linebacker Dick Butkus.

Afterwards, I practiced kickoffs and extra points with a couple of other guys. Later, I ran pass patterns against the linebackers and defensive backs. We would simply tell the QB what we wanted to run and then do it. I was amazed that the QB, Rudy Bukich, apologized to me for missing me after I had broken wide open on a crossing pattern. I never remotely expected that. The team had four future Hall of Fame players on the '66 roster: Doug Atkins, Dick Butkus, Mike Ditka, and Gale Sayers.

In 1971, a made for TV movie, "Brian's Song," told the story of the friendship between Sayers and another '66 player, Brian Piccolo. One thing captured in the film that I personally witnessed was the opposite temperaments of the two. Brian was always chatting and joking, while Gale was as quiet as a wall.

Two of the Bears were from New Orleans: Richie Petitbon and Rosey Taylor. Two others played for the New Orleans Saints after they entered the league in 1967: Doug Atkins and Dave Whitsell.

After my workout with the team, I ran dozens of pass routes for Billy Wade. He was a veteran who joined the Bears in 1961, after seven seasons with the Los Angeles Rams. Wade had led the Bears to the NFL championship in 1963, but was now something of a mentor to the Bears starter, Rudy Bukich. Billy's body had taken a beating after 12 years as a NFL quarterback. He was a tough runner and rushed for both Chicago touchdowns as they beat the New York Giants 14–10 in the '63 NFL championship game. In deference to the condition of his knees, Billy wore uncleated tennis shoes. He was to retire in the following season.

Wade and Jim McMahon are the only quarterbacks to have won a championship with Chicago since 1947. What stood out to me was the accuracy of all the quarterbacks. When passing in skeleton drills (without defensive opposition), they never made you stretch or even break stride. They put the ball right in your hands.

SEMI-PRO FOOTBALL

Mr. Halas drove me back after practice to his office, where I met with John Johnson for our trip to the Cubs game. Mr. Halas told me to play with a semi-pro team in my area to gain more experience. I was actually able to play with two different teams.

I only played in one game with one team that was assembled to play in the Jefferson Parish Doll and Toy Fund Bowl. It was a popular annual fundraiser played at East Jefferson stadium. One of the star attractions was a player dubbed "Tiny," who was nearly seven feet tall and weighed close to 400 lbs. He posed for pictures with a lot of fans but only played a couple of snaps.

Most of the players were from the New Orleans area or the Mississippi gulf coast. I actually played with the team that was given a Mississippi name. Many of my students from Rummel came to the game. Prejudice reared its ugly head, after I entered the game to attempt an extra point. As the ball was snapped, I noticed out of the corner of my eye a player rushing in from my left completely unblocked. We only had 10 men on the field. I was forced to rush my kick and the ball took off like a low line drive and scattered the band seated on some bleachers behind the end zone. When I returned to the sideline one of the players thought to console me with "Don't worry. You missed the kick but you hit a nigger." Seething, I just kept my cool and did not reply. You can't argue with prejudice. Some sloppiness could be expected, as neither team had ever assembled or practiced prior to the game.

The other team I played with was the Hammond Eagles, a semi-pro team that played in the Southern Football League. This team also participated in the Doll and Toy Fund Bowl. We practiced only once a week and played home games in Slidell, LA. Our most distant road game was against a team in Anniston, AL. We operated on a shoestring budget, carpooling to practices and game sites. The team only provided our uniforms, and we were not paid.

The two organizers were both coaches and players. They were the twin brothers, Tiny and Tubby Doyle, whose brother, Ronnie Doyle, was a coach and colleague of mine at Rummel High School. Allan Trosclair, mentioned previously, was on the team. Nearly everyone had played football in both high school and college. A few had played in the NFL.

1966 Hammond Eagles—I am in the front row, far right (#28)

THESE HAMMOND EAGLES from New Orleans area will see action against the Oklahoma City Plainsmen in Saturday evening's Jefferson Parish Doll and Toy Fund Bowl game in East Jefferson Stadium at 7:30. The Eagles will be after their second straight victory in the charity classic whose proceeds go to making Christmas happier for needy children. The Crescent City Eagles are (top row), ROWLAND ENGERRAN, HARRY DAIGLE, RONNIE MARRETTA and PAT ORLANDO. Kneeling are JOHN HANSON, ALVIN DOYLE, ELBERT DOYLE and HARRY NUNEZ.

Doll and Toy Fund Bowl newspaper clipping—
I am in the front row, far left (#28)

FILLING THE SHOES OF GEORGE BLANDA

I also received invitations to try out with the Dallas Cowboys and the Houston Oilers. The Cowboys offered no financial support for a trip to Dallas, so I never went. The Oilers were members of the American Football League and competed against the NFL to draft players. I preferred to play in the NFL, but I thought it would be good experience to go to Houston and work out for them ... and, unlike Dallas, they were paying my expenses. I made the relatively short drive to Houston accompanied by Jo-Jo Bertrand, an ex-Christian Brother like myself. Jo-Jo had been one year behind me in the Juniorate.

As per instructions, I called the Oilers office and was directed to their practice facility, where I met Jack Spikes and Charlie Toler, the former a coach and former player and the latter a current player. There were two practice fields beyond their field house that ran end to end. I did a number of kickoffs from a tee before doing a number of extra points from the ground with Tolar holding the ball. Noticing that I was wearing ordinary cleats, Spikes had Tolar fetch George Blanda's shoes from his locker. Blanda's right shoe had a squared off toe. Since they were two sizes larger than my shoe, I put on two thick socks over mine and kicked some more.

Jo-Jo positioned himself to fetch the balls and relay them back to me through Tolar. Jo-Jo couldn't hit the side of a barn, much less Tolar. Tolar would just shake his head and run down Jo-Jo's relays, which invariably landed at least 15 yards off to his left or right. The look on Tolar's face was not that of a happy camper.

At least, I can always say that I played in George Blanda's shoes. George is in the College Football Hall of Fame of both the AFL and NFL. Some years later, the AFL and NFL merged, and, in 1999, the Houston Oilers moved their franchise and became the Tennessee Titans. A new franchise, the Houston Texans, began operating out of Houston in 2002.

ECOLE CLASSIQUE AND THE CURTIS FAMILY

In the spring of 1966, I traded in my VW and purchased a Ford Custom four-door. I was familiar with this car, having driven the '59 through '64 models while in Opelousas. Al Hirt's brother, Andrew Hirt, was on the Ecole faculty. Unfortunately, he was mugged and knocked into a vegetative state.

One of my colleagues at Ecole Classique was an attractive woman from Mississippi (are there any other kind?). We had gone out a few times, and she was spending the summer as a counselor at a summer camp for rich girls near Hanover, NH. One of my students spent her summers at her home in Gloucester, MA. While in New Orleans, she and her older sister (a student at Loyola University) lived in an uptown apartment with their aunt. I became friends with both girls and their aunt.

The younger girl shared an adventure with me, when we both joined the cast of a musical presented at the Municipal Auditorium. We learned of the production from an ad in the *Times-Picayune*, seeking singers and musicians. I remember auditioning at the home of the producer in East New Orleans. I sang "Old Man River" to his accompanying me on the piano. My student didn't have a car or driver's license, so I'd pick her up to go to rehearsals.

A few times, we practiced our parts at Ecole Classique after school. She played the piano at these sessions. The musical we performed was a romantic comedy named "The New Moon." The costumes were of French Revolution vintage, and the story partly took place in New Orleans.

We performed to a packed house, but only once. The subsequent scheduled performances were canceled. To say we were a flop is too kind. At one point in a scene, the entire chorus of some 50 men and women were to come bouncing on stage from the wings to join the leading man and woman soloists. We were cued by a woman named Johnnie. Johnnie just happened to cue us in about 50 bars too soon. The look on the faces of the lead singers, who were in the middle of their duet, was one of total surprise and shock. We stormed in singing "Stout-hearted Men." It was a difficult situation from which to recover, which we did not. Our premiere was our only performance.

A SURPRISE VISIT

Early in the summer of '66, the father of one of my students, a "Captain of Industry," drove up to my rental at 406 Hillary St. I was up on a ladder painting the weather boards. Mike Aymami and I had contracted with the owner to paint the entire exterior. You would think that greeting these very rich yankees in my painting garb would not make a good impression, but the Captain liked the fact that I could do manual labor, as well as teach physics. He even offered to help me obtain paint. He happened to own a marine paint manufacturing business and profited greatly from government contracts.

He invited me to join him, Vannie, and his daughters at the International Club of New Orleans for dinner. Members of the private International Club enjoyed similar facilities in many cities. Only members and their guests could enter these clubs. I dressed in my best suit and got a glimpse of how the wealthy entertained themselves. After dining in the finest fashion, we hit the dance floor, where the older daughter and I danced one lively polka after another. The band played classical instruments and was dressed in tuxedos. I also was invited to visit the family in Gloucester later that summer.

MY TRIP TO GLOUCESTER

I drove my new Ford to Gloucester to spend a week with the Captain's family. When I got to town, I called the Captain's residence, and, within a few minutes, my student and her mother, a physician, met me at an eatery on a marina, where we had clam sandwiches. I stayed a few days in a guest room at the Captain's home, a multi-storied mansion with its own tennis court. From that location, one had an unobstructed view of the Atlantic Ocean, which was just a couple hundred yards away.

The Captain had a son about 13 years old. The Captain's wife arranged for their son and me to go out into the Atlantic aboard a charter fishing boat. We joined about 10 other folks who paid the fee to go fishing. The rods, reels, bait, and any necessary equipment were provided by the boat's captain. We fished on the bottom. It took a while to lower our bait and reel our fish to the surface. After we would fish a spot for a while, the boat's captain would sound a loud bell, and all hands would reel in their lines. After moving to another spot, the bell would signal us to start fishing again. I caught the most fish and the largest, a 35-lb haddock. We brought home a nice supply of fresh fish for the Captain's freezer.

One night, the Captain's wife took her younger daughter, son, and me to an expensive restaurant right on the Atlantic. She recommended lobster, and I've never enjoyed such a tasty lobster before or since. One day, we visited the historic sites of Salem, MA. One afternoon, the son and I waded out into the ocean below the Curtis residence. I have never been in colder water, and it was summertime. Another afternoon, we went out into a bay in a yacht. I remember diving overboard and giving a big yank on the son's fishing line.

When I left to make a camping trip through New Hampshire, Vermont, and Maine, the Captain's wife asked if I would take her son along. I was glad to have his company and teach him the ropes of camping. After settling him at a campsite near Hanover, NH, I made a date with my Ecole faculty colleague, who was working as a counselor at a nearby summer camp for rich kids, and we went to a movie on the campus of Dartmouth College. My young camping companion was proud to be on his own for a few hours and was none the worse for wear when I returned from my date.

We camped the next night in Vermont and the following night in Maine. In Maine, we slept beside a fast-flowing stream that emptied into Sebago Lake. I set out a fishing line, and the next morning, we roasted fresh fish. After returning a thrilled young boy to his home in Glouster, I said my goodbyes and started the drive back to New Orleans. I got lost in Boston and would probably still be driving its streets "like the man who never returned," if not for a hooker who approached me and gave me directions.

I found New Englanders to be as nice a people as those of any region, but they had a natural wariness of strangers and took a little time to warm up to you. Fortunately, hookers everywhere warm up to anybody right away. I returned to New Orleans after driving most of the day and all night. It had been quite a long drive, as I went out through Mississippi, Tennessee, Kentucky, Ohio, and New York on my way to Massachusetts. I made a short stop in Oxford, MS to visit with Mr. Horton. I also crossed the border for a short ride into Canada at Niagara Falls. The return trip took me down the east coast states and the gulf coast states. There were no interstate highways then.

"NIGGER" IN MISSISSIPPI VS. "BLACK" IN CHICAGO

When I stopped in Oxford, MS, on my way out to Massachusetts, Mr. Horton told me a story that contained a lesson on racial prejudice. One day, Mr. Horton asked his black yardman if he had ever left Mississippi. He explained that he had gone to Chicago to live but soon returned to Oxford because he would rather be a "nigger" in Mississippi than a "black" in Chicago. In Mississippi, he knew where he stood, but in Chicago, his acceptance by whites was usually all pretense.

In the fall of '66, I began my teaching career at Rummel, teaching four classes of physics to seniors. Before I left Ecole, I had the opportunity to coach a young man on Ecole's 8th grade basketball team. At one of our games, his father, who had made his mark in football, introduced himself to me. His name was Hank Lauricella. Hank had made every All-American team in 1951, after leading the Tennessee Volunteers to 20 consecutive victories in his junior and senior years. He was runner-up for the Heisman Trophy in 1951. One of his rivals for the honor was Rudy Bukich, whom I had practiced with on my trip to Chicago. Small world.

My first year at Rummel, I continued to teach one physics class at Ecole Classique. Both schools accommodated my schedule to allow it. Physics teachers were in demand then, and I didn't want to leave Mr. Federico of Ecole Classique in a bind. He had given me my first job after I left the Christian Brothers.

6

MATRIMONY: JANUARY 28, 1967

PATTY CALLEGAN, R.N.

That fall, I met my future wife, Patricia Ann Callegan. She was a head nurse at Charity Hospital. My longtime friend, Mary Lynn Aymami, who also worked at Charity, introduced us. This meeting led to our engagement. While courting, I sometimes stopped by Charity to see Patty. Patty was amazed that I was able to pass through security unquestioned. The guards never stopped me. I simply wore a suit and carried myself as if I were a doctor.

When I proposed to Patty one night and gave her an engagement ring, it put her on cloud nine. When she went to work the next morning, she was one distracted nurse. She excitedly showed her ring to everyone. Making rounds with one of the doctors, she was asked to hang an IV bag. Patty opened the bag and held it unconnected above her head. The doctor shook her out of her dream by asking, "Nurse, are you through yet?" The contents of the bag were slowly dripping onto Patty's nursing cap and hair. Patty's thoughts were so far away that she had not noticed. Both aware of and sympathetic to Patty's enthrallment at being engaged, the doctor gave Patty the rest of the day off.

On our first date, Patty and I stopped to visit my Mom, who was hospitalized at The Hotel Dieu on Tulane Avenue. From there, we dined at Ye Olde College Inn on Carrollton Avenue before dancing at the Fountainbleu on Tulane and Carrollton. These two establishments became stops on nearly all of our subsequent dates. The College Inn remained a favorite with us long after our dating time, while the Fountainbleu became only a fond memory after marriage.

In the fall of 1966, I taught four classes of physics at Rummel every morning, before driving across town to Ecole Classique to teach one afternoon class in the same subject. I only dated Patty at that time, and she accepted my proposal in December. At first, Patty wanted to marry me in June of 1967, but she moved up the date to January 28th. I was 30 years old, and Patty was 27, when we were married in Patty's parish church, St. Louis, King of France, in Metairie, LA. It was the only time I ever spent in that church. We usually went to either Mater Dolorosa or St. Dominick's before we married.

OUR WEDDING DAY (AND HONEYMOON)

Patty had some anxious moments on our wedding day, as the limo her dad had leased to carry her to the church arrived very late at her house. The wedding guests, bridesmaids, groomsmen, best man, groom, and priest all cooled their heels, while the frustrated limo driver was delayed by a passing Mardi Gras parade.

After the ceremony, we were chauffeured over to Messina's Restaurant on Williams Blvd. in Kenner, LA. Mr. Callegan had rented Messina's reception hall on the second floor. Billy Arthurs captured everything on film and produced a beautiful album. His wedding photography business supplemented his Rummel teaching salary. I must say the women enjoyed the dancing as much as the men enjoyed the drinking. One of Billy's pictures is of Mr. Callegan pulling out his empty pockets. He was only to have one daughter marry, and he spared no expense to make her wedding a special occasion.

Patty in her wedding gown

Patty and me with our parents on our wedding day

Patty used a change room to get into a regular dress, and we met Roy and Susie Ellzey in the parking lot. They drove us to their house where we had stashed and packed our car. From there, we drove to a dude ranch in Ocean Springs, MS. It had a great restaurant, and we got there before it closed.

After a romantic dinner, we retired to our cottage in the woods. Because neither of us had experienced intercourse prior to that night, there was a little anxiety. It was no match for our passion, however, and we had been counseled by a priest and a married couple on what to expect at the obligatory Cana Conferences, sponsored by the Catholic Church for those seeking the sacrament of marriage. We enjoyed one another so much that, except for a brief horseback ride, we spent the whole week in only two places: the restaurant and our bedroom.

Patty had handed me an envelope earlier on our wedding day. On it was handwritten:

John Thomas Hanson
(Read when you are alone, but before you go on your honeymoon.)

I have kept the letter all these years. It was dated Jan. 28, 1967 and read:

To my Darling Husband,

I give to you on this our wedding day, my heart, my love, and my life. You are more lovely to me than hundreds of sparkling diamonds. More valuable than thousands of pieces of gold. More wonderful than a lovely spring day. More precious than the sweet smell of May.

You are my eyes, my heart, my dreams, my hopes, my inspiration. Everything that I am you have made me. You have brought me closer to God, taught me how to pray, helped me to see the good in others and overlook the bad, taught me to love and understand those who trouble me. You have given me a gift more precious than any other—your love and understanding, and so, in turn, I want to give you a gift. My love, my life, and all that I am. I will love and cherish you always, stand by your side through good times and bad. I will love you always—not only in this life but also in eternity. The love I feel for you is stronger than any force in this world, and nothing can move it from its course. My love (and I quote Carl Stanberg) is like a little bird—singing with all its heart in the lovely spring.

I love you my darling

Patty Hanson

Forty-seven years later, Patty handed me another letter on our anniversary. She had been fighting cancer for three years at the time, as well as recovering from a fracture of the neck of her right femur for two months and some 10 days. We later learned that she had also fractured three vertebra and two ribs. Truly, I can say that Patty's love for me is "as constant as the Northern Star."

So here we are 47 years later. We have had the good, the bad, and the ugly. We always rose above it all. There were times it could have ended, and times we carried on. We are two people with a lot in common, and some things that we cannot agree on. What has carried us on is love.

Love is such a small word that means so much. I could not imagine my life without you. All the good things I did in nursing would not have been done if I did not have the support you gave me.

When I look back at my life to this time, love is the shining star. The most important thing in our lives is love of God and his people. This we always agree on. Now, we are in our old age. We have deteriorating bodies. My body just keeps getting sicker.

There you are my knight in shining armor. You lift me up to be more than I am. Sometimes, I smile when I think about how close we are. We finish each other's sentences.

My love for you is always growing. I forget to tell you how much I love you. There are no words to explain my love. We take care of each other. I keep you as healthy as possible by eating right. You are ready to leave the house in snow storms and sunshine to get me something I want to eat. I know how hard it is for you to move. Arthritis has taken a hold on both of us.

I know how much God loves us. We have got to be together in Heaven. It would be so fantastic if we both could die together. One of us will be alone for a while. I do not know how much time is left, but I take it one day at a time.

The second night of our honeymoon at the Dude Ranch, I penned a letter to Patty's parents on the resort stationery. It was a "thank you" missive for the grand wedding we had. It exposed our giddiness, as well as expressed our gratitude.

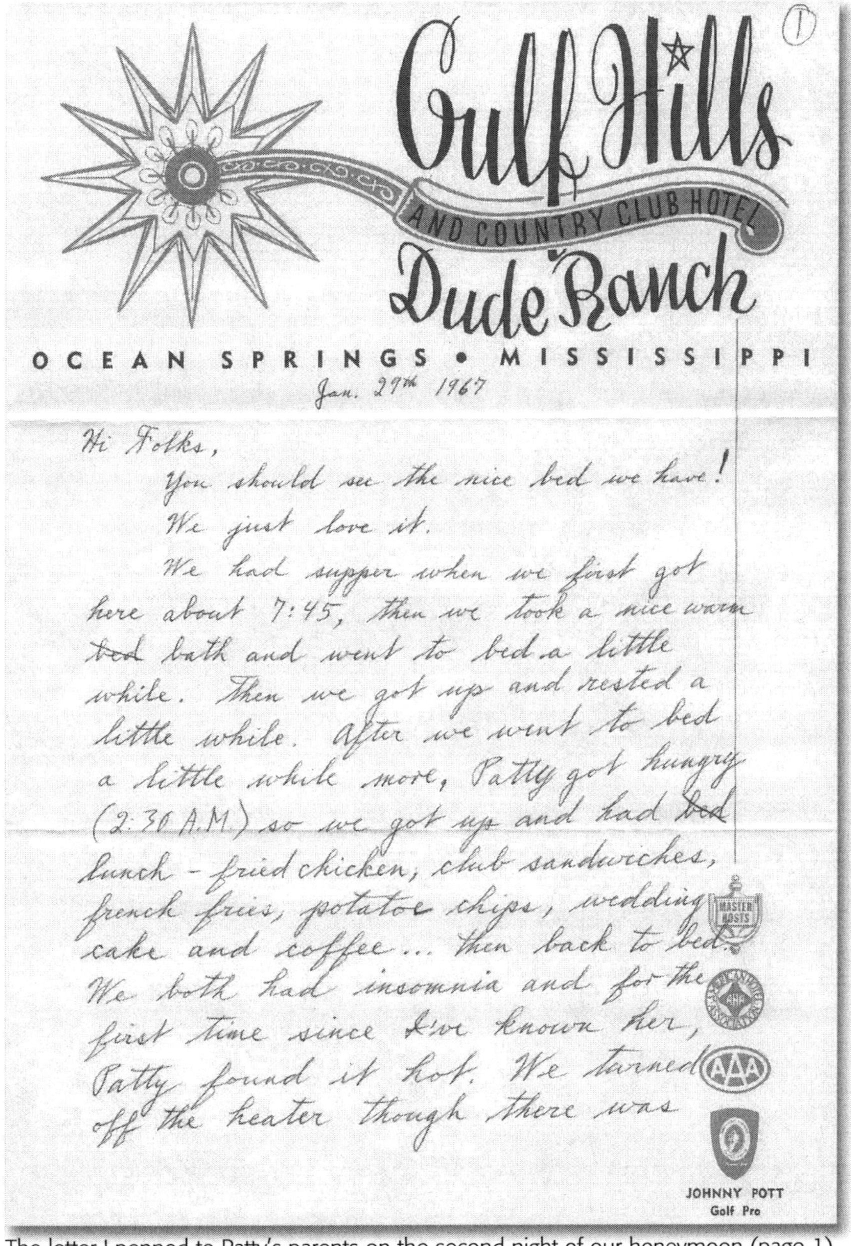

(1)

Gulf Hills AND COUNTRY CLUB HOTEL Dude Ranch

OCEAN SPRINGS • MISSISSIPPI

Jan. 27th 1967

Hi Folks,

You should see the nice bed we have! We just love it.

We had supper when we first got here about 7:45, then we took a nice warm ~~bed~~ bath and went to bed a little while. Then we got up and rested a little while. After we went to bed a little while more, Patty got hungry (2:30 A.M.) so we got up and had ~~bed~~ lunch - fried chicken, club sandwiches, french fries, potatoe chips, wedding cake and coffee... then back to bed. We both had insomnia and for the first time since I've known her, Patty found it hot. We turned off the heater though there was

MASTER HOSTS

AAA

JOHNNY POTT
Golf Pro

The letter I penned to Patty's parents on the second night of our honeymoon (page 1)

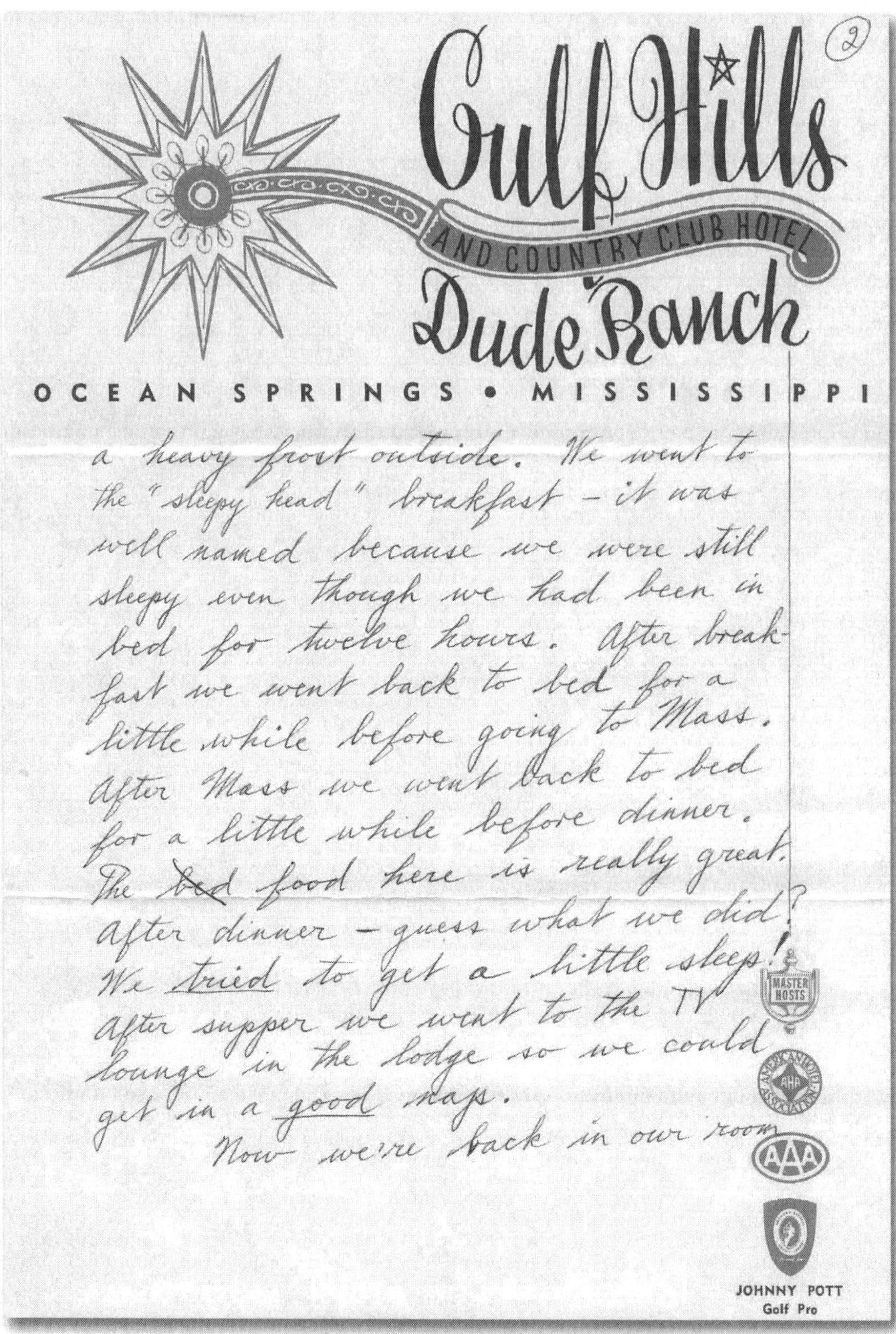

(2)

Gulf Hills
AND COUNTRY CLUB HOTEL
Dude Ranch
OCEAN SPRINGS • MISSISSIPPI

a heavy frost outside. We went to the "sleepy head" breakfast - it was well named because we were still sleepy even though we had been in bed for twelve hours. After breakfast we went back to bed for a little while before going to Mass. After Mass we went back to bed for a little while before dinner. The ~~bed~~ food here is really great. After dinner - guess what we did! We tried to get a little sleep! After supper we went to the TV lounge in the lodge so we could get in a good nap.

Now we're back in our room

The letter I penned to Patty's parents on the second night of our honeymoon (page 2)

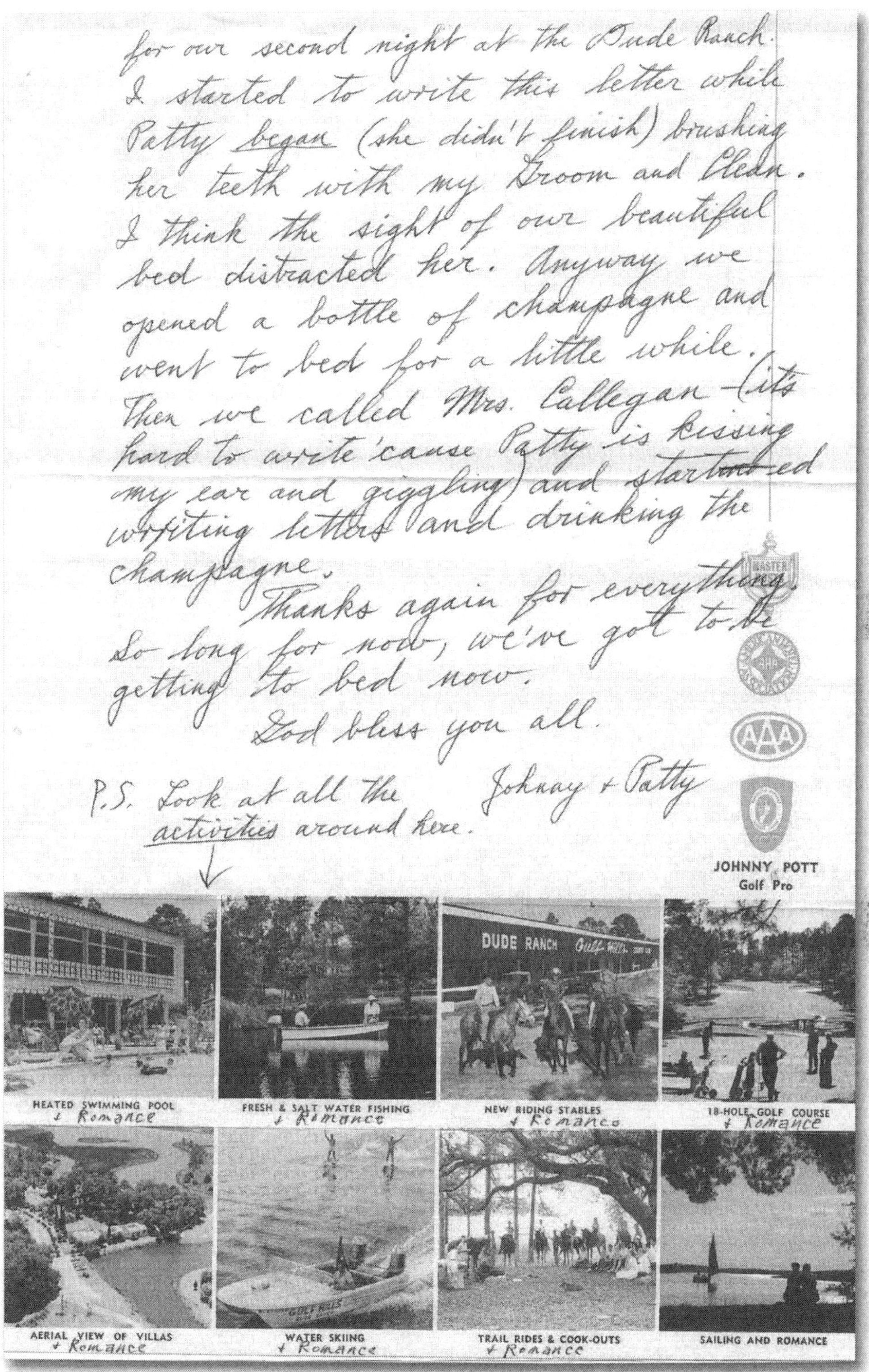

for our second night at the Dude Ranch. I started to write this letter while Patty began (she didn't finish) brushing her teeth with my Groom and Clean. I think the sight of our beautiful bed distracted her. Anyway we opened a bottle of champagne and went to bed for a little while. Then we called Mrs. Callegan (it's hard to write 'cause Patty is kissing my ear and giggling) and started writing letters and drinking the champagne.

Thanks again for everything. So long for now, we've got to be getting to bed now.

God bless you all.

Johnny + Patty

P.S. Look at all the activities around here.

The letter I penned to Patty's parents on the second night of our honeymoon (page 3)

We received many wedding gifts, but one that was especially dear to me was a silver-plated serving platter that was presented to me by my homeroom Rummel students. They were all seniors, and most of them were in my physics classes. I hired a physics student from the University of New Orleans to teach the lessons I had prepared for the week that I would be gone on my honeymoon. I could have just let the administration assign substitute teachers from our faculty pool, saving me money, but shortchanging the students. My way allowed for a single teacher, competent in the subject, to teach all the classes I missed.

OUR FIRST HOME

Shortly before Patty and I were married, I moved from my 406 Hillary St. address to a small apartment up the street, which is where Patty and I took up housekeeping when we returned from our honeymoon. I rented this garage apartment from the sister (Florence) of my landlord at 406. The apartment was located at the end of her driveway and secluded behind a six-foot fence.

It would have been very private, but for the fact that Florence was an inveterate busybody. This situation wore on Patty, given that she had quit her job at Charity Hospital and was a full-time homemaker. We had decided to get by on my teaching salary, because we wanted Patty to become a stay-at-home mom. We were hopeful that Patty would soon become pregnant, but it didn't happen for five months.

We were just over three blocks from the Aymami residence on Dominican St., and Patty and I would walk over to visit with them most afternoons. Mike was living back home after stints with the Trappist Monks and the Marines. Mary Lynn had returned home after leaving the Sisters of Charity. She soon afterwards married and moved to Westwego. We usually enjoyed a cup of coffee with Mike and his parents, and then took Fluffy for a walk. Occasionally, Mike stopped by our apartment, but would not come in if I wasn't home, because he knew the rumors that Florence would broadcast throughout the neighborhood, if he were alone in our apartment with my wife.

RIP COLLINS, USN, AND PELLEGRINI'S BAR

Mike and I worked some painting and tree-removal jobs when school was out. I had noticed that Mike was depressed, and I thought work would help him. The problem I had with Mike was he had trouble getting up in the morning. He was still a chain smoker, but he had taken to drinking, as many do who are suffering from depression. Mike's favorite drinking hole was Pellegrini's Bar at the corner of Dublin and Willow. Pellegrini's was only about a mile from Mike's house and just two blocks from Mater Dolorosa Church.

One of the characters who was a fixture at the bar was a navy veteran. This character knew no strangers and strode up to any newcomer, grasped his hand with a vice-like grip and said, "Rip Collins, U.S. Navy!" One night, Rip was telling an old war story and ended it with a thunderous slap on the bar. It startled the bartender, who was reaching under the bar, and he bolted upward, smacking his head on the underside of the bar. Infuriated, he came out aiming a wild punch at Rip. Rip never saw the punch coming. He just happened to spin away on his stool, as he ended his story and headed for the "head," oblivious to the mayhem that ensued. The bartender's wild punch clobbered the lady who had been on the stool next to Rip. Her escort took issue with the bartender, and they got into it with vigor, before order was restored. Rip missed the whole show.

SIDE JOBS

After departing the Christian Brothers order, I tried all sorts of ways to earn extra money on weekends and nights. Besides independently contracting to trim and remove trees or paint, I ventured into sales jobs. I was a sucker for the employment ads in the *Times-Picayune*. One of the jobs I applied for took me to a small office on Broad St. After filling out an application, I was immediately told to report for work the next day.

Upon reporting, I joined about 15 other new employees in a small backroom, lined with folding chairs. What a motley crew! Most of them looked like they were hungover, and they were obviously not college graduates. The leader demonstrated how the product worked and how to sell it. The whole meeting seemed like a motivational pep rally.

I decided I really didn't want to be associated with their salesmen and their sales pitch. As the meeting broke up, I met someone I had known at De La Salle High. He was still a student there and was surprised to meet me where he worked. We had had friendly chats at De La Salle, and he had briefly mentioned all the extra money he made selling vacuum machines, but I never made the association when I applied. He convinced me to give it a try, and we made a few calls on people in their homes.

It wasn't for me. For one thing I couldn't get past reporting for the morning pep talks. The manager was just sending out anyone with a pulse to sell his vacuums. He didn't mind the constant turnover of his sales force. He just ran his ad continuously and sent out anyone who applied to sell vacuums to people they knew. When their leads dried up, so did their sales, and they moved on. It was strictly a commission job. The manager made an override commission on every unit sold, and it didn't matter that his sales force was constantly changing. He was making money running an ad and conducting motivational rallies. Incidentally, the product was very good. My young friend did very well, until it was time to pursue his college education.

One summer, I provided him with an adventure of a lifetime. After sneaking into the vacant tennis courts at Tulane's Newcomb College for Women for some tennis, we went out to the Mississippi River batture a few miles upstream from the Huey Long Bridge. It was abreast of where Virginia Parkway in River Ridge dead-ended at the levee.

I invited my young friend to swim across the river with me. He was game and stripping to our shorts we eased into the current and headed for the other side. I kept him alongside me, in case he tired and needed some help. We didn't fight the current so we drifted downstream a good distance on the way over. I was fresh but my companion was worn out. We walked upstream along the west bank until we were directly across from where we had entered the river.

Concerned with my pal's stamina for the return swim, I found a suitable piece of driftwood he could cling to, as he slowly paddle-boarded his way. Seeing that he was OK, I set a course for our entry point where we had left our clothes. To maintain my course, I had to head at an angle against the current. I never realized just how slowly my friend would move, and he drifted several miles downstream before he reached the east bank. It took me a while to find him. To this day, he talks about swimming across the Mississippi. He is the only one I know who has made that swim other than myself.

A FRUITFUL SUMMER (1967)

Patty and I took a trip in the summer of 1967 to Lookout Mountain out of Chattanooga, TN. We had sold our cars and purchased a new Olds Cutlass, which we drove on our trip. Patty especially enjoyed visiting Ruby Falls, a 145-foot waterfall located within a cave in Lookout Mountain.

It was a very productive trip. Nine months after our trip, our son, John, was born. In anticipation of John's birth, we had moved from Florence's cramped quarters on Hillary St. We actually moved twice before John's arrival. Both rentals were near Bonnabel Blvd. between Veterans Blvd. and Metairie Road. Both residences were close to Rummel High and St. Catherine of Sienna Church. The second was just a few blocks from Lakeside Women's Hospital, where John's birth was scheduled to occur.

A SPACE AGE CAMERA

In the fall of 1967, I began my second year of teaching physics at Rummel. Three of my students would be my colleagues on the Rummel faculty, when I returned for an additional nine years at Rummel from 1977 to 1986. It was that fall that I inquired about a job advertised in the *Picayune* by a California corporation. What attracted me to the job most was the product they were selling. I had always been interested in photography, and they had a camera that was supposedly foolproof. They guaranteed it would shoot perfect pictures by simply activating the shutter with either a "near" or "far" button. All other settings were automatic. Digital photography did not yet exist, and the film had to be sent to the company for development. The turnaround time was about a week, but well worth the wait because the prints were gorgeous.

The regional manager for this company was responsible for developing sales in several southern states. His office was located in a prominent office building in the downtown central business district (CBD). He recruited salesmen and enjoyed an override commission on every sale in his territory. From the salesmen he trained in New Orleans, he would select the most successful to set up businesses in other cities. These managers would receive an override on all the sales made by their crews. Of course, he got a piece of every sale.

There was the potential to make a lot of money, especially if you worked your way up the management ladder. If you showed the potential to both sell and train and inspire others to sell, the company would fund the expenses of setting up and operating an office in one of the larger cities in a region. It was a way to set up your own business, without the expenses of rent and advertising.

The manager used a conference room to introduce his selected trainees to the art of selling the camera. The entire pitch was modeled on the canned pitch utilized by encyclopedia salesmen. It was quite a lot to memorize, along with demonstrating the camera. All married persons had to have their spouse present for the presentation. After going over the presentation on a Thursday and Friday, Howard gave us the weekend to prepare to make the presentation to the rest of the trainees on Monday. Come Monday, I was the only one who made the pitch from start to finish flawlessly. I also bought a camera for my own use and took pictures to bring with me on sales calls.

The psychology of the pitch was to ask a series of questions to which the customer would answer "yes." This sequence subsequently led to the final "yes" to an order. The price of the package was just over $1,000, which was a lot of money back then. The company offered incentives for referrals, along with financing. They also had an artist render a large framed portrait in oil from a photograph submitted by the buyer.

The financing contract called for a $10 deposit. We were told that if the customer didn't have the $10, we could take something of greater value as collateral. Once I gave a presentation to an old man who lived in the Fisher Housing Project in Algiers, a notorious hot spot for drug-dealing criminals. This lead came from one of our magazine ads and was given to me to work. I felt bad about taking this old man's TV, but by the end of my pitch, he was drooling for the camera and insisted that I take his TV. I walked out of the project with the TV on my shoulder. Fortunately it was mid-afternoon, and most of the criminals lay low until after dark. The manager and the crew just shook their heads, when I brought in that order with a TV for the $10 collateral.

A PROFITABLE WEEKEND

One weekend, Patty went to Houston with my Mom and Louie Lapuyade to take in the sights, particularly the Astrodome. I went to Houma to work some magazine leads. About 9 a.m., I started with one that was in a trailer park. Beside the target trailer, there was a carport. In it, two men were working on the fuselage of a small airplane. When I inquired of them if they knew the name on the lead, one of them informed me that his name was on the lead, but he wasn't interested in any camera. He said I should knock on the trailer door beside the carport and ask his wife if she had sent in the inquiry.

The woman desperately wanted to see the camera, but I informed her that I couldn't show it to her unless her husband watched with her. She badgered him to the point where he agreed to listen with her under the carport, while he continued to work on the plane. His friend and helper would listen too.

I quickly saw that the man and his friend were intent on disrupting me at every turn. My experience at controlling students, intent on disrupting my lesson, stood me in good stead. Not only did I make the sale, but the helper, who lived in a trailer across the road, wanted the camera too! When I told him I couldn't sell him one because his wife wasn't there for the demonstration, he practically begged me to return that evening when she would be home from work.

I did return, but the wife wasn't about to listen to my pitch after a hard day's work. I could still hear them arguing as I pulled away. I made $460 that weekend. That was about a month's pay as a teacher.

Soon, I was offered the Baton Rouge district. I wanted the position, but I wasn't going to break my teaching contract. By the spring of 1968, the Baton Rouge vacancy had been filled. I was offered the State of Tennessee with a downtown office in Memphis. I could make the move after school let out. It would be a new challenge and an opportunity to make 10 times as much as I did in teaching. Patty, as always, was on board with whatever I wanted to do.

THE BIRTH OF OUR SON, JOHN T. HANSON, III

We were still living on Hesiod St., when John was born on April 1, 1968 at the Lakeside Women's Hospital. We arrived late at night, and the frequency of Patty's contractions rapidly increased. I don't think our doctor was anxious to come out in the wee hours, because he ordered a medication that slowed Patty's contractions to a near halt.

At a more convenient (for the doctor) time that morning, John made his entrance into this world. He must have been working out in the womb because he exhibited muscular definition from birth. Louie Lapuyade gave him the nickname, "Little Man." Soon after we brought John home, Patty experienced severe bleeding and had to be returned to the hospital. So, it fell to me to care for my newborn son mornings and evenings. Little Man stayed with my Mom and Louie during the day, when I was teaching, but I had him the other 18 hours of every weekday. I can truthfully attest that there is no more rewarding experience than tending to the needs of an infant.

LEARNING TO CROCHET

During the months of Patty's pregnancy, I crocheted a blue baby blanket for John. I didn't start this project. Patty did. When she became frustrated translating the instruction booklet, I began reading the directions and wound up making the blanket. The whole process consisted of using a crochet hook to tie three different knots and keeping a count of them. There was the chain stitch, the single crochet, and the double crochet. I showed Patty what to do, and she picked up immediately what the written word failed to communicate to her. She became adept at crocheting, knitting, and sewing. The only crocheting I ever did after that was collaborating with Patty on producing a bed spread. We still have it.

A WRECK ON THE CAUSEWAY

Other than a minor wreck in Oxford, MS, I hadn't been involved in any vehicle accident since my college days in Santa Fe. On that occasion, I was a passenger and escaped unscathed, as our school bus rolled over on its top on the road between Pecos, NM and Camp LaSalle. My luck ran out one morning when I was driving to Rummel from my apartment on Hillary St. As I drove west on River Road, a driver going east suddenly turned left (north) at Labarre Road.

There was no way to avoid hitting him, though I had a little choice as to where I hit him. I chose to hit him more toward his back door to minimize harm to the driver. I was found to be without fault by the police. Not so the other driver. Again, my guardian angel was on the job, and I was unharmed and able to teach my classes that day.

Later, I went to purchase the Olds Cutlass that Patty and I took on our trip to Tennessee in the summer of 1967. It was bought new from Royal Oldsmobile. I hadn't learned yet to save a bundle by buying certified pre-owned vehicles. Because Patty loved that Cutlass, I really hated it when I got rear-ended on the Causeway.

The Cutlass did a 270-degree counterclockwise rotation, as it went from facing south to facing west, before stopping short of the guardrail. My guardian angel saw to it that he didn't have to pull me out of Lake Ponchartrain. The other driver was found to be at fault, and no one was injured. I wound up replacing the Cutlass with a new blue Plymouth sedan.

APARTMENT LIVING AND SCUBA DIVING

After John's birth, Patty and I changed our living quarters again. It was our third move, but only John's first. We found a unit in a large apartment complex near Causeway and Veterans. We received free rent and utilities in exchange for some simple managerial duties. We basically took care of maintenance problems that the other tenants had from time to time and collected rent.

We really enjoyed the large swimming pool the complex had. The residents frequently had parties at poolside, and Patty and I brought little John to them. He was an instant hit. I believe it was due in part to John's exposure to many personalities and age groups that he never went through that "shy" stage, typical of most babies and children.

It was in this pool that my cousin Donald taught me the basics of scuba diving. It was the least he could do after inviting me to go diving and spear fishing beneath oil rigs in the Gulf of Mexico. My guardian angel must have been very nervous about my going from swimming in a shallow pool to swimming 55 feet down below an oil rig 12 miles offshore.

On my first and only spear fishing trip with Donald, we went out from Grand Isle on the boat of one of Donald's friends. Donald and his friend were experienced divers. It didn't seem to bother them that I had only token experience. After they had gone down and returned one or two times, Donald's friend directed me to put on the scuba gear and follow him down. I was told to use one of the cables anchoring the rig to the bottom as a guide.

I didn't follow him very far. Two things persuaded me to come back up. For one thing, the pressure on my eardrums became painful, and the water became so murky that I couldn't see more than a couple of feet. This situation was no fun at all, and if a shark or barracuda took an interest in me, I wanted to see it coming. I shot back up the cable to the boat.

In a few minutes, my buddy surfaced and asked why I had not followed him. When I told him, he explained how I could equalize the pressure in my ears and how the water would clear up after I descended below the murky top layer. He was right, of course, but how was I to know if no one told me?

The pressure problem never arose in the shallow pool where I had practiced breathing with the scuba regulator, and I knew nothing of the alternating layers of clear water in the Gulf. Well, I descended again and entered a whole new world. Coming out of the top murky layer, I entered a deep clear layer that extended nearly to the sea floor, which was hidden by a murky layer about five-feet thick.

I was hunting for a fish to spear, and it was like squirrel hunting, except there seemed to be squirrels on every branch. Fish were everywhere, and I hid behind a stanchion and waited for one to swim past me. After a while, I selected one, speared it, and returned to the boat. I never made another diving trip, but when it comes to scuba diving and spear fishing, I can always say, "Been there. Done that."

7

MEMPHIS, TN AND PRESTONSBURG AND LEXINGTON, KY: 1968–1973

A MOVE TO KENTUCKY BY WAY OF TENNESSEE

True to its promise, the camera company gave me the Tennessee territory in which to develop sales. After the spring semester at Rummel concluded, we packed up and followed the manager's car to Memphis. He had leased space for my office in downtown Memphis, along the Mississippi River. The company covered all of my telephone and advertising costs. I began recruiting and training salesmen. We found a nice apartment on North East Parkway. Patty had only our two-month-old baby for company most of the day, as I managed my business.

One day, I was playing peek-a-boo with John. He was sitting on Patty's lap on our sofa, and I was ducking down behind it for just a second or so before popping up in John's view. John laughed with delight each time I reappeared. Then, I did something unexpected. I stayed down for maybe 10 seconds before popping up. Startled, our little John was furious. He was flushed red with anger, letting out a long groaning sound and raising both of his tightly clenched fists. Patty and I have never forgotten at what an early age John showed the emotion of anger. It was a hilarious moment.

After a few weeks in Memphis, I became aware that I could not continue working for the company. My problem was getting them to fix problems our customers were having. They were laid on my desk but I was dependent on them to make things right. I just could not work for a company if I had to make promises that I could not keep.

Patty and I were in a new city with our three-month-old baby, and I had to find another job. We took a trip to visit Mr. Horton, my graduate school adviser and friend, at his home in Oxford, MS. I showed him the camera and told him of my dilemma. Mr. Horton told me of another former student who went through the same master's degree program that I did. This man was Joe Jeffries, who was now the academic dean at a community college in Prestonsburg, KY. Joe had asked Mr. Horton for help finding a physics teacher. Mr. Horton called Joe, and Joe called me and offered me the physics teaching position. I accepted the job, and resigned my position with the camera company. Patty, John, and I then drove into the mountains of eastern Kentucky. We would be there for the next five years.

THE YEARS ON ABBOTT MOUNTAIN

We stayed with Joe and his wife for a day or so, before we found a place to rent. It was in a very old structure that housed the local post office on the first floor. We were on the second floor, and the rats were in the attic above us. We set out traps that would slap shut with a loud clap at all hours of the night. We also adopted a young smoky grey male cat and soon the sounds of scurrying rodents in the attic and the snapping of our traps subsided substantially. We named the cat "Smoky." We quickly found a house to rent.

The Levisa fork of the Big Sandy River flows north through Prestonsburg, which had a college named Prestonsburg Community College (PCC). Nearly the entire town was built on the east side of the river, and a single main street paralleled it. The cross streets extended only a few blocks from the river and up the hollows to the east side.

In 1968, there was only one traffic light along the road through town. The cross street at this light ran west into a cluster of small shops, anchored at the river by the hospital (Prestonsburg General) and bank (The Bank Josephine). Maloney's, the largest (and only) general merchandise store in town was at the southern end, while PCC was at the northern end. Prestonsburg High School lay between the traffic light and PCC.

The high school gym was the largest structure in town. Prestonsburg was the eastern terminus of the Mountain Parkway, a modern road that ran about 75 miles to Lexington, KY. Archer Park was located on the west bank of the Big Sandy on the north side of the Mountain Parkway. The park had ball fields, a swimming pool, tennis courts, and a general recreation building, which housed a basketball court on the second floor. Jenny Wiley State Park was just a short distance east of town. It featured a summer theater, golfing, and boating.

THE SPRADLIN HOUSE

A secondary road that led past the west entrance to PCC crossed the Big Sandy and wound its way up Abbott Mountain. There was one old farmhouse along the west bank at the base of the mountain and two houses at the pass over the summit, but only one other house halfway up. There was nothing but a guardrail on the left to retard vehicles from a steep drop off.

The house we found was the one halfway up Abbott Mountain. The road from the highway up to the house was a one-way dirt switchback. It was so isolated that one could shoot a rifle off the front porch. In the winter, it was only partially visible from only one turn of the main road.

We rented the house from a Mr. Combs, who had plans to subdivide the surrounding acreage and sell parcels for building homes. That never happened, because the plan was contingent on having city water, and that service never reached the mountain. Our nearest neighbors were a mile up or down the mountain. In good weather, it only took five minutes to drive to PCC down the curvy mountain road. Another 10 minutes, and you could drive all the way to Maloney's on the south end of town.

The house we moved into was known as the "Spradlin House," after the family who had occupied it originally. A short walk of a hundred or so yards took one through the forest to a small cemetery, mostly inhabited by Spradlins. A little further along, one could look down at the Big Sandy and Prestonsburg. The screen of the town's drive-in theater could be seen just over the Big Sandy Bridge. Movies could be watched with binoculars, but the sound was inaudible. Beside the path to the cemetery, there was a fenced-in chicken yard, with a hen house. The road up to the house continued uphill along the east side of the house, past a small storage shed and on to a dilapidated small barn.

The house was a home-improvement project in waiting. It was a two-story edifice, wrapped in weather boards and topped with a tin roof that extended over the front porch. Its heating system was pretty primitive. There was a fuel-oil heater in a large central room on the first floor and a fireplace in the front room. The room with the fuel-oil heater was used as our main bedroom, and the room with the fireplace became our parlor.

There was no insulation in the floor, walls, or ceiling. The door in the parlor led out to the front porch. Our back door led from the kitchen to a small back yard. There was a company we could call to fill a large fuel-oil tank on the east side of the house. Another company would deliver coal by the ton.

Cutting my own firewood from the forest on the mountain proved impractical, given that the time it took me to cut the wood equaled the time it took to burn. I only had an ax and a handsaw. We used bottled gas to fuel our kitchen stove and a small open-flame heater.

One drawback to our fireplace, besides keeping it going, was the occasional downdrafts. These currents of air would carry fine flakes of soot out of the fireplace into our parlor. Once Patty left John tucked and strapped in his carrier in front of the fireplace, after bathing and dressing him. Attracted by John's oohs and aahs she came into the parlor to find John happily grasping at the black "snowflakes." He was covered with the black stuff.

OUR FIRST HOME PURCHASE

After we settled into our jobs and living on the mountain for a few months, Mr. Combs offered to sell the house to us for $10,000. We obtained a mortgage from the Bank Josephine for no money down and monthly notes of $95. It didn't affect our budget, since we were already paying $95 a month for rent. It just meant that all the improvements I would make to the house would add to its value and our comfort. So, the Spradlin House became our first house, although I had purchased some investment lots in Ocean Springs, MS, before getting married.

Our new home had seven bedrooms. The landing at the head of the stairway led to a large room that overlooked the roof of the front porch and faced south, with a view of a long wide valley far below. The room opposite looked out over the kitchen roof and provided a view of the terraced vegetable and fruit garden that I later installed behind the storage shed.

The east-facing room had a narrow view of our tree-shrouded chicken yard. The view from the west-facing room was all trees, forming a canopy over the switchback road up to the house. We nicknamed that driveway "the green cathedral," because it reminded us of the nave of a grand church.

At the foot of the stairs, a door to the right led to the bedroom at the southwest corner of the house. The door straight ahead opened onto our front porch that ran the width of the house. The parlor was at the southeast corner of the house. Besides its exit to the front porch, it had an exit to a hallway that ran north past two bedrooms to either side, a dining room to the west, and a bathroom to the east, before ending at the kitchen. There was a door that led from the hall down to a root cellar that was under the southwest corner of the house. There was only a small crawl space under the rest of the house.

HOME IMPROVEMENTS

I became quite the handyman by necessity. In order to eliminate the fuel-oil heater, I elected to install electric baseboard heaters, which could be individually regulated. I ran all the properly gauged wiring under the house to each heater. I replaced the old fuse box with a higher capacity breaker box. My department chairman, Jack Cudaback, connected my breaker box to the Big Sandy Rural Electric feed. In order to make the increased electricity demand affordable, I insulated the outside walls and flooring. I painted the weather boards white and the roof green. Most of this work occurred over time, after we had been in the house for a year or two and had experienced the eastern Kentucky seasons, especially the winters when the temperature dipped as low as eight below zero.

FACULTY FRIENDS

Jack Cudaback became good friends with me and Patty. One afternoon, Jack took Patty for a ride in his small plane. Jack kept his plane at a small airstrip, just north of Prestonsburg. There wasn't room for two passengers, so I remained on the ground. It was a thrill for Patty (what wasn't?), who had never been in a small plane. I had flown in one, while I was in Lafayette and Opelousas. It seemed a waste of fuel for me to repeat the experience, though I recommend everyone try it once.

Another couple we became good friends with was Dr. Ken Blick and his wife. Ken had replaced Bob Blackledge in chemistry. Ken and I had a natural affinity, given that he also loved basketball and was a fine player. Ken and I played touch football with the students on the PCC campus.

THE WORLD THROUGH THE EYES OF A CHILD

One day, when John was about two-years-old, he witnessed Patty's reaction to being stung and bitten on her hand by a large wasp. Patty screamed out, "You son-of-a-bitch" several times. After that our toddler would point to every wasp he saw and identify it with "Summa-ma-bitch, summa-ma-bitch." With time and experience, he grew out of it and called a wasp a wasp, but it was comical for a while.

John developed another childhood perception that carried with it the potential for much greater embarrassment. John began to see black people as monkeys. One day, we were having lunch at Wise's Cafeteria in town and a large black man ambled down the sidewalk, clearly visible through a picture window. John pointed at the man and shouted out, "See the monkey! See the monkey!"

Of course, all the patrons looked out the window and saw only the passing black man. Upon trying to correct John's perception of blacks, we realized that he had never seen a black man, since he left New Orleans as an infant. He had seen the children's books that taught youngsters to identify animals and letters from their pictures, and his perception of monkeys and gorillas had been transferred to blacks. It took a couple of years for John to see the difference. There were no black residents living in Prestonsburg and very few in Floyd County. The passing of the black man outside Wise's Cafeteria was an isolated event.

Every year, we had a festival that attracted the students of community colleges from Kentucky and West Virginia for fun and competition. Many of these students were black basketball players whom I knew from coaching our own team. I decided to take John to the talent show that was part of the festival's activities. This setting would give me a chance to introduce him to some of my young black friends and let John see that they were not monkeys, but people like us.

Carrying John in my arms, I explained John's problem to a handful of blacks gathered near the entrance to the auditorium. They took no offense and sought to help by talking and playing with John like anyone would with a child. Thinking that this experience had cured John of his misperception of blacks, I took my leave and turned for the exit. I had only taken a few steps, when John looked back over my shoulder and shouted, "Bye, monkeys!"

Later, I had to drive to New Orleans with John, and every stop for gas in Mississippi was a flirtation with embarrassment and possibly worse, as a black attendant would lean over the front of the car and clean the windshield. Of course, I put all the windows up and hoped the black man wouldn't notice John pointing and exclaiming, "See the monkey!" John finally realized the distinction between blacks and monkeys, when I took him to the Audubon Zoo, where he saw both black and white visitors feeding the monkeys in their cages. Prejudice is pre-judgment or judgment without knowledge. How are the races to know one another if they never interact?

CHICKEN FARMERS

We had a man named Don Johnson on our faculty who taught biology. He and his wife became friends with Patty and me. One day, he noticed our chicken house on the mountain. A country boy, he suggested we buy some white leghorn hens and a couple of roosters. We would get enough hens to supply both our families with fresh eggs, plus extra eggs, which Don would sell to his neighbors to buy chicken feed. I would just feed the chickens and collect the eggs.

Patty was thrilled no end when I told her what Don and I were planning. Soon afterwards, Don delivered some two dozen hens and two roosters. When Patty came home from work (she had taken a head nurse position at the hospital in town), I told her the chickens had arrived. She ran to the chicken yard all excited. She was, after all, a city girl who only saw chickens after they were dressed and delivered to a super market.

After watching the chickens for a few minutes, I noticed a worried look on Patty's face. "What's wrong?" I asked. Patty said, "They're awful dirty." She had noticed that the feathers under their tails were soiled. I thought she was kidding me and remarked, "Yeah, we'll have to give them a bath." The next day, Patty had the day off. When I returned from school, I found her at the kitchen table. She looked exhausted and depressed, so I asked, "What's wrong, Honey?" She replied, "I tried. I tried to wash the chickens, but I just couldn't catch one!"

She went on to explain how she had filled our bathtub with warm water and planned to pass the hens through the window above the tub. To a city girl, this plan seemed a practical approach, though it failed to take into account that the chickens would probably die of pneumonia. Patty described how she cornered hen after hen in the hen house, only to have each hen flap loose from her grasp with great squawks of protest. She imitated the flapping and squawking for me to my great amusement. I had her do this imitation many times when we told this story. Maybe chickens have guardian angels too!

Patty continued to be fascinated by our chickens. When one of the hens began to set on a clutch of eggs, I told Patty we would be getting some baby chicks in about three weeks. She began to enter the chicken yard and keep a close watch on the nesting hen. At first, she was chased out by Hank our largest and dominant rooster. I had learned as a child stealing eggs on Mr. Clu's place how to fend off a rooster with a broomstick and taught Patty how to handle Hank. Joe, our smaller rooster, was never a problem. In time, Patty started hearing chicks pecking at the inner side of their eggs and was there to witness them breaking out of their shells. She was totally thrilled to witness the hatchings and observe the new chicks grow to maturity. When she left the house with a broomstick, I knew right where she was going.

THE MONSTER/MOTHER

One day, as I was leaving work, I noticed an opossum on the side of the road. I hit the brakes and jumped out to grab it by its tail. Far from going into a catatonic state, the possum did all she could to bite me. Holding her upside down and swinging her to and fro prevented her from curling up to reach my hand. I noticed that the possum had babies in her pouch. They were still hairless and blind. Opossums give birth prematurely and complete the development of their offspring in a pouch on their underside. I decided to bring the possum home so Patty could observe the coming out of the babies.

I had, in a concession to our snowy winters, traded in our Plymouth for a new four-wheel drive Jeepster Commando. As a result, it was something of an adventure to drive the standard transmission vehicle up the mountain with my right hand, while suspending the furious possum out the window with my left hand. When I reached our house, I found a large cardboard box, which could hold the possum for easy transport. I placed the box on our kitchen table and waited for Patty to come home from work.

I knew the first thing Patty would do when she saw the box would be to say, "What's in the box?" She did and approached the box to open it. "No, Honey. Don't open it. There's a monster in there."

She ignored me and proceeded to open the top flaps. The possum let out a hideous hiss and showed Patty its impressive array of teeth. Patty practically flew across to the other end of the kitchen and exclaimed, "It is a monster."

I replied, "She has babies." Patty's expression immediately changed, and she said, "Oh. It's a mother!" So, in a flash, Patty's perception of the possum changed from monster to mother. "I want to see the babies," she pleaded. I explained that the babies weren't fully developed and would have to remain in their mother's pouch for a week or so.

I transferred our visitor to a wire cage in the storage shed. I used a length of 2 x 4 to pin the possum back when I had to reach in the cage to deliver food and water. When the baby possums began to crawl all over the mother, I would pin her down the same way and remove the babies.

The monster turned mother

When Patty realized I was bringing the babies in the house to play with John, she got the idea that she had better give them a bath and brought out her pail and Ivory soap. I discouraged that action. Patty reached the point where she would go out alone and remove the babies in order to bring them in for observation and play. John was still crawling, and the babies would crawl on him. He objected strenuously when they got in his hair.

Eventually, I released the possums far away in the woods when they were able to fend for themselves. As with the chickens, Patty experienced with the possum what very few city girls ever do. I learned that Patty loved all beasts, great and small, as long as they were babies … or mothers.

STRANGE VISITORS

One day, Patty was looking out the windows above the kitchen sink, when what was to her a mysterious and intimidating animal passed slowly by in full view. I could hear the anxiety in her voice, when she called me for an explanation of the nature of the beast. It was Mr. Wright's plow mule, who had wandered up the mountain from the Wright farm on the Big Sandy. To Patty, the large mule seemed as big as an elephant. I called Mr. Wright and helped him recover his mule.

On another occasion, Patty was startled by a snake on the west side of the house. It was a harmless, but aggressive, Blue Runner. I was on the slope below the house when I heard her scream. She was trying to run, but it appeared she was afraid to put her feet on the ground. As soon as a foot touched down, she hopped upward. She traveled the entire length of the house with leaps and bounds, her legs pumping uselessly away while airborne.

SMOKY TALES

When we moved from the apartment above the post office, we took the cat we had employed to help with the rats. He sat calmly while unrestrained for the ride up the mountain to the Spradlin House. Smoky was an unusual cat in that he greeted me like a dog when I came home and would go for walks in the woods with Patty and me. He was a great tree climber and, fortunately, the kind that could come down on his own. Smoky regularly deposited one of the chipmunks he caught in front of our front door. One day, I observed Smoky swallow a rabbit he had caught. I had never seen anything like it. Smoky began with the head. I was amazed as the rest of the rabbit followed the head into Smoky until the entire rabbit disappeared. Of course, the rabbit was well masticated, but it seemed impossible that Smoky could devour an animal close to his own size.

One evening, I was sitting in a stuffed chair near the front door. It was a chair that could swivel 360 degrees. John, who was not yet walking, came crawling along, chasing Smoky. When he cornered Smoky at the front door, Smoky raised a paw in self-defense, and I had visions of my young son's face being shredded. In one lightning reflexive move, I spun the chair, grabbed Smoky across his shoulders with my right hand, completed a full turn, and flung Smoky across the room toward the door leading to the hallway. Smoky wrapped around the door frame, fell into the hall, and disappeared for a day or so. When he finally emerged from his hideout under the hot water heater, Smoky was a changed feline. He never ever threatened John again, no matter what John would do to him. John could pull Smoky's tail and even carry him by that appendage when he started walking. Smoky would just go limp.

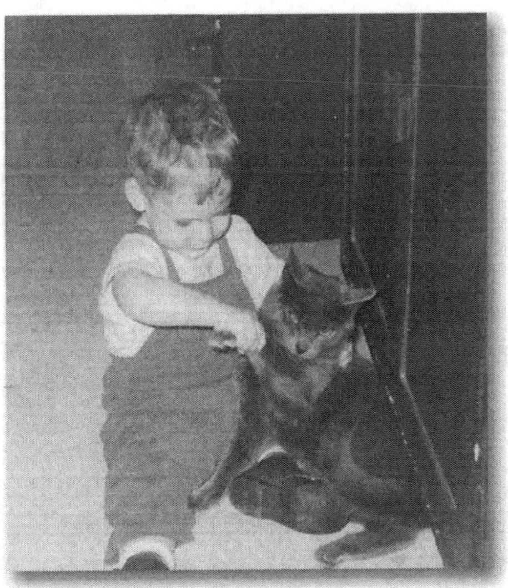

John with Smoky

EL LOBO BLANCO

Our favorite animal was a large male German Shepherd. He was registered with the AKC as El Lobo Blanco (white wolf). Lobo was solid white. We purchased him just after he was weaned from a farm-family litter in the valley just south of Abbott Mountain.

Lobo was a great watch dog and very protective of Patty and little John. When John began to play outside, Lobo would shadow him along the edge of the steep slope on the west side of our house, staying between John and the edge. One night, I heard voices outside in the middle of the night and observed the headlights of a VW bug parked on the east side of the front porch. Silently, Lobo and I slipped out the back door and observed our visitors from the west side of the porch.

One young man exited the vehicle and walked up to the front door. As the man stood on the porch in front of our front door, I sent Lobo to check him out. When Lobo silently approached our visitor, the man opened our storm door and lodged himself between it and our main door. He cried out to his companions in the VW, "Help! He's going to eat me!" No one left the VW to aid him.

I allowed the kid to cringe between the doors for about a minute, before I called Lobo off with a whispered command. Lobo returned to me, where we continued to observe our visitors unseen. The boy on the porch raced to the VW and rejoined his companions, who had thoroughly enjoyed his predicament. I think they all were a little intoxicated.

As the VW headed down my driveway, I headed down the west slope to intercept them. As I hid behind a tree alongside and above the road, I held a bundle of small branches I had scooped up. As the VW passed my position I dropped my branches through the open moon roof of the VW. I can only imagine the panic this caused to the occupants of the VW, given that they never stopped to figure it out.

DR. COOK

When Patty began working at Prestonsburg General Hospital, she assisted Dr. Cook in surgery. She was so impressed with Dr. Cook's skill that she later refused to have her hysterectomy performed by anyone else. The need for her hysterectomy was diagnosed at Oschner Foundation Hospital in New Orleans, one of the most renowned medical institutions in the world. Without the surgery, the probability of Patty developing ovarian cancer was very high. Because we both wanted to have more children, the decision to have the surgery tore at our hearts. Patty had already been associated with many doctors, including the renowned Dr. Michael DeBakey, but she returned to tiny Prestonsburg General to place herself in the hands of Dr. Cook.

While Patty was away, I took care of John. During the day, I dropped John off with Julie Clark, our regular babysitter. Julie loved taking care of John and took him all over town. Townsfolk began to know John better than me. Often, when I met someone from town, and we talked for a while, they would comment, "Oh, you're John-John's father." Julie had coined that nickname, and it stuck with my son our whole time in Prestonsburg. Julie's husband and son doted on John. Julie's son was attending school at Morehead State University on a football scholarship. "Wimpy," as he was nicknamed, was a placekicker (to which I could relate).

TEACHING JOHN TO FEED HIMSELF WITH A SPOON

When Patty came back from being diagnosed in New Orleans, she was surprised to learn that John was feeding himself with a spoon. He had attempted to do so every time Patty fed him in his highchair, but Patty would take the spoon away because John repeatedly missed his mouth. I figured John would learn if he were allowed to keep trying, so I let him have at it. Initially, he got most of his food on the table, the floor, the wall behind his chair, and his hair, face, and bib, but he managed to get enough in his mouth to satisfy his appetite. I would just clean up everything after John finished. By dint of trial and error, John began to consistently bring his spoon to his mouth. When his Mom came back from New Orleans, he could eat on his own. He mastered that before he could walk.

PATTY, DR. DEBAKEY, THE DUKE OF WINDSOR, AND THE KING OF GREECE

Patty was an accomplished registered nurse before we met. After being awarded a scholarship, she trained at the Touro School of Nursing, which was affiliated with Tulane. Upon graduation, she was employed at Touro Hospital. Soon afterwards, Touro opened the first intensive care unit in Louisiana. When the head nurse quit shortly after the unit opened, her assistant, Patty, became the head nurse.

It spoke to her maturity and competence that as a nurse right out of nursing school, Patty was able to run the first intensive care unit in the state. While there, she became intrigued with cardiology and left Touro to study cardiology nursing in Houston under the famed heart surgeon, Dr. Michael DeBakey. Impressed with her skill, Dr. DeBakey most often chose her to be at his side in the operating room. He even entrusted the Duke of Windsor and the King of Greece to her for their post-operative care. Dr. DeBakey had a few things in common with Patty. Though 30 years her senior, both were born in Louisiana and completed their basic medical education at Tulane.

FARMING OUR HOMESTEAD

We had an apple tree behind the storage shed back of the kitchen. A large patch of the slope below the tree had been cleared of trees and was overgrown with weeds. I removed the weeds, and with a shovel, I turned the soil and shaped the slope into steps. Every other step became a row for planting. Soon we were enjoying sweet corn, leaf lettuce, tomatoes, potatoes, strawberries, watermelons, et al, according to the season. Patty delighted in being able to walk out to the garden and pick the fresh ingredients for our salads.

Occasionally, I would put one of our chickens on the chopping block and dress it for the pot or pan. As a city girl, Patty was a little averse to eating chickens we had raised but had no qualms about eating their eggs. There are so many folks who never have any association with cows, pigs, chickens, and such until the animals make it to the supermarket. I feel blessed to have experienced the planting, tending, and harvesting of foodstuffs and the rearing of livestock. It reveals in a special way the hand of God as creator.

FAMILY VISITS

We had visits from my Mom, Patty's Mom, and my sister Ann, as well as her four kids, over our stay on Abbott Mountain. My Mother-in-Law was a precious lady named Annette Callegan. We had about six inches of snow, after we all retired for the first night of her visit. When Annette awoke, she peered outside at the winter wonderland surrounding our house. She was so childlike in her enjoyment of the snow. She had never seen anything like it in her years in New Orleans. We took her for a long drive in our Jeep to the Breaks Interstate Park. Patty had the same endearing childlike enjoyment of life as her Mom. She dressed herself and John in warm clothes and built a snowman. She also used a plastic washtub as a sled.

Annette enjoying the view just southeast of our home (visible in the background)

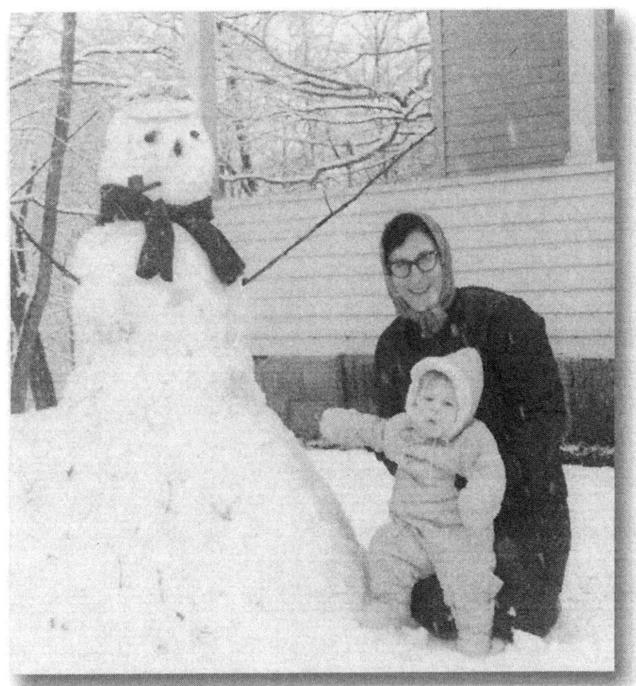

Patty and John with their snowman (The west side of our front porch is in the background.)

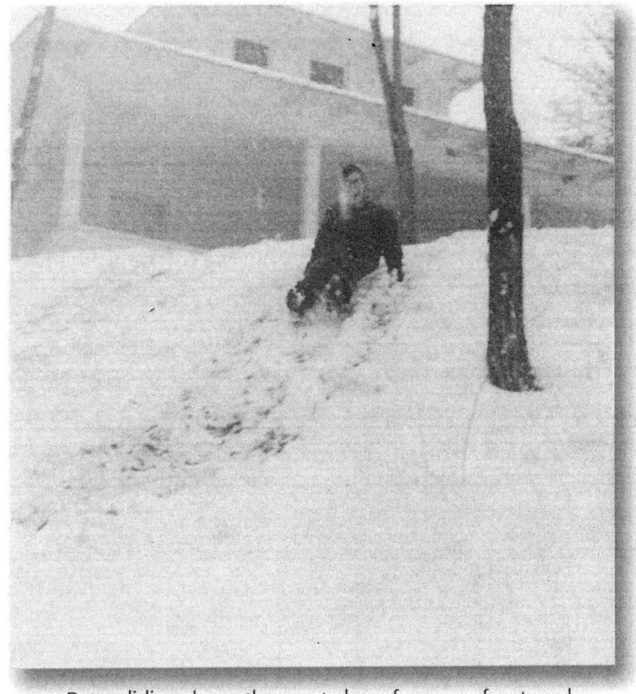

Patty sliding down the west slope from our front yard

Patty on the east side of our house (Lobo is in the background.)

THE UK COMMUNITY COLLEGE SYSTEM

PCC enabled men and women high school graduates from Prestonsburg and nearby towns to enroll in the University of Kentucky, without the expense of living in Lexington, KY … at least for their lower-division courses. PCC was one of some 15 community colleges spread throughout Kentucky that provided this service. The community colleges offered the same courses as the main campus. In addition, they developed two-year degree programs that trained graduates to work in local industries like forestry, mining, and nursing. Some short non-credit courses were offered to accommodate our local populace's interests.

I once gave a short series of lessons on unit conversions to some of our students enrolled in our two-year practical nursing program. Some were grandmothers who had been out of school for years. Our main focus was always to start off students toward a four-year diploma from UK.

I got to know my students on another level by participating in our school's intramural basketball league. My first semester at PCC, there was only one other faculty member who played—Dr. Blackledge, our chemistry professor. Dr. Blackburn was 6'9" and had played college ball at the Citadel. We were on the same team.

Once the kids got to see me play, they invited me to play in outside leagues with them. We played in gyms in little towns all over Floyd County. My play gave credence to the rumor that I was a former small college, All-American basketball player. Of course, I was not, and despite my denials, there are some who probably still say I was.

THE TURKEY BOWL

Some of the graduates of Prestonsburg High School started a tradition of choosing sides from former high school football teams and playing a tackle football game on Thanksgiving Day. The game was dubbed the "Turkey Bowl." The players wore no protective gear. In an effort to try to minimize injuries, the field was flooded by the fire department, if it hadn't snowed. I played in three Turkey Bowls. Each time, Patty hosed me down when I came home covered in mud.

VIETNAM AS ACADEMIC MOTIVATION

A goodly number of our students had been d rafted and served a tour in Vietnam before enrolling at PCC. I remember one of many individuals, who had only enrolled at PCC to get a student deferment from the draft. When he flunked out of school, he lost his deferment and wound up in Vietnam. Upon returning, this veteran came back to PCC with a new attitude toward work and study. He made straight A's and wound up becoming a medical doctor. We had a few faculty members who were "hippies" and anti-war activists. They were not popular in the community.

OUR BOOTLEGGING DAYS

Patty and I became friends with an older married student and his wife. Philip Meek had been an MP in the Canal Zone in Panama. I was still attracted to the tropics of Central America, as I had been, when Brother Ignatius mesmerized me and the students of De La Salle with his stories of his adventures in Nicaragua. I toyed with the idea of teaching the kids of military families in Panama. The pay and benefits were much better than available to stateside teachers, and I was still drawn by the flora and fauna of the tropical jungle.

It was Philip who enticed me into helping him with his bootlegging business. Because Floyd County was dry, it was, consequently, attractive to bootleggers and preachers. Philip would drive to Lexington and buy a load of beer, which I allowed him to store in the cellar of my secluded Abbott Mountain home. From there, Philip would distribute the booze to his customers. I was compensated for the use of my cellar space with beer. I have never felt that my participation in Philip's enterprise entitled me to add "bootlegger" to my resume.

OUR SECOND SON, PATRICK

Unable to have more children, Patty and I decided we would adopt a little brother to raise with John. The whole endeavor had a tragic ending. We went through the whole process set up by the state of Kentucky to adopt a child and journeyed to Louisville to receive our child, a six-month-old baby boy, whom we named Patrick.

Within a couple of weeks, we noticed that Patrick was not acting like a normal baby. He seemed to be suffering from headaches, and he was inconsolable. I remember sitting up in the middle of the night in our Morris chair, holding both Patrick and John, each in the crooks of my arms.

John in my right arm and Patrick in my left

Both babies were hospitalized at Prestonsburg General, where Patty worked. John had double pneumonia, while Patrick had it in one lung. You could not tell John was sick the way he ran around the hospital. Patrick lay in his hospital crib restless and in apparent discomfort. Our case worker, who was responsible to see that Patrick was a fit in our family, decided he should be returned to the care of the state and transferred to a more up-to-date hospital. Though we had Patrick only a short time, he became in our hearts our second son, whom we lost without the closure of a funeral and burial. We still mourn for our lost son. Tears still well up in my eyes when I think about Patrick. Patty and I prayed and thought about another adoption, but decided against it.

HALLOWEEN AND GERALDINE

We were invited to a faculty Halloween party our first fall in Prestonsburg. It was hosted by Joe and Neleta Jeffries. Joe, our academic dean, had hired me. It was a costume party, and I decided to dress up in black face, as I had with my Mom for a New Orleans Mardi Gras. I remember my Mom danced in a bar on Magazine St. with one of her brothers, and he didn't even recognize her.

None of the faculty at Joe's party recognized me either. I introduced myself in an affected voice as "Geraldine," a character borrowed from the Flip Wilson TV show. I had blackened my face with soot from our fireplace, and Patty had dressed me up in some of her clothes. I wore black panty hose, a short skirt, a long-sleeved blouse, a heavily padded bra, and a black wig. Geraldine was the life of the party. Aristotle says the essence of humor is incongruity, and the faculty in attendance found the incongruity between Geraldine and my true persona to be hilarious. To think I had been a bashful child.

PCC BASKETBALL

My involvement with the PCC basketball team was only that of a fan for the '68–'69 season. I had been advised by Bob Blackledge not to expect too much, but the '68–'69 team won about two-thirds of their games. Expecting more would have been too much. Basketball was big in Kentucky, considerably more so than football. PCC was a member of the NJCAA and, as such, was eligible for, if not capable of, competing for their national championship.

Our coach, Dickie Hall, had graduated from PCC and was an insurance agent. Dickie did the best he could with what he had, which wasn't much. He couldn't offer anything much in the way of scholarships, and his pay wasn't much more than expenses. Like the players he could round up, he was there for his love of the game and his alma mater. There were good eligible players in school, but between commuting and working, they could not commit to the practicing and traveling demanded of playing a 20-game schedule.

Since I attended all the games, I was able to keep shot charts for Dickie, which I would bring into our locker room during halftimes. Dickie would look at all the missed shots and enter into a tirade saying, "I can get you all these shots, but you have to make them." It was like telling the players that losing was all their fault. I thought to myself that shaming the players for missing shots was destructive of the confidence they needed to make them. I noticed that our players never made any adjustments to being trapped by their opponents' defenses. I knew that the best thing I could do was keep my mouth shut. Accordingly, I bit my lip and said nothing to Dickie, the players, or the fans.

During the '69–'70 season, I began to practice with the team. It was great exercise for me, and I was able to make the starting players work harder in scrimmages. I also made it a point to outrun everyone when we did sprints, hoping they would hustle more, knowing there was no way I should be beating them if they were giving 100 percent. I can't say I helped the team much as they went 0–20 for the season. I had to bite my tongue, but never once did I offer any advice to Coach Hall or his players.

With only about three games left to play, I was asked by the dean to accompany the team to Somerset, KY for their game with Somerset Community College, a powerhouse among junior colleges. Dickie was unavailable, and the team had to be accompanied by a faculty member. I met with the team before the game in the visitor's locker room. I wanted to be as helpful as I could, so I drew up a simple continuity pattern on the blackboard and asked the players if they could run it. They had been trying to run 15 different plays under Dickie, and they couldn't do any of them well. Moreover, I didn't know them, so I wouldn't be able to tell them what they were doing wrong. The players assured me they could run my pattern, and we took the court.

During the introductions, I knew the crowd assumed I was the regular PCC coach. Soon after the game started, I had to call time-out, as we were being beaten soundly. My players didn't have a clue how to run the pattern I had given them. After every time-out, we just got worse and worse, and I could feel my neck turning red with embarrassment under the stares of the Somerset crowd, who thought I was the PCC coach. We lost by over 50 points.

Unable to afford to stay overnight, we drove back to Prestonsburg, arriving in the wee hours of the morning. I hate to miss class, so I showed up to teach my 8 a.m. physics class. After class, as I was walking to the faculty lounge, a student approached me and asked how we had done against Somerset. In something of a foul mood, I replied, "We lost. But if I had our team for a few practices, we could have won." It was a very bold remark. It was just the way I felt, perhaps arising from the success I had in turning around the basketball fortunes while teaching at AIC in Opelousas.

MOUNTAIN DEW BASKETBALL

As fate would have it, Dickie resigned as coach with a couple of games to go, but then changed his mind and finished the regular season. A sign of immaturity? I guess. But then Dickie quit for good and left the team facing our annual Mountain Dew Tournament without a coach for its basketball tournament. It had become an annual tradition for PCC to sponsor a festival for the community and junior colleges in Kentucky and West Virginia. These schools sent student representatives to compete in activities, ranging from a beauty contest through various sports. Points were awarded for the top finishers in the various events, but the highest point score was given to the basketball tournament champion, giving the school they represented a leg up on the overall festival championship. The basketball tournament was definitely the central event of the Mountain Dew Festival.

Faculty members were expected to sponsor one of the events. My first year, I had run the table tennis competition, and in 1970, I was scheduled to run it again. Patty and I were sitting at home on a beautiful spring afternoon, just three weeks before the start of Mountain Dew, when the phone rang. It was Bob Allen, PCC's academic dean. He opened with, "John, we want you to sponsor the basketball tournament for Mountain Dew." "I can't," I replied. "I'm doing the ping pong." "Don't worry. We have someone else for that. Dickie quit, and we want you to do basketball." "You mean you want me to coach the team?" "Not really. All the referees have been hired and the brackets drawn up. All we ask is that you play host to the visiting teams, show them where things are, collect the All-Tournament and MVP ballots and present the awards … and sit with our team when they play their game. Bobby Akers, our student manager, can send in the plays."

At this point, my mind wandered back to Somerset, where I had sat with our hapless players, and I was loath to go through that embarrassment again in my own town. After a prolonged silence, Bob asked, "John, are you still there?" "Yes, Bob. I'm here," I replied. "Well, will you do it?" I said, "Bob, I'll do it under a few conditions. First, I want you to rent the gym (the Prestonsburg High gym) each school day between now and the start of the tournament. Second, I want full authority to cut any current players and to add eligible players from our student population."

This time, Bob went silent. I knew he was thinking the $150 to rent the gym would be wasted. He confirmed this when he said, "Do you think you can do any good?" "Well, that's the only way I'll do it," I said. Bob agreed to humor me, and I hung up. Patty asked, "Who was that?" "Bob Allen," I said. Patty followed with, "What does he want?" "He wants me to coach basketball for the Mountain Dew Tournament," I said. Always one to go directly to the point, Patty asked, "Are you going to win?" "Yes," I predicted and began planning to pull off a sports miracle.

There were 12 teams competing in basketball—ten from Kentucky and two from West Virginia. Four of these teams had defeated us home and away during the regular season.

One of these teams, Alice Lloyd, was ranked #1 or #2 in Kentucky on the two major polls. Another, Logan, was ranked #1 in West Virginia on both major polls. Logan had the #1 seed and Alice Lloyd the #2 for our tournament. It was a single-elimination tournament. The champion would have to win four consecutive games.

At our first team meeting, the old players noticed that there were two new faces seated among them in the first two rows of the bleachers. I announced to them that I wasn't there to go through the motions of being a coach. I was there to show them how to win the tournament. I told them that I knew how to win it, and all they had to do was to listen to me. If they did, they would win, and they could have all the credit. I added that if they listened to me and lost, I would bear all the blame, but that wasn't going to happen. To dispel from their minds that our team would no longer be the losers they had been all year but a new team, I collected all their uniforms and informed them that we had some new players competing with them for a spot on our tournament team. If an old player made our new team, he could get his uniform back. As it turned out, all of the old players got their number back, but one of the starters lost his place to one of the new guys. I could see a monumental change in attitude come over the players during that meeting. I could see in their eyes that they believed in me, and that signaled they were ready to be molded into a team. Practice could begin.

I did not have a lot of talent or height. In fact, we did not even have a player who could jump high enough to dunk the ball. I mention this factor, since it put us at a disadvantage in rebounding against the taller, high-flying opponents we would face. As such, I knew that this would make each of our possessions the more precious, so we would have to minimize turnovers. My goal was to get an open shot with each possession. Because of my physics background, the continuity offense I designed for my players was dubbed "the slide-rule shuffle."

Without getting into too much detail, four of my players ran between the backcourt and the forecourt in roughly circular patterns, while my best player moved about in the lane area. Each revolution presented three options to pass/shoot. Pass, if covered;

shoot, if open. Even if the defense reacted to each option, we would gain a step and a half as we ran each shuffle. If a shuffle didn't create a shot, a new shuffle was immediately begun. As it turned out, we seldom had to repeat a shuffle to get open. Our openings appeared quickly, and we never passed them up. Dribble penetration was never in our plan to create shot opportunities.

As one player put it at a team reunion, some 36 years later, "You took the air out of the ball." The player was Ronnie Bradley, who was short in height but long in conversation and shooting range. At the time, I was running the players through the shuffle to familiarize them with it, this same player commented, "Mr. Hanson, we're running around in circles." "That's right. And it will get the defense running around in circles to cover us," I replied. We would be running in circles by design, while the defense would be doing it by necessity.

A major factor in making our shuffle successful was having each of our players take the first shot that presented itself. I explained that shooting the ball at the basket was the easiest athletic move they would be asked to do. It would require much less athleticism than the footwork required to defend and rebound. Passing up an open shot was just widening the window of opportunity for the defense to produce a turnover … "a bird in hand is worth two (or three or four) in the bush." Every time we took an open shot in a player's range, I complimented the team on the teamwork that earned that scoring opportunity. In doing this, I ignored whether or not the shot was made or missed. Once in an early practice session, we had run the shuffle to perfection, and Greg Ratliff launched a long open jump shot that hit nothing but the floor. "Great shot!" I bellowed with excitement, and proceeded to describe how each player had contributed to creating the opportunity.

I sensed from the expression on the faces of the players that they suspected I might be speaking with sarcasm and was about to lower the boom on Greg. They had grown accustomed to their coach berating them for missed shots. When I paused in my tribute, Ronnie Bradley (who else?) broke the silence with, "Mr. Hanson, he missed the shot." "I know, Ronnie," I said. "But if we take 10 shots like it, we'll make eight or nine of them. I've seen Jerry West miss a lay-up. Would you have him stop taking lay-ups?" They all knew of Jerry West, one of the greatest basketball players from Appalachia.

Soon afterwards, my best player, Keith Hicks, tripped over a defender's foot and, while falling, threw up a long hook shot from the foul line extended. Nothing but net. I blew the whistle and began to speak very slowly and softly, but with emphasis on each word. "Keith, I don't ever, ever want you to take that shot again. You could have easily passed the ball to Ronnie." "But I made it, Mr. Hanson," said Keith. "OK," I said quietly, "here's the ball. I want you to take the same shot 10 times. How many do you think you'll make? We can't win against our competition taking shots that we can only make one or two times out of 10." Keith immediately got the point and declined to repeat the shot 10 times. He realized he had just been lucky.

For me, it was a great teaching moment. Following my praise of Greg's missed shot and my condemnation of Keith's made shot, the team realized my only concern was that they take good shots. Our success was dependent on everyone taking the good shots and not taking the bad ones. They knew that I would get on them more for making a bad shot than missing a good one. They all began to take their good shots relaxed, and without any fear of missing.

It makes it tough on a defense when they have to defend five equal opportunity scorers. It is much easier to defend a team that is reliant on one or two scorers for offensive production. Very few young players can overcome a coach's lack of confidence in their scoring ability and have the self-confidence necessary to make a high percentage of their shots. When a coach doesn't give the green light to take open shots to all his players, he is declaring his lack of confidence in their shooting ability. It is human nature that a teacher gets from his students what he expects of them. As John Wooden of UCLA fame declared, "Coaching is teaching, nothing more."

One thing I taught my players was to respect the game officials. If they did not, the officials would not respect them. When an official made a bad call that went against them, they were to immediately follow the official's direction without any facial expressions or verbalizations. Basketball officiating is very difficult, and all officials make mistakes. Showing them respect can earn from them a future close call in your favor. Showing them up will never endear you to them. I went beyond just telling my players these things. When I officiated our scrimmages, I would deliberately throw in some bad calls to test them and make the necessary corrections. It was too much to expect that they would behave toward officials under game pressure in a manner we had not practiced in the gym.

A GOLDEN OPPORTUNITY

On Thursday morning of our first week of practice, I received a phone call that was a Godsend to our tournament preparations. The caller was Coach Goth of Logan Community. They were the #1 seed in our approaching tournament. They had defeated us handily home and away and hadn't lost a game in two months. Logan was a feeder school for Marshall University. Marshall supplied the Logan team with beautiful uniforms and warm-ups in Marshall green colors. Because of their team size, PCC had nicknamed them the "Jolly Green Giants."

Coach Goth asked if I was the basketball Coach, and I told him, "No, I'm the physics teacher." Coach Goth said he had been told I was the basketball coach now that Dickie had quit. "Oh, I'm just sponsoring the team for the Mountain Dew Tournament," I explained. Coach Goth continued, "Well, I have a favor to ask. Would you bring the team to Mann (Mann was a small town in West Virginia) to play us? The local Kiwanis Club is sponsoring a double-header fundraiser that has two high schools playing first, followed by a college game. We are scheduled to play in the second game, but our opponent had to withdraw at this late date." "Coach, I don't know. It's a long drive over the mountains, and I have no idea what budget constraints are in place," I stalled. Coach Goth offered, "Look, we'll cover your expenses and put you up at a motel, so you won't have to drive back until the next morning." After feigning reluctance I agreed to bring the team to Mann for the fundraiser.

I met with the team that afternoon for practice and announced that we would be playing Logan in Mann Saturday night. The players were all excited. I immediately calmed them. "Don't tell anyone this, but this game will be no more than a glorified scrimmage for us. I've been observing you play, with no officials and no crowd, and this game will give me the opportunity to see who listens to me under real game pressure. Remember, our purpose is to win the Mountain Dew Tournament. In the game in Mann, I will give each of you equal playing time, regardless of how the game goes. The results will determine who starts for us in the tournament."

At Mann that Saturday, Logan opened as they had all season in a 1-3-1 zone defense. We had been practicing our shuffle, which was designed to attack a man-to-man defense. It was difficult to the point of being foolhardy to run our shuffle against the Logan defense, but that is exactly what I had our team do. It accomplished two things: It showed me clearly which of my players would listen to me no matter what, and it convinced Coach Goff that I didn't know what I was doing, and we would be no threat to him in the tournament. That is what I wanted him and his "Jolly Green Giants" to think.

Coach Goff poured it on for the whole game, giving me a good look at his 1-3-1 half-court trap and his full-court 2-2-1 press. The following week, I showed my players how to attack the Logan zone, trap, and press. It got to the point where my players loved going against the Logan defense.

OPENING GAME IN BETSY LANE

In the opening round, we were scheduled to play the second of two games to be played in Betsy Lane, KY. The quarters, semis, and finals were to be played in Prestonsburg. My team and I sat together to watch the opener between the #1 seed, Logan, and Hazard Community College. Like PCC, Hazard was part of the University of Kentucky system. Logan treated Hazard like they had us. Even though they were easily beating Hazard, they poured it on with their trap and press. "See what they're doing?" I asked my players. "You know what we'll do to them if they try that again with us." Their smiles and nods assured me they were confident they could handle Logan's defense.

After Logan's lop-sided victory, I approached Coach Goff and congratulated him. "Great game, Coach. Are you going to stay and watch our game with Williamson?" "No," he replied. "We're going to get started on our trip back. It's a long ride over the mountains." I thought to myself that if he had any concerns about us, he would stay and scout our game.

Coach Goff showed he was concerned about the team from Somerset by asking me if I had seen them. I explained that I had taken Dickie's place when PCC played Somerset. "Coach! They have this guard whom they pop out above the circle with a down-screen and ... nothing but net!" Coach said, "No!" and a worried look came over his face. "That isn't all," I added. The worry wrinkles in his forehead deepened, and he said, "What?" "They have another one just like him come off the bench," I explained. His face showed that his worry had grown even more. Coach Goff probably had Somerset on his mind all the way back to Logan. He need not have been concerned, since Somerset had withdrawn from the tournament. I knew that, but he had only asked me if I had seen them play, so I let him stew over facing them.

Coach Goff might have stewed a little more had he stayed to scout us. We scored 105 points and beat Williamson handily. A turning point came at the start of the game, when Ronnie Bradley hesitated with the ball above the key, when his defender backed off. I yelled to him to shoot it. After a surprised look, he launched a 25-footer, which swished cleanly through the net. I had affirmed in a game what I had told them in practice. They had the green light from me to take any and every open shot within their range. The kids left the game, elated over their first victory of the year, as well as scoring over 100 points.

Our next game was in Prestonsburg, and it was well-attended, as were the other three games that Thursday. All the schools were in town for the festival, and the basketball coaches could scout their opposition at one location. I'm sure the coaches for the top two seeds, Logan and Alice Lloyd, gave one another a good look, as each advanced to the semis. We played Jefferson Community College, and I doubt there was enough concern over either of us to draw the attention of the seeds. We defeated Jefferson 98–93. It was our only game where we failed to score at least 100 points.

We came out against Jefferson with enthusiasm and intensity and established a substantial lead. They just were not a very good team. Gradually, our intensity waned, as our opponents didn't really challenge us, and we got sloppy. It was too easy, and Jefferson did not elicit our best.

The reason our margin of victory was reduced in the final few minutes to five points was two-fold. Jefferson stopped the clock by sending us to the foul line, and, uncharacteristically, we couldn't buy a free throw. And when Jefferson got possession after a missed foul shot, the long desperation shots they put up were going in. Maybe, our game against Jefferson was a good thing. It helped keep us "under the radar," so to speak.

Friday, Logan advanced with another easy win, and Coach Goff came to watch Alice Lloyd against us in the other semi-final. He fully expected to meet Alice Lloyd in the finals on Saturday. What he witnessed really shook him up. Though Alice Lloyd was seeded second, I felt they were a better team than Logan, and I sought to have us peak against them. I was confident that we could take Logan if we made the championship game.

Alice Lloyd would not be easy. We expected a battle, and we got one. We took a razor-thin lead from the start and never relinquished it, though we added to it in the tiniest of increments. At halftime, we led 56–50. We had won the first 20 minutes by only six points, a lead that could easily be erased by an Alice Lloyd run. The game continued without the usual changes of momentum between well-matched teams. We just never had a letdown and outscored them by eight points in the second half to win 122–108. We shot 85 percent from the field and 75 percent from the foul line. It was my finest moment as a teacher. Remember, coaching is teaching, nothing more. Coach Goff had come to scout Alice Lloyd, but now had to concern himself with us.

That Friday night, I went over to the PCC auditorium. I knew most of my players would be there to see the festival talent show. I wanted to remind as many of them as I could find to go home and get a good night's sleep. We were not finished. We had to beat Logan Saturday afternoon to be the Mountain Dew Basketball Champions.

As fate would have it, the first person I met in the lobby was Coach Goff. Coach Goff shook my hand and congratulated me on the good game we had played against Alice Lloyd. I stared him right in his worried-looking face and said, "You know, Coach, that game we played you in Mann was just a scrimmage for us, but tomorrow we're coming after you."

I turned away and began finding my players. I did not stay for the talent show, but one of my players, Morton Adkins, did and sat right behind Coach Goff. Morton told me the next day that Coach Goff was drawing basketball diagrams throughout the show. I wasn't worried, given that there was not enough time for Coach Goff to make any changes to what his team did all year, and we were thoroughly prepared for that.

I stopped by our nearly vacant school Saturday morning and chanced to meet another faculty member. "John," he commented, "The team has really come a long way. Too bad they have to face those Jolly Green Giants now. How do you think we'll do?" I replied, "Anything can happen in sports. We might have a terrible shooting day. Someone may be injured or get sick. But, if we have a normal day, we will win."

My colleague looked at me like I was crazy. He was happy that we had just made the finals, but never dreamed we could win it all. Few beyond my team and I believed we would beat Logan. Coach Goff (I learned of this about a year later) had purchased a case of champagne to celebrate his victory in a joyous Logan locker room. It was never opened.

THE CHAMPIONSHIP GAME

Excitement was high the day of the finals. Even Patty came to the game. Shortly before the game began, she asked one of our players, Jack Watkins, if we were going to win. "Yes," Jack answered. "How do you know?" Patty queried. "Mr. Hanson told us so," Jack said.

The game didn't start like we were going to win, as we quickly fell behind 9–2. I called time-out. The Logan players ran to their bench, while leaping and pumping their fists with enthusiasm. I was often asked what I said to our team during that time-out. I told them that I just wanted to break Logan's momentum and that they should not change a thing. We were playing perfectly. We were getting our shots, and they would start to drop as the game went on. Moreover, Logan got some lucky offensive rebounds, in spite of our blocking them out. So, the message was, "Don't change a thing."

Logan called the next time-out, with the score 11–9 in our favor. With us leading by a dozen points near halftime, Coach Goff called time-out again. When my players came to me, I told them that when we went back out, Logan would be in their full-court press. "You know what to do." I reminded them of how we had practiced against it.

When an official handed Ronnie Bradley the ball to inbound it from our end-line, he looked up and saw Logan in a full-court press. Ronnie not only revealed no concern in his expression, but made eye contact with me and broke into a big smile. He knew we had them where we wanted them. It was at that point, that we broke the game wide open. We steadily added to our lead until we led by some 30 points with five minutes to go. At that point, I put in some of our players, who had worked hard in practice, but hadn't played much. Logan quickly knocked 15 points off our lead, and I had to put our starters back in to stop their rally. We won handily and broke 100 again.

When the horn sounded the end of the game, I rose from the bench to do the traditional handshaking. I had not taken two steps, when I was hoisted up upon the shoulders of my players, who led a bevy of fans in a victory lap around the court. Shouts of "We're number one, we're number one!" bounced off the walls of the gym. I was finally lowered to the floor and shook a lot of hands. I could not find Coach Goff or a Logan player. They had retreated to their locker room during the spontaneous celebration of the PCC players and fans. Our students continued to greet one another with "We're number one!" for some time. My young son was just learning to count, and he would out of the blue say, "We're number one … we're number one, two, three, four."

I remember some of the people I met at school the following week, particularly their comments about our team. I met the tournament MVP, Keith Hicks, one morning outside my physics lab. We shook hands, and I said, "You made me look like a coach." Keith gave me one of his rare smiles and replied, "You made us look like a team." Earning the MVP award confirmed that I was right to think that Keith was our best player. He averaged 40 points per game against Alice Lloyd and Logan. I don't remember his rebound stats, but he was a bear on the boards. By having Keith be the third option in our shuffle cycle and remain in the lane area, the defense was drawn away from Keith, and he was in position to rebound any missed shots taken by his teammates off the first two options.

I also met Nancy Campbell, our president's wife, one morning in the faculty lounge. The success of our basketball team was still the talk of the town. Nancy asked me as soon as I entered the lounge, "John, how did you do it?" I answered, "I'll be right back." I went to my office and returned with the detailed plans I made for each practice. "Here," I said to Nancy and handed her the plans.

Everything we did in practice was laid out in detail, with regard to the players, the drills, and the times allotted. Behind the plans, I had devoted much thought to motivating the players and instilling confidence in them. In essence, I taught basketball the same way I taught physics or any other subject. My results with the PCC basketball team bore out the truth of John Wooden's observation, "Coaching is teaching. Nothing more." I succeeded in coaching the PCC basketball team, because I was already a good teacher.

I was surprised by one thing in the tournament. I thought we would win but only by small margins like maybe 60–56. I really thought we would have to "work" the shuffle longer to get open. I knew we would be out-rebounded, and I expected our opponents to defend us better. We could repeat three shuffle cycles in 10 seconds. Since we seldom had to repeat a cycle to get someone (anyone) open, we usually got a shot off in less than five seconds into our possession, once we were past mid-court. As a result, we got far more field goal attempts than I expected in our 40-minute games.

In our four games, we scored 430 points or 107.5 points per game. That's better than what most NBA teams average in their 48-minute games. Much better. My basic theory proved correct. Give the players an offense that requires only the basic skills to avoid turnovers and have each player shoot at the first opportunity. In my shuffle offense, the basic skills were running, passing, and catching the ball. My players caught the ball on the move and immediately either passed it to a teammate on the move or shot the ball. No putting one-on-one moves on a defender to get open. Dribbling the ball was an unnecessary liability. We weren't there to produce the highlight moves that fans found so entertaining, but to win games. For every highlight moment produced by dribble penetration by an average player, there are many more turnovers produced.

Mostly through the coaching grapevine, word of the performance of our players got around. One of our players, who wanted to obtain a four-year college degree, was offered a scholarship to play for a college in Georgia. The story of Morton Adkins is an unusual one in sports. He loved basketball, but his Mom wouldn't allow him to play on his high school team. She feared he would get hurt. So, Morton was the manager of his high school team. Ironically, he starred for two years at PCC and went on to earn his undergraduate degree, while starring on his college basketball team.

I left PCC three years after that tournament. Thirty-six years later, it is a memory cherished by me and the PCC community, particularly the players. We had a reunion in 2006, and it was as though we had only been separated for two weeks. A couple of the players had died, and several were grandfathers. We shared our memories of that special time and rejoiced with one another. None of us will ever forget our miracle on the Big Sandy.

My PCC welcome home party attendees in December 2006

SUBSEQUENT COACHING AT PCC

I was asked by the administration to coach our basketball team during the 1970–1971 season ... gratis, of course. I was able to get a nice collection of players together and start them practicing. My problem was keeping them. It was just too difficult for my commuting and non-scholarship players to continue coming to practice. By the time the season started, we were down to a couple of decent players and warm bodies. We just didn't have enough depth to play my system for more than a half. We were usually leading at halftime, but were gradually worn down by our larger and more talented opponents by game's end.

1970–1971 PCC basketball team, cheerleaders, manager, mascot (John, center), and me (back row, far right)

From the 1970–1971 PCC basketball team program

Early on, we played an AAU team, consisting of former college players, who were led by the younger brother of Wesley Unseld of NBA fame. We were leading them at halftime, and one of their players told me after the game that at halftime, they "didn't know what they could do." They only had to wait for fatigue to set in.

At the end of the regular season, we faced the 1971 Mountain Dew tournament, and, as in 1970, we were expected to lose. I got some of the players who had to leave the regular team early on to commit to practice only a couple of weeks and play with us in the tournament. We won the tournament again, when we beat Alice Lloyd 98–93 in the finals. The added quality and depth made all the difference.

SUMMER SOFTBALL AT ARCHER PARK

One summer, I played on a team mainly made up of PCC students in the Archer Park softball league. I remember three things from the season. Once, I brought Lobo with me and left him in a shady spot with the windows halfway open in our Jeep. I returned from the game to find my seats all torn up. I guess Lobo suffered from some sort of separation anxiety and took it out on the upholstery. I remember also that I made the league All-Star game, but did not play in it because either I was unaware of the scheduled date or it skipped my mind.

The last thing I remember is a hitting streak I had. In consecutive games, I went five-for-five and in the following game, I was three-for-three before coming to bat with our winning run on third. I had made my streak by hitting line drives and being lucky enough to find a gap 13 times in a row. Rather than press my luck, I decided to hit a fly ball. With only one out, the runner on third could tag up and score. If I hit a line drive, and it were caught by an infielder or the rover, our winning run could be stranded on third. My fly-ball out ended my streak, but it won the game. My Mom was visiting during my hitting streak and came to the games. I give credit to her for my hitting streak. I did not dare make an out with her watching.

INTEREST IN TENNIS RENEWED

It was in Prestonsburg that I began to take tennis seriously. Russell Music was the best player in town. Russell never wore shorts. He would take the court in khaki work pants and a tee shirt. With a cigarette dangling from his mouth, he would take on all comers and usually win.

Another player of note influenced me to buy my first Arthur Ashe Head racquet. The Head was one of the first popular composite racquets. Tennis has increased so much in popularity from those days that the cost of a can of balls is actually lower now. The price of a three-ball can has dropped from around $2.30 to $1.90. I taught my first tennis lessons at Archer. One thing I learned is that some women who took lessons could care less about tennis. They were more interested in the teacher.

A SUMMER AT TEXAS A&M

In the summer of 1970, Patty, little John, and I packed up our Jeep and headed for College Station, TX. I had received a grant to take some graduate classes at Texas A&M. College Station is where Patty and I became good friends with Paul and Norma Niemi. Paul was in the same graduate program as I was, and he is the one who persuaded me to work out with weights and pose for pictures he used in a couple of his freelance articles.

Paul also added "humongous" to my vocabulary by referring to my "humongous" calf muscles. It was these muscles that drew Paul to introduce himself to me. He assumed that I must be a bodybuilding enthusiast like he was. He seemed disappointed to learn that I had never trained with gym weights.

We still communicate regularly. Paul drove a VW bus, and I wound up trading in my Jeep for one after I returned to Prestonsburg. Paul and Norma and their young children visited us on Abbott Mountain for a few days one summer. They lived in Fitchburg, MA. At the end of my stay at A&M, we drove to Boulder, CO to visit with Jerry Dotson. Jerry had been a Christian Brother, just a year behind me in the formation process. He now had his doctorate in biology and was a professor of biology at the University of Colorado. After we returned to Louisiana in the fall of 1973, Jerry visited us. We also had a visit from Paul.

JOHN-JOHN AND THE STEWARDESS

Patty, John, and I took only one commercial flight between Lexington and New Orleans during our time in Prestonsburg. I was sitting in an aisle seat on the right side of the plane, and Patty had the window seat. John, still a toddler, had my lap. He was at an age when bare skin fascinated him, and, given the opportunity, he would frequently reach out and squeeze it. As a stewardess paused in the aisle just ahead of us, John seized on the opportunity and grabbed the back of her right thigh. Quickly, but belatedly, I pulled John's little hand back. The stewardess whirled around, spotted my hand moving away and gave me her best "you dirty old man" look. I pointed at John and looked to Patty for support. I got none. She just let me stew. I guess this incident ranks right up there with some of my most embarrassing moments.

KEEPING SECRETS

One day, I was walking down the main corridor of Prestonsburg General, when a nurse and friend of Patty pulled me into an empty patient room. She seemed ecstatic as she cautioned, "John, don't tell anyone, but I'm pregnant." I congratulated her and didn't tell anyone, including her good friend, my wife, Patty.

About a week later, Patty was grilling me, "Why didn't you tell me?" "Tell you what?" I asked. "That my good friend was pregnant!" Patty exclaimed. I explained, "She told me not to tell anyone." Patty chided me, "She didn't mean me!" I had had many people confide in me over my years in teaching, and I simply took Patty's friend at her word. I counseled many folks, especially students and their parents, and it was my practice never to betray a confidence.

THE POTTERS

Arlie Potter and his wife Jackie moved to Prestonsburg about this time, and Patty and I became good friends with them. They had two young boys. Arlie had been a police officer in Detroit and attended PCC with a view to a career change. Later, Arlie returned to Detroit and suffered from a depression that led to his blowing his brains out with a handgun. Jackie remarried and opened a bar in Detroit. We still trade Christmas cards with her.

When Arlie's brother, Dr. Ira Potter, learned that I was interested in going to medical school, he took me to Lexington to visit the Albert B. Chandler medical school at UK. The highlight of that visit was an interview with the dean, Dr. Roger Lambson, chairman of the committee on admissions. We made the trip in Dr. Potter's customized Pontiac, which was one of the first with computerized features. I thought that I might accomplish more good in Appalachia as a doctor than as a teacher, and make a huge leap up the economic scale in the process.

MEDICAL SCHOOL

As always, Patty was on board with whatever I wanted to do, even though she well understood the difficulties imposed on the families of doctors. When I researched the qualifications for admission to medical schools in the U.S., it was evident that most of them would disqualify me for my age alone. All would disqualify me for my lack of the minimum credits in quantitative analysis and/or organic chemistry. The earliest admission date for me would be the fall of 1973.

As it turned out, the UK medical school was one of a few that accepted older students. Moreover, because I was a resident of Kentucky, my tuition was only half of that for out-of-state students. The University of Louisville was the only other medical school that offered the same tuition break. It was for these considerations that I made applications to only UK and U of Louisville. Part of the application process was taking the Medical College Admissions Test (MCAT) and making formal visits to the schools, which I did in the late fall of 1972. What I learned in the whole application process continued to help me advise many of my students who were interested in becoming doctors.

As part of my application, UK required me to write out a statement about my health, philosophy of life, and motivation for attending the Albert B. Chandler Medical School. I'm including what I wrote in my memoirs to help my children and grandchildren to understand my outlook on life. The following is what I wrote:

> *My health is excellent. When I was a child of pre-school age, I was hospitalized to have my tonsils removed, but I have never been hospitalized since starting school. I played all sports in school and never sustained serious injuries. In my senior year in high school, I played every minute of every football game as a center on offense and a linebacker on defense. That would not have been possible, if I had caught just one bad cold. I eat a well-balanced diet and I exercise regularly. Lately, I have been going through the entire practice session (including wind sprints) with the local college basketball team. This indicates to me that I am still in excellent health.*
>
> *I think that happiness is having what you want or being reasonably on your way to fulfilling your desires. However, a man who has no integrating principle of life, whereby he can control his desires and order his activities, is in for a frustrating unhappy time of it. There is a lot of truth in the old saying, "Happiness is not so much getting what you want, but wanting what you get."*
>
> *On the other hand, I don't think it should be interpreted in a passive or fatalistic sense. A man should actively seek to shape his life and not sit around waiting for something to happen. It is so important that a man knows himself, if he is to set reasonable goals for himself and select appropriate means to achieve his goals. I think a person's maturity is*

directly proportional to his unselfishness and self-control. A person's desires will range from animal to spiritual, from ridiculous to sublime. They will frequently conflict with one another and with whatever life principle that integrates one's person.

The man who lacks self-control will be a fragmented person, chasing the whim of the moment. I do not think that one can achieve perfect happiness given the human condition, but the greatest measures of happiness go to those who are men of principle, striving to develop their talents to the utmost.

My relationships with other people have been of a great variety as to both the kinds of people and the activity involving me with others. When I was 12-years-old, I became a route newspaper boy in New Orleans. My routes served people of every economic level and walk of life. I dealt with people of many races, creeds, and dispositions. I kept that job for over two years, and it was a wonderful education in public relations.

For much of my life, I have been active in team sports as either a player or coach, and it has demanded maintaining good relationships with all types of people, under all kinds of circumstances. My most extensive relationships with other people have resulted from my being in the teaching profession. These relationships have been too innumerable and profound to adequately comment on them in this letter, but I would be delighted to discuss them in my interview.

Most people will respond favorably to someone who is sincerely interested in them. Others most often describe me as being very kind, and I like to think that kindness is at the basis of my relationships with other people. My friends frequently comment on how calm I am in tense situations. I think that being kind and calm inspires others to have confidence in you. This confidence is what enables others to profit optimally from the service you render.

I think that good relationships with others demand that one make sensible commitments and be faithful to them. A good sense of humor can be a wonderful asset in relating to others. A very valuable element in establishing good relationships is the ability to listen, an essential ingredient of the art of conversation.

There are many others. Within the confines of this letter, suffice it to say that all of them relate to my personal philosophy regarding maturity as I expressed in the aforementioned.

The most compelling reason that I desire to attend the University of Kentucky College of Medicine is that I think this college can best relate my medical education to the health needs of the people of rural eastern Kentucky. This is where I live. This is where I desire to practice medicine.

I also have an eye to the future. Your college has the stated purpose of providing continuing education to graduate physicians. It will be nice to return to familiar, as well as conveniently located, surroundings for postgraduate study. I also like the attention your curriculum and approach give to the individual needs and interests of the student and the emphasis placed on relationships between the various disciplines.

I am aware of this through what I have read in the College of Medicine Bulletin and conversations with Dr. Ira Potter, one of your graduates. I find the physical set-up of the Albert B. Chandler Medical Center very attractive. I found it modern and conveniently arranged when Dr. Potter took me on a tour of the Medical Center early this fall. These are the main reasons that I desire to attend your college for my medical education.

I received two letters of acceptance, dated February 27, 1973 (U of L) and March 15, 1973 (UK). Though it was very exciting to be accepted by both schools, both offers were conditional upon my completing some coursework. U of L required that I complete a course in quantitative chemistry and one year of organic chemistry, including laboratory. That couldn't be done in one summer. UK only required that I complete the organic chemistry course. That would be difficult enough to do, even if a school that offered 12 hours of organic chemistry over a summer session could be found.

I found that Transylvania University, right in Lexington, KY, offered the 12 hours in organic in three consecutive summer sessions. I arranged for married student housing at UK and enrolled in the Transylvania organic course. I would spend mornings in class and afternoons in lab, five days a week all summer, but I would complete the 12 hours in organic just in time to join the UK Medical School class of 1977.

THE JAGUAR DROP-HEAD COUPE

In the months preceding our departure from Prestonsburg, we acquired two used cars. We got a sporty green Karman Gia, which was mostly used by Patty. I traded our VW Bus for a 1957 XK-150 drop-head coupe Jaguar. Gene Wright, the son of our neighbor with the wandering mule, had moved to Prestonsburg to take an administrative position with the new hospital being built to replace Prestonsburg General. Gene suggested the Jaguar-VW trade, and we made the deal on the condition that any major repairs required in the first year would be the responsibility of the previous owner. This was a "handshake" deal, and we both honored it, given that both vehicles suffered serious breakdowns within a few months.

Me with my XK-150 Jaguar circa 1978

GOING AWAY PARTIES

Dr. Blick arranged a small bon voyage picnic for Patty and me shortly before we were to depart for Lexington. Jack Cudaback was in attendance at this cook-out, which was held in Jenny Wiley State Park.

We had a much larger going away bash at our Abbott Mountain retreat. Nearly all of our friends we had made from outside the PCC community showed up. I had filled a large punch bowl with Brother Daniel's "nothing" concoction. A ladle was provided to pour the punch-like concoction over glasses filled with small ice cubes.

The men mostly imbibed regular highballs, but the women couldn't get enough of "nothing." The delayed effect of the sloe-gin ingredient in "nothing" hit the women in about 45 minutes. They all began to cross the line between sober and drunk as though some switch had been thrown. Patty actually became ill for nearly a week with alcoholic gastritis. Folks were all over the house and outside.

Arlie backed up to the border of our backyard, unaware of the slope he was approaching and went head over heels down the incline. Completing a totally involuntary and completely relaxed back flip, Arlie landed on his feet, unharmed, as we rushed to his aid. Thankfully, he needed none. Smiling up at us Arlie quipped, "Wanna see me do it again?" I was able to see that everyone had at least one reasonably sober driver for the trip down the mountain. Arlie insisted on driving his vehicle, but had to be replaced when he rubbed his car into the side of the mountain near the end of our driveway. It was comical to watch Russell Music's companions struggle to fold his long frame into the back seat of his VW Beatle.

The purchase of the Abbott Mountain house turned out to be a good investment. We had paid nothing down for our mortgage and made monthly payments on our loan equal to what we had been paying in rent. We sold the house to a young couple who had joined the PCC faculty for $10,000. This transaction turned out to be a good reserve against unforeseen expenses over the coming months.

THE MOVE TO LEXINGTON

Arlie and Jackie Potter helped us make our move to Lexington. We loaded up a U-Haul truck with our household goods and headed for Lexington. I drove the U-Haul, followed by Jackie in the Potter car, Arlie in our Jaguar, and Patty in our Karman Gia.

The order of our procession resulted in a comical inconvenience. Arlie pulled the Jaguar to the side of the road with engine trouble and stood frantically waving, when Patty passed by. Not getting Arlie's distress message, Patty cheerfully waved back at our marooned and frustrated Arlie. When the three lead vehicles stopped further up the road, we became concerned when the time went by with no Arlie. I took the Karman Gia and drove back to where Arlie had last been seen. He was still there of course. Along that desolate stretch of highway, there was nothing to do but wait for us to figure out what had happened and come to his rescue. We continued our journey in the other three vehicles and sent a tow truck to bring the Jaguar to a repair shop in Lexington. Cell phones would have come in handy, but they weren't on the market yet.

When we arrived at the UK married students housing complex and began unloading our stuff, we were carefully observed by one of the residents, a young (dumb?) blonde. We were four adults and three young children going in and out of our one bedroom apartment during the unloading process. The blonde advised, "You should have got a two bedroom."

MY FREUDIAN SLIP

The complex was known as Shawneetown, but the residents had nicknamed it Shantytown. UK ran a bus between the complex and its campus. Of course, I drove myself to Transylvania U during the summer to complete my credits in organic chemistry, but I began to ride the UK bus to medical school in the fall.

I like to tell a story about one trip on the bus. The bus was usually crowded at my stop, and students were standing in the aisle, holding onto straps suspended from an overhead bar. I was struggling with an armload of heavy medical texts and school sundries, but thought I saw an empty seat about halfway to the back of the bus. I could only see the head of the short woman occupying the seat, as I began making my way over. I made eye contact with the woman and I'm sure she realized that I intended to sit next to her.

When I reached the woman, I realized that I might have caused her some embarrassment because her bottom was too large to allow for anyone else in her seat. After a few awkward moments, the lady sweetly offered, "Can I hold your books for you?" Really touched and grateful, I passed her my books and said, "Lady, you're all ass." I meant to use the common expression, "You're all heart," but I've been told I made a Freudian slip. Anyway the books hit the fan, and I don't believe I recovered all of them in my haste to get off the bus.

MEDICAL SCHOOL PRESENTATIONS AND FLAG FOOTBALL

There were 110 students in my class, and we all followed the same schedule of classes and labs. Our main lecture hall had theater seating, providing clear sight lines for all to the lecturer and all the video aids employed. In one of the courses given in this hall, we were asked to form three-to-five member groups to research and present lectures on different medical topics.

I volunteered to do the very first presentation, which was on sickle cell anemia. After dividing up the work, a classmate and I were given the task of going into a low-income housing project to interview a young man suffering with the sickle cell anemia condition. We were to return to bring him back on the day of our presentation, so he could tell his story to the whole class and answer their questions.

On our first trip into the project, we got lost. Spotting five or six young black men standing around on a corner, I pulled up to them in my Jaguar (top down) and said, "Hey, boys!" My companion cringed. It was a time when most blacks took offense at white folks calling them "boys." Many still do. My buddy froze, expecting us to be attacked. I can only surmise that they sensed that I didn't mean any offense, because one of them stepped up to me and gave me the directions we needed. Or, more probably, my guardian angel was still on the job.

UK sponsored an intramural flag football league for all its colleges, and a group of us from the medical college entered a team. After our first practice, I was chosen to play quarterback on offense and middle linebacker on defense. Our team was called the "medicine men," and we had a blast, while playing together, and formed close friendships. At Saturday afternoon home UK games, we would sit together in the newly opened Commonwealth Stadium to cheer on the Kentucky Wildcat football team.

MY RESIGNATION FROM MEDICAL SCHOOL

I was having a blast in medical school, but things soon soured for me. Patty was having a hard time with us not spending the time together to which we had become accustomed. She was working at the Veterans Hospital in cardiology, John was in child care, and I was consumed with my studies and school activities.

Sensing Patty's unhappiness, I had a heart-to-heart conversation with her. She revealed her own dissatisfaction with our new lifestyle, but the kicker was that she revealed my young son's anxiety. He had summed it up with, "Daddy's always looking at books." The three of us had pretty much been inseparable for over five years, and now we were pretty much going our separate ways.

I told Patty that I didn't have to be a doctor. I could quit medical school and return to teaching. I did wonder though why, knowing what she knew about the medical profession, she had supported my going to medical school. It was a long and difficult process just to apply. She explained, "I didn't want to be the one to spoil your dream, but I honestly didn't think you'd be accepted into medical school. It wasn't that I didn't think you were smart enough. I just thought you were too old."

I submitted my resignation to Dr. Roger Lambson just before mid-term exams. He called Patty into his office and asked her to persuade me to stay. He told her that I was at the top of my class, and they didn't want to lose me. Patty told him he was talking to the wrong person. She was the one who wanted me to leave.

8

METAIRIE, LA: 1973–1977

BACK TO METAIRIE

Patty remained in Lexington to serve out her two weeks' notice with the VA Hospital, and I drove to Louisiana and shopped for a house to buy. In a few days, I found one in Metairie, which I described to Patty over the phone. She liked it, so I signed the agreement to purchase and returned to Lexington to collect Patty and John. We traded in our Karman Gia to a Lexington dealer for a Chevy station wagon and hired a mover to bring our household goods to New Orleans and store them until notified. Upon arrival, we rented a room at the Imperial Hotel on Causeway Blvd., until our act of sale for 701 Caribou Ct. was executed a few weeks later.

OUR FIRST JOBS UPON OUR RETURN

Patty worked at Montelepre Hospital on Canal St., while waiting for an opportunity to take a position with the dialysis department at Oschner. In just a few months, an opening came along, and Patty served Oschner in dialysis and several other departments for 28 years until her retirement in 2002.

Two of my former colleagues in the Christian Brothers had left the order and become the superintendent and assistant superintendent of the Archdiocese of New Orleans School System—Howard Jenkins and Jo-Jo Bertrand, respectively. They added my application to their files and began looking for an opening, though one was not likely to occur until the start of the spring semester. Because that was still a couple of months away, I took a job as a retail clerk with Hill-Behan in Harahan, LA. They sold both lumber and construction products to contractors and the general public.

One of the physicians at Montelepre took great pride in not allowing his patients to suffer any pain. One of his patients was complaining of pain one night, but had taken the limit of pain medication prescribed. When the patient's nurse called the doctor, he ordered that an increase in the prescription be given. When the nurse sought the approval of her supervisor, who was Patty, Patty refused to authorize the dosage. When informed of Patty's refusal, he got Patty on the phone and raised hell with her. Patty stood her ground, knowing that to give the amount of narcotic the doctor ordered would send the patient into cardiac arrest.

In a huff, the doctor rushed over to the hospital and administered the narcotic himself. The patient immediately began to go into arrest, and the doctor bellowed for the antidote medication. Patty had quietly prepared the antidote before the doctor arrived and was standing at the door in anticipation of the coming emergency. "Is this what you need, Doctor?" Patty asked as she handed him the antidote. It wasn't the first time Patty had refused to administer a lethal dose of medicine ordered by a doctor. A nurse is liable for any medication she gives under a doctor's order. "The doctor ordered it" is no defense.

AN AMBULANCE CHASER

We had an experience with an attorney of the "ambulance chaser" ilk while Patty was still at Montelepre. On the way to work, she was broadsided by a large commercial truck, as she entered the intersection of Veterans Blvd. and Causeway Blvd. Thankfully, she was driving the big Chevy and suffered no serious injury, though the Chevy was totaled. Patty has a guardian angel on the job too.

Lawrence Trahant, recommended an attorney to us. We didn't realize then that Lawrence was a man who was quick to sue and would work the court system with a cooperating attorney. The attorney we saw set up a doctor's appointment for Patty, who made several visits to this quack's office. Patty had suffered some whiplash pain that had subsided, and she told the doctor that she was fine.

The doctor insisted she continue to come see him for a number of further visits. When she asked him, "Why?" the doctor said, "So we can get more money." Patty never saw that doctor again. She realized that the doctor and her attorney were in cahoots in a fraudulent scheme.

Her attorney convinced us to settle with the trucking company, as their defense would force us to sue the truck manufacturer for a latent brake defect, and it would be hard to beat them. As a result, the attorney and the doctor made out like thieves, while we only got enough money for another used car. They never compensated Patty for her lost days of work. This unethical arrangement between lawyers, doctors, and insurance companies is far too common. Later, I would face the practice up close and personal, when I worked as a private investigator.

FIRST STAY AT BROTHER MARTIN HIGH SCHOOL

Brother Bryce, the principle of Brother Martin High School in New Orleans, gave me a call shortly before the start of their spring semester and offered me a teaching position. He explained that his physics teacher was going on a 100-day retreat, and he needed a physics and general science teacher to replace him, but only for the spring semester. I accepted the temporary job, knowing the odds favored other positions opening up in the archdiocesan system for the next school year, since most faculty changes occur over the summer.

That spring of 1974, I didn't get much involved beyond teaching my physics and general science classes. Most of a teacher's interaction with other faculty members takes place at the start of the school year, so I had already missed many of the faculty meetings and social gatherings and had no club moderator or coaching duties. Furthermore, my classroom was just inside a side entrance to the school, so I didn't meet other faculty in the hallways at the start of the school day. Moreover, I was always one of the first to arrive.

Faculty members are usually required to stand by the entrance to their classroom between classes, so they can monitor the students in the hallway and at their lockers. One of the seniors who had a locker right outside my classroom really stood out. He was nearly seven feet tall.

I had several short conversations with him and learned that he was on the Brother Martin basketball team. I observed him at practice occasionally and nicknamed him "Showboat." He was anything but that, so it got under his skin a little.

This young man accomplished something very unique in basketball. He starred on a highest classification state (Louisiana) championship basketball team, a NCAA division 1 national (Kentucky) championship team and a NBA (Boston Celtics) championship team. His name was Rick Robey. I spoke with him by phone many years later, when I was advising his parents on moving their household goods from Rick's childhood home in Algiers, LA. Rick had settled in Kentucky after retiring from professional basketball.

JOB HOPPING

I was hoping to get my old job at Rummel when I returned to Louisiana from Kentucky, but it was held by an old confrere from my days in formation at Lafayette, LA and Santa Fe, NM. He used to cut my hair in the Juniorate. He had also left the Christian Brothers after a few years. Three years later, he left Rummel and I got my job back in 1977. During this time, Patty and I were living at the house we purchased at 701 Caribou Ct. Until my old job at Rummel opened up, I taught one year each at Archbishop Shaw High, Archbishop Chapelle High, and St. John Prep. That three-year stretch must have made me appear to be quite the job hopper.

ARCHBISHOP SHAW HIGH SCHOOL

The problem with teaching at Shaw was logistical. I had to drive a long way through heavy traffic. Part of the route was the Huey Long Bridge, which occasionally hosted an accident that backed up traffic for miles. The daily grind of this commute had me hoping for a closer teaching position on the east bank. This opportunity came up for the following academic year (1975–1976), when I was offered a position with Chapelle, which was just a couple of miles from my house.

The drawback to teaching at Chapelle was having to teach all girls, something I had never done before. They are very different to deal with. I wanted to get back to an all-boys school. As fate would have it, I was offered a position for the 1976–1977 academic year at the all-boys St. John Prep School. So, I wound up teaching at four different high schools in three and a half academic years, before I returned to Rummel for nine years (1977–1986).

Archbishop Shaw High School was on a large tract of land at the southwest corner of the West Bank Expressway and Barataria Boulevard. An order of priests and brothers known as the Salesians had cared for orphaned boys there in an institution known as Hope Haven. They had specialized in training their charges in trades. In establishing Shaw, they were venturing into formal college prep education, which was a calling new to them. The campus was one of the newest of the Archdiocesan high schools, and they had great athletic facilities, as well as classrooms and labs. They even had a swimming pool.

I taught four sophomore geometry classes and one senior math. Of course, I had a homeroom and helped supervise certain assigned areas, like the cafeteria. The principal was a priest named Father Wolfram. We got along very well, even though we differed a lot on school policy decisions. We were able to disagree agreeably, and that is rarely possible.

At one faculty meeting early in the first semester, Father Wolfram presented his idea that every student should participate in extracurricular activities. He noted that in perusing the yearbook, many students had no such activities listed under their pictures. He explained that this was understandable, since many students had long commutes and jobs and could not stay after school for the meetings and practices of the various established clubs and teams.

He proposed to canvass the student body to determine in which type of club or activity they would like to be involved. He would then have each faculty member choose one or more of these pursuits to moderate. He referred to these pursuits as hobbies and said that 30-minute "hobby periods" would be incorporated into the schedule three days a week. He said that the regular six periods would be shortened by five minutes to provide the time for the hobby period.

I immediately got the floor after Father Wolfram finished his proposal and strenuously objected to it. What he had proposed was the equivalent of a huge expansion of the curriculum, and it could only be implemented on paper. Twelve hundred students couldn't be checked into and out of an unlimited number of activities of their choosing and located over a 50-acre campus in 30 minutes.

In the real world, spatial and temporal limits would prevent its realization. "Now, John, let's give it our best and we'll see," Father Wolfram countered. "Alright, Father, but I'm telling you it won't work." After the meeting adjourned, a Salesian priest from England told me I should have gone into law.

Since I had publicly opposed Father Wolfram's proposal before the entire faculty and administration, I was determined to give it my best effort so no one could say I had a part in its inevitable failure. I ran the "archery club," which had about 25 students. We set up targets on bales of hay in the field outside my homeroom, and I planned our activities for every scheduled "hobby period." I also had to keep order among some 150 students, who signed up for the "magic club." They met in the cafeteria and watched one of the Salesian Brothers botch one magic trick after another.

A few weeks after Father Wolfram's project was launched, he began to cancel the hobby period in the morning announcements. I found myself preparing my archery classes, only to have them cancelled. After suffering this frustrating waste of time for a few weeks, I walked into Father Wolfram's office for a tête-à-tête. "Father Wolfram, are we ever going to have hobby period again?" I probed. He admitted that he needed to announce its permanent demise and stop cancelling it one day at a time. Thus, the space beneath student pictures in the yearbook remained as devoid of activities as ever.

MORE CLOSE CALLS

One afternoon, as I drove home from Shaw, my guardian angel came to my rescue again. I had just driven across the Huey Long Bridge and around the traffic circle onto Jefferson Highway, when the brakes on my Jaguar gave out. Because there was a line of cars stopped ahead of me, I turned onto the grassy median to coast safely to a stop. Had my brakes failed a few minutes earlier on the long down slope of the bridge, I would have had no room to maneuver and would have accelerated to a high rate of speed entering the traffic circle. This occurrence would almost certainly have resulted in a horrific accident. My guardian angel was still on the job.

One morning, I was in the Shaw faculty lounge, when a male faculty member suddenly leaped up and ran out of the room, screaming and wildly waving his arms. I ran after him, thinking he would surely bring harm to himself if he weren't subdued. I caught up with him just outside the main entrance and was soon joined by a couple of other faculty men, who had given chase. Together, we held him securely until someone gave him some sugar to counteract the diabetic imbalance that had caused his seizure. I guess his guardian angel gave me the opportunity to act as his assistant.

One night, I joined some of the Shaw coaches for a basketball game against the football players. They were a group of very large young men. Our coaches weren't exactly small either. We had a referee to avoid the game becoming a brawl. It nearly did anyway. As one of our players took a foul shot, I lined up next to a very big football player, who had the inside-rebounding position. I had learned that if you time a quick shove of an opponent just as the ball strikes the rim, the referee seldom catches the foul. I did just that to the player on my left and sent him under the backboard, stumbling out of bounds. The miss came down right to my waiting hands, and I put it back up for an easy score. The player I had displaced was mightily upset and came at me with a vengeance. Fortunately, my guardian angel got an assist from one of our very large coaches, who stepped between us and defused the volatile situation.

Shaw was located near the edge of the Barataria wetlands, and one day we had a strange visitor to our campus. Wildlife and Fisheries was called to capture and remove a six-foot alligator from the ditch in front of the school.

ARCHBISHOP CHAPELLE HIGH SCHOOL

An opportunity to teach on the east bank and avoid the long commute to Shaw came my way, and I signed a standard one-year contract to teach the 1975–1976 school year at Archbishop Chapelle High School. I knew the principal, Ralph Mahan, who had been a Christian Brother. Teaching at Chapelle involved some major adjustments, but the school was just a five-minute drive from my house. One of the adjustments was teaching in an all-girls high school. The other was teaching an honors class in organic chemistry.

At Chapelle, I missed the sports played in the boys schools. My homeroom was composed of juniors, most of whom were in my general chemistry classes. They got me involved in their "rally" competition. Once a year, each homeroom would dress up in some theme or other and engage in a cheering competition held in the gym. At the time, there was a popular TV show named "Happy Days," and my girls decided they would dress up like the girls on this show. They would dress me like Fonzie in jeans and leather jacket, accessorized with a motorcycle. We won the competition, and I forever was the "Fonz."

Fonzie and his "Happy Days"—
my niece is next to me

REFRIGERATION SCHOOL

During my one year at Chapelle, I attended training at the New Orleans Refrigeration School on Mazant Ave., near the industrial canal in New Orleans. The knowledge and skills acquired could help me earn extra income in the summer, when school was out. So, for nine months, I drove across town and back two nights a week and spent four hours in classroom instruction and shop work. The students came from all walks of life, but I was the only one with college degrees.

I accomplished something no student had ever done when I took the final exam to earn my HVAC diploma. I made a perfect score. Our instructor had mistakenly marked two of my answers "wrong," but he corrected himself when I pointed out his errors. In one instance, the error resulted from using an incorrect answer sheet. I've often wondered how long that answer sheet had been in use, and how many students had a correct answer marked incorrect. So much of the material was based on the concepts of physics, and having majored in physics in graduate school, I had a distinct advantage in absorbing the course material. I did a considerable amount of work in the field over the following years. I worked in both installation and service for St. Pierre's Heating and Air Conditioning out of Destrehan, LA. I became good friends with the St. Pierre family, with whom I still stay in contact. I love them all. Good people.

ST. JOHN PREP HIGH SCHOOL

During my tenure at Chapelle, I moved one step closer to returning to Rummel, my original goal upon returning from Kentucky to Louisiana. Joe Rossolini, a former Christian Brother who joined a few years after me, had left the order and become the assistant principal at St. John Vianney Prep. Joe offered me a faculty position for the '76–'77 year, and I took it. This school prepped students from 8th grade through high school for entry into the Seminary of the Archdiocese of New Orleans. The students lived at home, but at school, they were oriented toward attending the seminary and becoming priests. Only a small percentage of St. John's graduates entered the seminary, and I could see that the school would not stay open more than a few more years, but I figured my old position at Rummel would open up.

The school fielded teams in one of the lower classifications, due to their small enrollments. There were less than 100 boys to draw on for our football, baseball, basketball, and track teams, but I preferred that to teaching in a school of 1200 high school girls.

The St. John's football coach was Kevin Trower, who had been a postulant while I was in the Novitiate. He never did stay to receive the habit. He went on to continue being one of the most successful basketball and baseball coaches at Jesuit High in New Orleans, winning state championships in both sports. At St. John's, he coached baseball and basketball, in addition to football. Kevin was very old school and was the only coach in our area to run the single wing in football. One of our star athletes was the son of Dr. Norman Francis, the president of nearby Xavier University. I became good friends with Dr. Francis and his wife, as well as with several of his children. I even went to his house to repair his air conditioner. I did this gratis, but when I installed a water filter in his kitchen, he insisted on paying me the full cost.

TURNING THE TABLES AT INITIATION

My homeroom was the 8th grade boys, who were the lowest on the status totem pole. Every year, the seniors would get to "initiate" the freshmen, and our juniors were salivating at their upcoming chance to haze our 8th graders. I thought of a way for my 8th graders to get in a first lick on the juniors.

With my suggestion, the 8th graders made a list of the juniors who were most obnoxious toward them. I devised a plan for the 8th graders to execute at an upcoming "talent" night in the gym. They would be on their own, because I could not attend. Each class would have the floor to perform an act or acts of their choosing, before the entire student body assembled.

When our turn came, our class president announced that we were going to conduct the famous "Pepsi taste test," featured in TV commercials back then. A cart was rolled out in front of five folding chairs. A tablecloth covered the lower shelf of the cart. On top of the cart was a large bottle of Pepsi and two bottles of other sodas, as well as a stack of paper cups. The targets were called down to participate, seated in the folding chairs and blindfolded.

After each of the contestants was given a cup of soda to taste by an 8th grader, one of them folded back the tablecloth, and they all took a paper plate loaded with whipped cream and quickly positioned themselves behind each junior. "Now taste this!" our emcee bellowed, and the pies were rubbed into the faces of the unsuspecting juniors. I wasn't there to see it, but I was told a near riot ensued, with juniors chasing 8th graders all over the gym. There was nothing the juniors could do to the 8th graders to top what had been done to them.

RETURN TO RUMMEL

In the spring of my year at St. John Prep, I was offered the teaching position I had been waiting for by Brother John Fairfax, the principal at Rummel. Brother John was a young brother who contracted polio in Mexico, while I was in the Novitiate in Lafayette. Brother John had braces to stiffen his paralyzed legs and used two canes to swing his legs alternately forward. He walked with his unique gait everywhere without assistance.

He had the remarkable ability to remember the names of all the students and alumni. He was a humble man with a sense of humor. After teaching all the physics classes for a number of years, Brother John called me into his office to ask me to be the chairman of the science department. I had just had a hemorroidectomy. With a straight face, I feigned offense and said to the chief administrator of the school, "Now! Now, that I'm a perfect ass, you want me to be an administrator!" We both cracked up, and I became chairman of the science department.

I remained at Rummel until my son graduated from the school in 1986. At the start of my second stint at Rummel (the '77–'78 school year), I made another big move. Patty and I sold our house on Caribou Ct. and purchased a house at 401 Little Farms Ave. We would live there until April 29th, 2006, when we left to occupy our home at 814 Fairmount Ave. in Bristol, VA. I have a few memories of our three years at 7 Caribou that stand out and many more of our 29 years at 401 Little Farms.

7 CARIBOU CT.

7 Caribou was part of a horseshoe-shaped street that looped out from Lynette Dr. It was about three blocks long. The Jefferson Parish Recreation Department operated Delta Playground, which was just three blocks away and fronted West Metairie Ave. The playground had a gym, two tennis courts, and football and baseball fields.

John participated in the pee-wee football and baseball programs as a six- and seven-year-old. He also took boxing lessons there and was on the card in the fights held at the gym. The New Orleans Parish Prison always sent a team to compete with older fighters in the various weight divisions. At one of these competitions, I recognized a former De La Salle student who had a bout with one of the inmates. Ned Konke had been boxing as a New Orleans Athletic Club member since his high school days, where he starred for the DLS basketball team. I had played many a pickup game with Ned in the DLS gym. Ned had become an attorney, but remained active in both boxing and basketball. I would later compete against him in basketball in the "over the mountain" league.

John was a diminutive six-year-old, when he first signed up for pee-wee football at Delta. When he asked me for permission, I told him that he could sign up, but once he did, he would not be allowed to skip practice or drop out, unless he was sick or injured. I explained that a commitment is a commitment, and one must be true to one's word.

John was excited when we got him his pads, helmet, and shoes, but his enthusiasm soon waned when his time after school was no longer free. It didn't help that he was competing with boys who were larger and had a full year of experience under their belts. He soon asked me for permission to quit. I refused, reminding him of our agreement. I told him that if he chose not to play the following season, that would be fine, but he was "in it" for the duration of the current season.

John grew larger and improved that first year, and he eagerly signed up for the following year. There was no talk of quitting, and he made the "All-Star" team. At one practice, John asked the coach if he could play on the defensive line. He had become bored playing a safety position, where there was little action.

Grandma and John showing their "game" faces

1975 Delta Eagles—John is front row center

The coach, knowing John was one of his smallest players, thought he would let John see for himself that he wasn't meant to be on the defensive line. He placed John on the right side of the line and ran a play his way. The quarterback faked a handoff to a back headed straight at John and kept the ball to run it around the end. John was temporarily fooled and knocked the running back to the ground, before catching the quarterback behind the line of scrimmage. The coach kept John on the defensive line, but also played him as a running back.

Patty and I were seated with the parents of the players and other fans at one game, when John made a long run into the end zone. Patty jumped up and screamed excitedly, "John made a home run! John made a home run!" This outburst pretty well silenced the cheering, as the fans stared quizzically at Patty. At that time, Patty still had not become the knowledgeable football fan she was to become in time.

CHOOSING AN ELEMENTARY SCHOOL FOR JOHN

Our Lady of Divine Providence Church and elementary school was on the property on the west side of the Delta Playground. We attended church there, but we enrolled John in St. Matthew's elementary on Jefferson Highway in River Ridge. I had the inside scoop on the two schools from the superintendent himself, my former confrere, Howard Jenkins. St. Matthew's academic rating was well above Our Lady of Divine Providence. In addition, it was located only a few blocks from my sister Ann's house on Virginia Parkway. Patty would drop John off there on her way to work, and he would walk to school with Ann's kids. John got to spend plenty of time with his Aunt Ann and Uncle Pat and his four cousins. Patty picked him up on her way home from work.

When a house in our near neighborhood exploded due to a natural gas leak, we began to think of moving. Many of the subdivisions built west of Causeway Boulevard and between Airline Highway and Lake Ponchartrain were constructed over marshland. The lots were filled in with river sand and pilings, driven down to support the slabs of houses. In many areas, the fill subsided over time to the point that the pilings were exposed to view. Because the subsidence played havoc with the natural gas lines, explosions occasionally resulted.

On her commute to work at Ochsner, Patty fell in love with the house at 401 Little Farms Ave. She had driven past it twice every workday for over two years. When it went up for sale, near the summer of 1977, we arranged to buy it for $62,500. The owner set up financing for us with Gulf South Bank. We moved in, as I began my first year teaching back at Rummel since 1968.

9

RIVER RIDGE, LA: 1977–2006

401 LITTLE FARMS

The man who sold me my house on Little Farms was a very successful agent for Metropolitan Life Insurance. Subsequently, he planted in my head the idea of selling life insurance. I took no immediate action, but after meeting another agent with Prudential, I decided to give it a try. I met this agent playing tennis at the Little Farms courts, just 100 feet from my house. These two courts were part of the Little Farms playground complex that was operated by the Jefferson Parish Recreation Department.

It wasn't long before I finished training to represent Prudential and passed the exams given by the State of Louisiana to obtain a license to sell life and health insurance. Since I never stopped teaching full-time, I didn't spend much time writing policies. I wound up donating my commissions to the Rummel Scholarship Fund.

Our administration asked us to regard our staff as a community and to try to do some community service. I thought helping to advise faculty members regarding their insurance needs and donating my pay to the scholarship fund would be one way to take that advice to heart. I also arranged to have my annual raise donated to that same fund.

Moreover, since I had my training in air conditioning, I offered to fix the ACs of faculty members, when they had problems. This I would do without charging them for my labor and providing parts at cost. I considered this a valuable service to the community, and I only ran across one faculty member who didn't show any appreciation, when I serviced his AC system.

When I went to his house on a Saturday morning, he wasn't even home, so I communicated only with his wife. I probably spent two hours cleaning his evaporating and condensing coils, checking his high- and low-side pressures, temperature drop, and adding a little Freon to get his system operating at maximum efficiency. I charged his wife nothing, and she thanked me.

I didn't see or hear from her husband, until he came into the faculty lounge on Monday morning, when without so much as a greeting, he asked me what I had done at his house on Saturday. When I told him his only comment was, "Well, I could have done that." I bit my tongue, because in my mind, I was thinking, "Well, why in the hell didn't you, and I could have spent my Saturday morning playing tennis?" He never once said, "Thank you." Some of our native Indian tribes along the Mississippi told early missionaries that they considered ingratitude the greatest sin. When you think about it, there is a lot of truth to that opinion.

Another service I provided mostly gratis was to install water filters in kitchens and drinking fountains. Had I not been teaching full-time, I could have made a business doing this. Once you had initially installed the filters, they had to be replaced every few years. This step could be done in just a few minutes, though the original installation could take an hour. A force of salesmen/installers could be hired and trained, and there was no limit to the money you could make, except for your own interest and effort. My interest in teaching trumped my interest in business. I understood business, but I just didn't like it. I loved helping others, but not for a profit.

THE HANSON BROTHERS

In my first few years back in Metairie, my cousin Donald and I started up a painting business, which we named "Hanson Brothers." Donald had learned all the ins-and-outs of painting while in the navy. I only knew the basics, but I knew how to show up and work hard, and I could deal with the customers in selling the jobs and collecting payment.

We made some good money painting some commercial properties for a navy architect. For one of these, we hired some college boys to help us. This business had the potential to grow, since there was a lot of painting work, but I couldn't devote much time to it, except for the summer months when school was out. Donald continued painting on his own, when I returned to the classroom. Like an old soldier, Hanson Brothers faded away. It seems like every summer, I ventured into different ways to make money, but always returned to teaching.

RENEWED INTEREST IN TENNIS

My interest in tennis that had been spurred by friends in Prestonsburg was revived when I returned to Metairie. One of my wife's nursing buddies invited us to a party, at which I met a retired marine. The subject of tennis came up, and the marine and I set up a singles tennis match. Our first of many matches was played at Delta Playground, and my new buddy, Jim Demuth, destroyed me. We played again many times at Little

Farms, Harahan, and Jefferson playgounds. I gradually improved, until I owned Jim in singles. We even partnered up in some doubles-tournaments.

I met a tennis player at the Little Farms courts, who was a professor at Loyola University in New Orleans. Patty and I had dinner and exchanged gifts with him and his family every Christmas eve for years. We even travelled together to Sweet Briar College, near Lynchburg, VA to attend Dennis Van der Meer's weeklong Tennis University.

My attendance at Tennis University culminated with me becoming a certified teaching professional with the Professional Tennis Registry, an international association of teaching professionals. Prior to my certification, I was loath to charge folks who approached me for tennis lessons, given that I felt I was not competent in the subject. My success as a player was due to my athleticism and sheer effort. I really had no idea what I was doing, but realized I was not hitting the ball like the pros. Tennis U not only taught the biomechanics of every stroke, but also how to teach them to individuals and groups. Armed with the PTR training and support, I worked on my own strokes and began to teach lessons. In time, I became the tennis coach at Rummel. I also served as the head teaching pro at Cureton's Sports Club and an assistant manager of the Audubon Park Courts.

NEHEMIAH ATKINSON

Before I attended the Tennis University program, I came to know one of the greatest men and tennis players ever. His name was Nehemiah Atkinson. Nehemiah was the tennis director for the New Orleans Recreation Department (NORD). He managed the department's main facility at 4025 S. Saratoga St. in the uptown Garden District of New Orleans.

This facility was named the Stern Tennis Center, and I was closely associated with it for 25 years, until Hurricane Katrina ended all of my associations with New Orleans. This tennis venue first opened in 1897 as the private New Orleans Lawn Tennis Club. The city acquired the facility in 1973 and named it in honor of Edgar Stern, a local philanthropist. Nehemiah contributed so much to the development of tennis at Stern and in the city that when the center was later expanded and refurbished, it was renamed the Atkinson-Stern Tennis Center.

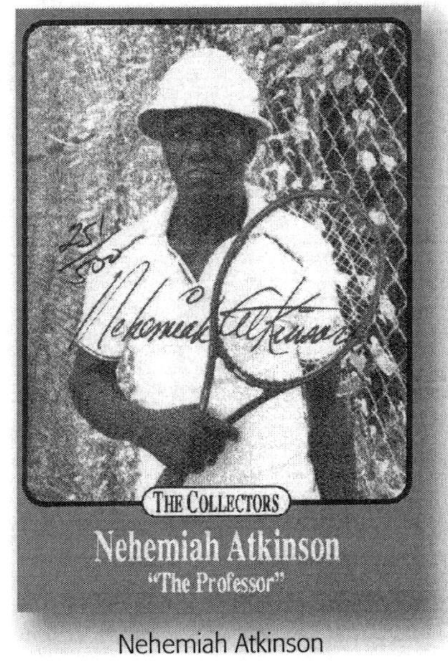

Nehemiah Atkinson

For his work with the inner-city (translation: poor black) children, Atkinson was the recipient of the Robert F. Kennedy "Ripple of Hope" award, presented to him on center court at the

1977 U.S. Open. At the tournament banquet, he sat at the head table with celebrities Ethel Kennedy and Howard Cosell. Nehemiah also served as a pallbearer at Arthur Ashe's funeral.

I first saw Nehemiah on TV when Channel 4 did a short feature on him during the sports segment of the news. I called the Stern Center, and Nehemiah invited me over for a lesson. He never really taught me any of the mechanics of tennis in my hour or so session with him on one of the rubico (clay) backcourts.

He did much more. He inspired me to want to be the best I could be. He saw me as a "natural" and encouraged me to enter the Louisiana State Closed Tournament, which was starting in about a week. He also introduced me to one of his protégés, named Lloyd Dillon, who would become a lifelong friend and doubles partner. Later, Lloyd served as director and I as assistant director of the summer tennis camps held at Stern.

At the State Closed Tournament at City Park, Lloyd told me he was having the first annual Nehemiah Atkinson Tennis Scholarship Foundation Tournament. Sanctioned by the USTA, it would be held at Stern for both adults and juniors. Its purpose was to honor Nehemiah and raise money to provide a bit of college financial aid to a boy and a girl participant. I would wind up raising money for and playing in this tournament for about 15 years. I collected quite a few trophies, plaques, and tee shirts with Nehemiah's image on them. I still have a few. More importantly ... I raised a lot of donations to fund scholarships.

Nehemiah was probably about 60 years old (young) when I met him. His complexion was very black, and he stood about 5'9". He seemed to have zero body fat, but he had a strong, wiry build. He was old-school and wore white tennis shorts, hats, and shirts, when playing and teaching. He always remained impeccably neat, as he "flowed" effortlessly and efficiently about the court. He loved tennis, and I loved him. Nehemiah was as perfect a gentleman as I've ever met. I used to tell him, "Nehemiah, you're so black, charcoal would make a white mark on you." He would reply, "John, are you still trying to pass for white?" and we would have a good laugh.

One day, Bill Cosby of "I Spy" and "The Cosby Show" fame visited Stern and wound up playing a match with Nehemiah. Bill had played tennis in his "I Spy" role, since that was his cover for his covert activities. Later, when he appeared on local TV, he was asked what he had been doing in New Orleans. He replied that he had played tennis and been soundly beaten by a little old black man. We all knew whom he was talking about.

LLOYD DILLON

Lloyd had played basketball and tennis at Grambling State University. He was about 6'4" and 215 lbs. He was given a tryout with an NBA team but didn't make the roster. He was my age and he was a teacher and coach in the Jefferson Parish system. We became best friends and played the Louisiana USTA tennis circuit as a 45-doubles team. We were ranked in the top five. Lloyd followed Nehemiah as the director of tennis for NORD. I am proud to say that in an interview with Billy E. Crawford on July 27, 2011, Lloyd named me, along with 22 other players, as a few of the most skilled players he had played against or watched in his career.

COMBATING SEGREGATION AND PREJUDICE

Martin Luther King did much to end the segregation I grew up with, but no one did more than Nehemiah to foster friendship between the races … and that is a giant step past simply passing laws that prohibit segregation. The ignorance that is the basis of racism isn't instantly wiped out, because the races are forced to mingle. It takes contact and interaction over time for a new generation to dispel the prejudice and hatred they have been so "carefully taught" (South Pacific) by their forebears.

In 1954, the Supreme Court ended segregation *de jure*, but not in the hearts of the people. You either loved your neighbor or you didn't. But, your neighbor was someone who lived in your neighborhood, and most blacks lived in their own neighborhoods. The integration process begun in 1954 took decades to reach today's levels. While the prejudice level has been much reduced, it still has a long way to go.

I didn't play tennis growing up in New Orleans. For the most part, only people who were white and rich did so. The same was true for golf. I was white, but poor. In spite of his color and the scarcity of facilities for blacks, Nehemiah started playing tennis with a small circle of his black contemporaries. They played at the tennis courts of the black Xavier University. They also played at the black YMCA on Dryades St.

Nationally, the black tennis players formed an organization that put on tournaments for black players. It was named the American Tennis Association (ATA) and still exists today, although blacks have long since been allowed to play in tournaments sanctioned by the United States Tennis Association (USTA). The ATA today has a few whites who play in their tournaments; maybe one in 50. Most of today's better black players play in the USTA tournaments.

Nehemiah played his way into acceptance by the white tennis community. White tennis players would seek him out as a doubles partner for their club tournaments. One such player was Dr. Paul DeCamp, a vascular surgeon at Oschner Hospital, who worked closely with Patty. Not only did this odd couple travel together for out of town tournaments, they also played a singles match every Tuesday morning at Stern for years.

Even after he could no longer be barred from tournaments because of his race, he was disrespected by many fools. Nehemiah never responded with anything other than his impeccable courtesy and impregnable dignity. He made them pay for their lack of civility when he played them on the court. In this way, he won the respect of all who would deny it to him.

LLOYD DILLON, DELIVERY MAN

One of the first trips Lloyd and I made to play in a tournament was to Shreveport, LA. The tournament was held on the grounds of a fancy private club that featured a beautiful golf course. Neither of us had ever been to this club, and we didn't know where the courts were. We followed signs to a building that looked like an upscale motel and entered the lobby. While I was wearing inexpensive, well-worn tennis clothing, Lloyd had on brand new expensive warm-ups.

We were only steps inside, when the manager approached Lloyd and inquired, "Are you here to make a delivery?" I covered my mouth to hide my grin, cast a knowing glance at Lloyd and waited to see his reaction. Lloyd reacted like a true protégé of Nehemiah. He calmly informed the manager with no sign of offense or rancor, "No, sir. I'm here to play tennis." Completely abashed by his racist faux pas, the manager fumbled with the directions to the courts.

For many years, when I would greet Lloyd at a tournament or some tennis setting, I would ask him, "Are you here to make a delivery?" and we would have a good laugh. When we attended the installation banquet of Nehemiah into the Louisiana Tennis Hall of Fame, Lloyd was one of the speakers and told this story to illustrate the prejudice Nehemiah and other black players had to face to make their way in tennis.

Our trip to Shreveport was an overnighter, and we stayed at the house of one of Lloyd's old girlfriends from his college days at Grambling. On the way to her house, Lloyd stopped to buy a bottle of her favorite liquor. After showering and changing, Lloyd got behind the wheel of his small "Z" car, and his old girlfriend climbed onto my lap as we headed for a nightclub called "The Grotto." The Grotto was a window-less, cinder-block building.

Lloyd's old flame strode proudly inside, with Lloyd on one arm and me on the other. The patrons sat around small round tables, enjoying their drinks of choice and listening to the live band. Every other band selection or so, Lloyd or I would take our lady friend for a spin around the dance floor. I was the only white person in the place and naturally drew a few stares. As the band would play, the patrons would clap their hands and snap their fingers to the beat. I pretended to not be able to get the timing right, and soon had folks from the neighboring tables helping me. That broke the ice, and I was and continued to be a homey. At a later date, I found myself the only white in a sea of black tennis players who came from all over the USA for an ATA tournament at Stern. The outsiders started to give me a frosty reception, until one of my black friends from Stern advised them, "Hey, he's a brother."

STERN, A MELTING POT

Under Nehemiah's management, the integrated Stern Tennis Center fostered friendship among the races, while promoting tennis among the poor black children in the inner city. A nucleus of white adults, whose families had been playing tennis at Stern (as members of the all-white New Orleans Lawn Tennis Club) for generations going back to 1897, continued to play at the integrated facility. Most moved on to play at the new club location on Laurel St., after integration.

Those whites who continued to play at the city-operated Stern were mostly of means, as were the blacks who came to Stern. So, the adult players at Stern became an integrated mixture of doctors, lawyers, teachers, accountants, businessmen, musicians, judges, and politicians. Their children grew up playing together at Stern, like their parents. The poorer children from the area were nearly all blacks.

They were gradually taught to love tennis through clinics organized by Nehemiah and Lloyd over many years. Lloyd's son, Lloyd Jr., became a ranked junior player. My son, John III, played on the Rummel tennis team. At Stern, I met and played with mayors, judges, professors, business owners, famous musicians, restaurateurs, etc. over the years. Many of the interactions between the races at Stern developed into lasting friendships. The law provided forced mingling of the races, but the influence of Nehemiah converted the mingling into friendships.

Before Nehemiah passed on February 9th in 2003, at the age of 84, he accomplished his dream of winning a USTA national tournament and earning his first gold ball at the 1999 80s hard-court championships in San Diego, CA. Many more titles followed. Atkinson was a member of the Gardnar Mulloy Cup team in 2001 in Perth, Australia, which won the Cup (and also a member of the Mulloy Cup in 1999 and 2000), and the singles world champion in 2001 in the men's 80 division.

SUMMER CAMPS AT STERN

My becoming a PTR-certified teaching pro inspired Lloyd to do the same. He extended his training beyond Tennis University to become a national tester for the PTR. This position enabled him to train and certify other teachers. He also incorporated all the PTR methods of teaching tennis into the summer tennis camps that he put on every summer for the inner-city kids.

I worked as his assistant director, Monday through Friday, from 8:30 a.m. to 4:30 p.m. We had about a dozen employees who were paid by the city. I was the only white employee. We had only two white children among 63 kids.

The kids were only charged $15 for the 40 all-day sessions. We only charged this small fee (about a nickel an hour), so the parents and kids would have something invested in the program. A few of the very poor kids were given "scholarships."

Once a summer, children from all over the city were bussed to Stern for fun and games. We set up nine courts with instructors to supervise nine different fun tennis activities and rotated groups through all of the courts. Saratoga St. was blocked off by the police to allow for the Saint's organization to set up some inflated stations for the kids to try their skills at passing and kicking footballs. We also had a waterslide. I had taken pictures all summer long, and my wife put together a slide show on a disk to the music from "The Power of One" film.

PURSUING A RANKING WITH ATRIAL FIB

Before I qualified to play in the men's 50-year-old division of USTA-sanctioned tournaments, I had stopped playing singles and only entered doubles competitions. Even the doubles wore me down to the point of shortness of breath and vertigo. I knew it wasn't the familiar heat and humidity of New Orleans, so I attributed it to a lack of conditioning. I didn't realize I was beginning to go into heart failure.

After Tennis University (TU), I realized that playing doubles with Lloyd limited my chances of success, given that Lloyd hadn't yet picked up on the strategy taught at TU. I decided to play with Richard Baron, who had attended De La Salle High like me. I had reacquainted with Richard when we met at different tournaments, and we agreed to partner up for men's-50 events. I was coaching tennis at Rummel and had become the pro at Cureton's Sports Center. Accordingly, I thought earning a high ranking in the Louisiana Tennis Association (LTA) would enhance my standing as a teacher. I didn't aim at a southern or national USTA ranking, since I could not afford the travel expenses.

Louisiana was divided into geographical regions by the LTA, and to qualify to be ranked, one had to play a minimum number of sanctioned tournaments, including two outside your own region. Richard and I played in the regions in which Shreveport and Jeanerette were located, as well as in our own region around New Orleans.

Richard and I won all but one of our tournaments. We finished second at City Park in New Orleans, when my heart acted up in the finals. I didn't know at the time it was my heart. I just knew I was faint and dizzy. Our record was good enough to have the selection committee of the LTA give us the #1 ranking. So, Richard and I will forever be listed as the #1 men's-50 doubles team in the LTA archives for the '86–'87 ranking year.

A GOOD START IN JEANERETTE

Richard also played singles when we entered tournaments. Our initial tournament was played in Jeanerette, LA, and I observed him play a match against one of the men we would eventually face in the finals of the doubles competition. This guy was a teaching pro from Scott, LA, and he and his partner were the reigning #1 doubles team.

It really bugged me that this guy was hooking Richard regularly and using stall tactics when it gave him an edge. Richard was a great sport and a really nice guy, who put up with his opponent's unsportsmanlike tactics without complaint. There was nothing I could do to defend him, until Richard and I played them in the doubles final.

Early on, they learned that I would not allow Richard and me to be cowed into changing our calls just because they challenged them. When they took to complaining about our calls, I invited them to call an official over to decide any contested calls. Of course, they declined, since they were the ones making the bad calls.

I had observed in Richard's singles match that this pro from Scott had used a certain stalling tactic as he prepared to hit his serve. As he bounced the ball before his toss, he would deliberately glance it off his foot, and then slowly retrieve it, as it rolled onto the next court. Everyone had to wait for his return for play to resume. Glancing at the fans, I could see that they didn't appreciate his shenanigans.

Later, he employed this tactic in our doubles match … once. The next time it was my serve, and this guy was all ready to return on a critical point. I bounced the ball off my foot and slowly followed it, as it rolled about 50 feet away. As I retrieved my ball, I saw that my opponent was furiously pacing back and forth, with both hands on his hips.

The crowd loved it. They knew what was going on, and now my opponent knew they knew and was too embarrassed to repeat his stalling tactic again. I had gotten into my opponent's head by using his own tactics against him. So, Richard and I got our payback. We started our season by defeating the defending champions.

WRAPPING UP OUR SEASON

When we played a Coca-Cola-sponsored tournament in Alexandria, we stayed overnight after the first day of competition at a home owned by one of Richard's relatives. Richard's wife was with us and gave both of us a professional massage to help us relax for the second day of matches. That was a first and last for me. The opportunity just never presented itself again. Another first and last was Coke presented us with $50 checks for winning the championship. Other than that tournament, we always got trophies or plaques. I am reminded of what Nehemiah said as he accepted a certificate of appreciation from Mayor Morial at a breakfast in his honor: "Silver and gold I have none … but I have plenty of paper."

Anne (masseuse extraordinaire) and Richard Baron

Another tournament that stands out in my memory that season was the one we played at the Stern Tennis Center. It was the Nehemiah Atkinson Tennis Scholarship Tournament. Richard and I defeated Lloyd and his new partner in the finals. Richard and I never competed as a doubles team again. Once I had achieved a #1 ranking, it was mission-accomplished for me. There was something of a "been there, done that" attitude, and it was more demanding of my time and finances than I was willing to bear.

GREAT DOUBLES PARTNERS

I had the opportunity to play doubles with Butch Seavey in a tournament held at City Park. Butch was perennially ranked at or near the top in both senior singles and doubles. We won rather easily. When folks asked me how I got Butch to play with me, I told them, "I asked him." One of the key elements to success in doubles is to get a really good player for your partner.

The best player in our senior age division was Lester Sack, a former tennis star at Tulane. He also was the pro at the New Orleans Lawn Tennis Club. He was ranked #1 in singles, both in Louisiana and the southern region of States. He was a regular entrant and winner of our annual NATSF tournament held at Stern. Since I was a part of sponsoring this event, I got to meet Lester.

I took a lot of pictures for our tournament. One year, I printed up one of Lester and presented it to him. In gratitude, he gave me a free lesson at his club. We became friends. Subsequently, I went to his house in Lakeview and serviced his air conditioner. He agreed to play doubles with me in our annual NATSF tournaments. We played together every year and never lost a match, even when we played some younger opponents. Lester's son and daughter were star prep players. His boy, Klein, played for Georgia on a tennis scholarship.

RALPH AND HELEN DAZET

Rummel had developed one of the top prep tennis teams. They won several state championships. One year, I took the Rummel team to a national invitational tournament that was held on the campus of Duke University. The 10 teams invited were the best in the nation. Our top player was Tim Siegel. In the finals, Tim lost in split sets to a player from California. Tim was awarded a full scholarship to play for Arkansas.

Ralph Dazet, the father of our star doubles player, Chris Dazet, sponsored our trip to Durham, which we made by motorcade, stopping at a motel overnight, going and returning. In Durham, I played a singles match with Ralph and beat him handily. He told me to give him a month, and he would beat me. What gave him that confidence was the fact that Ralph was better schooled in the mechanics of tennis. He, like his son, had taken plenty of lessons at the private Beach Club in Metairie.

When we returned to Metairie, I continued to beat Ralph at both the public Little Farms courts and at his private Beach Club. I had not yet attended TU. While Ralph had better strokes, I had far better movement. Ralph was also encumbered by some excess weight. Had Ralph had my athleticism and mobility, he would have crushed me.

Patty and I became good friends with Ralph and his wife, Helen. Ralph's accounting firm, Wegmann & Dazet, was one of the largest in Louisiana, and they became one of the largest sponsors of our NATSF Tournaments. It turned out that the young man who swam the Mississippi with me had become an important employee of Wegmann & Dazet. Our common friendship with his family generated an enhanced friendship with the Dazets. Patty and I were invited to parties at both their houses. Ralph took me fishing from his camp in the marshes across the Mississippi from Buras. I wired a circuit for the camp, so he could install an AC unit. Ralph's youngest son accompanied us on our fishing excursions.

Helen invited me to be her mixed-doubles partner in a Wegmann & Dazet Company tournament, held at the Hilton Hotel in downtown New Orleans. My Mississippi River swimming pal and his wife were there, and we had a great party. Later, when Rummel had a special day at school to get the community primed for a prep rally prior to a football game against one of our traditional rivals, Helen loaned me one of her tennis outfits.

Teaching physics class in Helen's tennis dress

The idea was to get a lot of faculty and students to wear costumes to school. When my physics students filed into my lab for classes that day, they were greatly amused, but settled down as soon as I began my lesson. I spoke before the entire student body assembled at the rally. I told them that I had been told during the day that I had a lot of nerve to wear my outfit, but that the folks who really had a lot of nerve were our opponents who would take the field against our Rummel Raiders. That got a big roar of approval.

CLUB TENNIS

There were a number of men, besides Ralph, who had sons at Rummel, who had received professional tennis instruction at private clubs in Jefferson Parish. As the tennis coach at Rummel, I got to know them and got invited to play as their guest. In this manner, I got to play at the clubs whose memberships I could not afford. Many of these members were regular entrants in our annual NATSF tournaments at Stern.

Many of the teaching pros at these clubs were regular winners of our open-singles division. Jan Buise of the Beach Club was one of these. Jan had emigrated from Belgium and played as a junior at Wimbledon and played for the University of New Orleans. We became friends and he taught both my son and me lessons at the Beach Club.

Tim Siegel's father, Bob, and I regularly played doubles at the Beach Club and both singles and doubles at the Chateau Golf & Country Club. Bob had memberships at both venues. We played doubles in the tournament sponsored by Chateau every year to raise money for St. Jude's Children's Hospital. St. Jude's has remained one of my favorite charities. Bob kept me apprised of Tim's activities. After playing for Arkansas, Tim played professional doubles, competing with the likes of Ivan Lendl, before becoming the tennis coach at Texas Tech.

I played in a number of different tennis leagues, sponsored by different organizations. One was an association of the various clubs in the region. The teams would follow a schedule that had you playing on either a weeknight or weekend schedule and at all the participating club sites. I wrote two long articles for one of these organizations that was based at the Beach Club. The articles discussed (what else?) the physics of the tennis ball and the racquet.

One group formed from a nucleus of players from the New Orleans Lawn Tennis Club formed a league that played all of its matches Saturday mornings on the clay public courts at City Park, Audubon Park, and Stern. I served on the board of this group, which usually met monthly at an uptown restaurant. I was the driving force to get this group to donate a golf cart to Stern for dragging and brushing their clay courts. This charitable act was much appreciated by Nehemiah, since his small tractor had completely worn out.

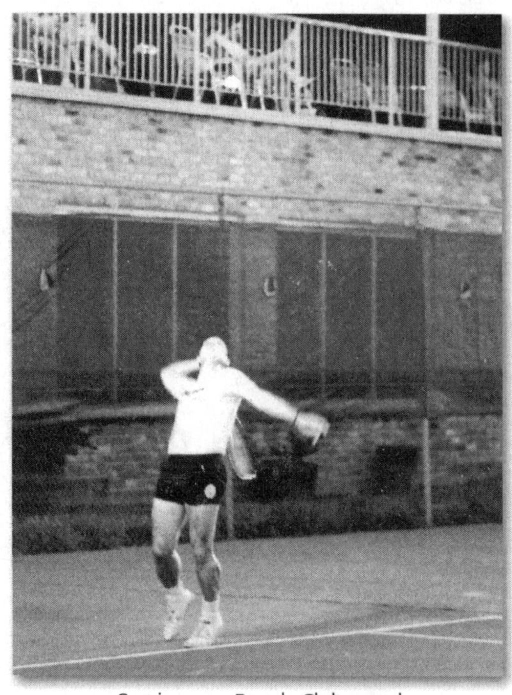

Serving at a Beach Club match

TENNIS OFFICIATING

I also attended a USTA workshop given at the New Orleans Lawn Club that certified me to officiate USTA-sanctioned matches. This distinction put my contact information on a list of USTA officials, so schools and tournament directors could hire me to work their events. One season, I worked all of the ladies home matches of Nichols State University in Thibodeaux, as well as the Southland Conference tournament, which they hosted.

PLAYGROUND TENNIS

A lot of my tennis activities continued after I retired from Rummel in 1986 and pursued some other activities. With all of this tennis-related activity, I became well known in the metropolitan tennis community. Some of the best friendships I made were made right on the Little Farms courts on Little Farms Ave.

I got involved playing doubles there with players who met just for fun on regular days and times. Later, I did the same thing at Jefferson Playground. This chain of events went on for years. I also taught private lessons at the public Little Farms courts when I wasn't teaching at a private club.

One of my students at Rummel had a younger sister whose father agreed to pay me to teach her as a birthday gift. The young lady was only 15, and because she was a bit shy, she recruited one of her friends to take lessons with her. As fate would have it, she didn't like tennis and quit after one lesson, but her friend, Celeste Mule, who had tagged along, fell in love with the game. She couldn't get enough lessons. Celeste played varsity tennis the following year at Chapelle High, and after graduating, she played for the University of New Orleans. She continued to take lessons from me for several years. A lot of my tennis activities continued after I retired from Rummel in 1986 and pursued some other activities.

THE "COLLECTORS"

One of these activities was finding sports celebrities, particularly tennis players, whom I could get to agree to have their images and bios published on sports cards produced by a company known as "The Collectors." The company would produce only 25,000 of each card and have only 5,000 autographed. I signed up Tom Dempsey (New Orleans Saints), Billy Ray Hobley (Harlem Globetrotters), and Nehemiah Atkinson, as well as Gardnar Mulloy, Vic Seixas, Ilie Nastase, Bobby Riggs, Pancho Segura, and Frank Parker (tennis).

I was friends with Billy Ray Hobley, because he often played tennis at Stern and Chateau. Tom Dempsey lived in a townhouse in Metairie, so I arranged to meet him and his family there. Except for Nehemiah, with whom I was best friends, I had to call Mulloy in Miami, and he helped me with all the other tennis stars. I did get to play doubles with Vic Seixas at the City Park courts. I interviewed Nastase by telephone at one of his homes in New York. Besides giving me the time for his bio, he graciously took down the contact information for one of my nieces, who was a big fan of his and mailed her an autographed picture. For all these celebrities, I wrote the bios that appear on the backs of their "Collectors" cards. This achievement is acknowledged by the initials J.H. at the end of each bio. The Collectors didn't survive long, because their owner, Jeff Jeffries, soon died of cancer.

The cards of some of the people I signed up for The Collectors

DOGS OF OUR LIVES

Patty and I got our first dog, Lobo, a white German Shepherd, shortly after we moved to Abbott Mountain in Prestonsburg. Incidentally, it was during our stay there that we had our only cat, Smoky. When we moved to #7 Caribou Ct., we bought Petey from a pet store on Veterans Blvd. Petey was a little curly-haired dark brown dog. He loved people but was a little on the slow side. We had an in-ground pool on Caribou Ct., and Petey avoided it carefully as he moved about the yard. However, when an airplane flew over approaching the east-west runway of the nearby New Orleans Airport, Petey would chase it, while looking up at it and wind up in the pool. Subsequently, he would have the most disgusted look on his face, as he emerged soaking wet.

Petey died shortly after we moved to Little Farms, and we got a beautiful black and tan German Shepherd that we named Rocky. Rocky was a "trash-eater" that never survived the surgery that followed an intestinal blockage. I held his paw, as he was euthanized. Gus and Bitsy came next, followed by Murphy, Sammy, Tootsie, Mosa, Pepper, and Topsy. Gus's story is an epic as dogs go.

Rocky

Gus

Bitsy

Murphy

The only one of these dogs that stayed with us after Katrina precipitated our move to Virginia was Tootsie. We had to turn over Pepper, Mosa, and Topsy to the animal shelter, after being unjustly harassed by a neighbor woman who was forever calling the police over some trivial matter or other. The remaining dogs died of natural causes.

GUS, OUR GREAT DANE

Gus was the dog we chose to replace Rocky. I always preferred larger male dogs and was attracted by the Great Dane breed. Through an ad in the *Times-Picayune*, I located a man who had some pups for sale. In a phone conversation with him, I learned that he had only one male puppy for sale. He was keeping his pick of the litter for himself.

When I asked him to tell me something about the breed, he referred me to a couple who lived in my neighborhood. I called them and was invited over to meet their male and female Danes. The male, Nero, was an AKC champion and had sired Gus. Nero immediately sold me on his breed. Not only was he beautiful, he also had a wonderful disposition. As I sat on the sofa, Nero backed up and sat his rear in my lap, while his front paws rested on the floor. Over the years, Gus would repeat this move many times on me and visitors.

It turned out that Nero had a co-owner, a lady named Joan Brenes. Joan had spent her entire life training and showing dogs, and she prevailed upon me to put Gus in dog shows … at least for a while. I had only purchased Gus as a pet and never intended to have him compete in dog shows. Joan was considering the reputation of her kennel and champion, Nero, which could be enhanced by Gus doing well on the dog-show circuit. If Gus became a champion, Joan could command top stud fees for his sire, Nero.

When Gus was in the six-month class, Joan persuaded me to enter Gus in a dog show for Danes, sponsored by the Great Dane Society of Greater New Orleans. I only had to deliver Gus to the site, and Joan would handle Gus in the show ring. Set up under the moss-draped oaks of City Park on a sunny spring day, the setting for the show was beautiful.

It was obvious to me from their vehicles and dress that most of the folks in attendance were high-society. I really didn't fit in at this scene. Everyone seemed to know one another and their dogs, and I only knew Joan Brenes. I parked my Chevy Luv a ways off from the show ring and handed Gus off to Joan to show him. While Joan was parading Gus around for the judge, I sat on the tailgate of my truck. When Joan and Gus returned to the truck the first time, I was ready to load up Gus and get home, but Joan told me that Gus had to return for further rounds of elimination. Finally, Joan called me to the show ring, and we all posed for pictures as Gus had won 1st place.

I was ready to flee the scene and get home, but as I put Gus in my truck, a lady, donned in expensive clothing, furs, and jewelry, stepped up and introduced herself. She said she had never seen me around before. I explained that this was my first show, and I was not a member of her society. In fact, Gus was the first Dane I had owned. With the air of an expert, she said, "Let me tell you, that dog will finish!" I couldn't resist. Feigning ignorance, I said, "Aren't we finished yet?" She patiently explained the process dogs must finish to be registered as champions.

Acknowledging that Gus was my first Dane, she declared, "You surely know how to pick them!" Again, I couldn't resist. "Not really. I found Gus advertised in the *Times-Picayune*, and he was the only male the owner would sell." That must have given her food for thought. Folks who show dogs spend a lot of time studying pedigrees to find a champion. Then, they spend a lot of money traveling the show circuit.

THE GREAT DANE NATIONAL SPECIALTY SHOW

Joan was so excited at Gus's success that she urged me to enter him in the AKC-sponsored Great Dane National Specialty Show in Dallas, TX, May 29th–31st, 1980. She explained that it was the most prominent of Dane shows, and that it would be judged by three judges brought in from Europe. It attracted Dane enthusiasts from all over the world. This point was later verified to me, when two men in attendance from Japan offered me $5,000 for Gus, and two of the dogs who competed against Gus were flown in by private jet from Alaska.

Since I had finished my teaching duties by mid-May, I made the trip to Dallas to placate Joan. Gus and I drove over in our old Olds. It had only 440 air conditioning (roll down all four windows and drive 40 mph).

When we parked in the hotel lot, our vehicle really stood out among all the Cadillacs, Mercedes, and Lincolns. The campers housed the professional handlers, who cared for and showed the dogs for their wealthy owners. Gus stayed with me in my room. This step was allowed, as long as I put Gus in his kennel, when I left him in the room alone.

Our first stop was the "hospitality room." As we approached the door, it opened and a lady of stern visage stepped out and barraged me with a string of questions about Gus. I was completely taken aback, since most of the questions were about Gus's pedigree and I couldn't answer them. Finally, I just said, "Lady, I'm John Hanson, and this is my puppy, Gus."

At that moment, the door to the adjoining room opened, and Joan stepped into the hallway and rescued me. She knew all the answers the lady sought. Gus's pedigree traced back to the kennel operated by this lady. The name of the lady was Hazel Gregory, who was recognized as the grand dame of Great Dane society. What amazed me was that Hazel recognized at a first glance that Gus had the characteristics of her line of breeding … thus, all the pedigree questions. It was a good omen that this expert in the Great Dane breed was impressed with Gus. He would go on to win the 1st-place prize in his age group.

True to her promise, Joan handled Gus in the huge red-carpet show ring that was set up in one of the hotel's ballrooms. When the judge picked Gus, an official entered the ring to present the 1st prize, which consisted of a beautiful wood etching of a Great Dane head and a ribbon, to Joan. Joan was too short to hold the etching high enough over her head to keep Gus from getting his teeth on it. I quickly entered the ring and rescued the prize. Gus figured it was his and left some tooth marks on the etching as a reminder.

There was a formal banquet and dance in the ballroom after the show. I sat at one of the round tables with Joan and a group that included a couple from Fire Creek Ranch in Alaska. This couple had entered two black Danes, who placed 2nd to Gus. They had flown down on their private jet. This crowd had both position and money. While I had neither in the eyes of society, I had Gus, and he had kicked ass. It was a good feeling.

When the band started up, I invited each lady at my table to dance with me, until I had danced with all of them. When I had made all the rounds, I noted to those at my table that Hazel Gregory was sitting alone at her table, and no one had danced with her. When I said I was going to ask her, the ladies at my table strongly opined that she would never dance with anyone. It seemed to me that I detected an undertone of jealousy among them. Well, I went over to Hazel's table, and we danced the next number together. When I returned, I simply said, "She's nice." They couldn't believe what they had just seen. For me, it was another good feeling to see the jaws of snobs drop.

GUS HELPS A JUDGE WITH HER DECISION

Joan convinced me to enter one more show. It was an all-breed show that was held at the old racetrack in Kenner. The show rings were roped-off rectangles, along a cinderblock wall under the grandstands. Gus won against the other Danes in the competition and advanced to compete for the best of the working-class breeds. When Joan led Gus into the ring to compete against the other working-class breed winners, I noticed that folding chairs had been set within arm's length of the ring. The handlers were between their dogs on their left and the spectators on their right, as they guided their dogs about the ring.

After a lengthy process of elimination, the judge was in the process of picking the 1st-, 2nd-, and 3rd-place finishers from among some half-dozen of the original competitors, who had survived her scrutiny. In doing so, she had Joan take Gus directly away from her along the line of spectators and then return back to her along the same line. Since Gus was on Joan's left, nothing separated him from the spectators but a single rope. I immediately had visions of Gus stopping to fraternize with the crowd, but he headed straight for the judge, who was standing just past a folding table that held the prizes.

As Gus passed the table, he suddenly turned his head and snatched the box containing the 1st prize in his jaws. I had to enter the ring to get the prize from Gus and return it to the table. The crowd loved it. It was as though Gus was telling the judge he was #1 and to get on with it. I thought that Gus had ruined his chances, but after the judge continued to examine her finalists for several more minutes, she picked Gus for the 1st prize. I made my second trip into the ring to retrieve it. I never entered Gus into any more shows. He was already a champion in my eyes.

GUS IN HARNESS

Joan told me that working dogs that pulled sleds up north could also pull a cart fitted with reins, traces, and a harness. Within a few months, I taught Gus to pull such a cart. He loved it, and soon, he was giving rides to the neighborhood kids. He was the hit of some of the birthday parties for children of my friends. The *Times-Picayune* did a feature article on Gus pulling his cart, and WWL-TV did one of its "Dog Days of August" segments on the evening news. I also taught Gus to jump over barriers. I often took him with me when I played tennis, and Gus would jump over the three-foot net at my hand signal.

FETCH IT YOURSELF

Part of the time Gus was with us, we also had a small dog named Bitsy. What a contrast! Not just in size, but also in intelligence. Bitsy loved to play fetch with a tennis ball in our backyard. She would retrieve ball after ball, until she was exhausted. When I first showed a ball to Gus and threw it across the yard, he dutifully retrieved it. When I immediately threw it away again and asked Gus to go get it, he looked at me as if to say "Look, I just went and got it for you. If you are dumb enough to throw it away again, you can go get it yourself." Gus just didn't get the point of Bitsy's favorite game.

A SIGN OF CANINE INTELLIGENCE

Gus was so smart that he seemed almost human. Once when Patty and I were sitting in our enclosed front porch, Bitsy was lying on the carpet between us, chewing away on a large Nyler bone that we had purchased for Gus. Bitsy had her own smaller bone, but at that moment, she was helping herself to Gus's bone. After a while, Gus came in, saw Bitsy with his bone, and approached her. It was obvious that Gus wanted his bone and, just as obvious, that Bitsy wasn't about to give it up to the giant dog towering over her.

Gus could have easily slapped Bitsy across the room with his paw, but he never once pulled muscle on her. Gus just moved his head pleadingly from side to side, while Bitsy growled stubbornly. After this stalemate continued for a minute or so, Gus turned and abruptly left the room. I commented to Patty that it wasn't like Gus to give up. After several minutes, Gus returned, carrying Bitsy's ball in his mouth. He released it, so that it rolled tantalizingly in front of Bitsy's face. Patty and I were stunned that Gus had thought of a way that might get Bitsy to voluntarily release his bone. It was a thought process on Gus's part, not something I had taught him.

IN BUSINESS WITH JOAN BRENES

My association with Joan Brenes, who handled Gus in his dog-show appearances and introduced me to dog carting, led to another activity that supplemented my teaching income. Joan had her own kennel at her home on the northeast corner of Maryland and West Metairie, where she trained dogs to sniff out narcotics and explosives. Her star dog was a Golden Retriever, aptly named "Columbo."

Most of Joan's income came from leasing a narcotics-trained dog to detective agencies, which would conduct searches on oil rigs that had crews, who lived on the rigs for two-week shifts. This endeavor could be quite lucrative, since the agency was paying us $10 an hour from the time they picked up a dog until they returned it. Trips to the rigs in the Gulf of Mexico would typically bill for $700, while a trip to Alaska could generate $1,600. Joan also taught obedience classes on weekends and showed dogs. I was not involved in either of those activities.

I did, however, help train our dogs to sniff out substances that were hidden to all their senses, except smell. Initially, we only trained the dogs to sniff out narcotics, which we obtained from the police department in only the small amounts needed. Eventually, Joan learned that dogs were being trained to sniff out live termites, and we began to train a Golden Retriever that Joan purchased for $40 in unpaid kennel fees.

We named the unregistered bitch "Charlene," and started training her to find termites. We kept a colony of live termites in an aquarium and fed them wood. After three months of training Charlene, we sold her to a company in New England that sold termite poisons and exterminating services. They flew down a lady whom I took around demonstrating Charlene's abilities. She was impressed enough to have her company shell out $8,500 for Charlene.

Working with Joan's dogs was something I could do, while still teaching full-time at Rummel. I would go feed the dogs and clean the runs after school, and then work with Joan training the dogs on the weekends. This work would never support me though, given that Joan was in no position to grow the business in the economy we faced. She also had some serious health problems and was well past her prime physically. So, when I retired from Rummel in 1986, I looked to do something else.

A TRIP TO NASA IN HOUSTON

In my last two years at Rummel, I got my physics students involved in a competition sponsored by NASA. Students from all over the country were invited to design a scientific experiment to be performed by astronauts, while they're in orbit in the space shuttle. The students who won were rewarded with an all-expenses-paid trip to the space center near Houston. Because their teacher got to go too, I went back to Houston for the first time since I had worked out for the Houston Oilers.

For a couple of days, I mingled with other teachers and their winning students. We crawled all over the shuttle. It turned out I had more student winners than anyone there (three), and my students were the only winners from Louisiana. The following year, several more of my students won the trip again but I picked one of the science teachers in my department to go with them, because I had been there and done that. Furthermore, it was a great opportunity for any science teacher.

THE DENOUX FAMILY

My association with Rummel brought me in contact with O'Neil DeNoux. O'Neil, the son, was never confused with O'Neil, the dad, because the latter always went by "Frenchy." Besides serving in Europe in World War II and in the Korean War with the 101st Airborne, Frenchy worked undercover in military intelligence. It was a natural transition to the New Orleans Police Department, when he returned to civilian life. Eventually, his son, O'Neil became a homicide detective with the NOPD.

When I first met Frenchy, he headed up the crime-scene photography department for the Jefferson Parish Sheriff's Office. Through mutual associations at Rummel, Frenchy learned that I did air conditioning work and asked me to help repair his house unit. In the process of doing so, I met his wife and his son, O'Neil. I didn't charge anything for my work, but Frenchy insisted that I let him produce a formal photograph of my family. I still have that framed photograph of Patty, my son John, Gus, Bitsy and me. We're posed in front of the fireplace in the DeNoux living room.

At this time, the older son, O'Neil, was the manager of the AAA Detective Agency and working on his first novel. They both did very well. O'Neil has published at least a dozen books and taught writing at the local colleges. Just Google "O'Neil DeNoux" to get his story.

A RETURN TO HUNTING

Frenchy and I both loved to hunt, though we were members of different hunting clubs. At that time, I had been away from hunting since my days in Opelousas, where I enjoyed hunting rabbits, dove, and ducks. I had introduced my son to shooting (and gun safety) in Kentucky, when he was four years old. When he entered Rummel, I felt it was time to take him deer hunting. My hunting buddies always said "It's better to go hunting with your son than to have to go hunting for him." Over his high school years, I spent a lot of time with my son. Much of that time was spent riding back and forth to Rummel and to tennis matches, as well as on the long drives to hunting camps.

One of the hunting clubs I joined was only about a half-hour drive from the one Frenchy joined. It was just out of Church Hill, MS … hardly more than a crossroads, about 20 miles north of Natchez. The club was family-oriented, and many of the hunters brought their wives, girlfriends, and kids with them. There was a rustic farmhouse, surrounded by large pastures and heavy stands of hardwoods. Some bunked in the farmhouse, while others brought campers and hooked up to the electric and water lines provided. My marine buddy, Jim Demuth, loaned me his trailer for the deer season. There was a small pond behind the farmhouse, and many streams flowed in the bottoms of the very hilly property. A four-wheel drive vehicle was needed to get around on the dirt roads. Only foot trails led to the deer stands. Hunting dogs were forbidden by our club rules.

John and I got to spend more time at the camp than most of the club members. We had a week off from school at Thanksgiving and two weeks for the Christmas break. For part of the latter, we had the lease to ourselves for a few days. John took advantage of the privacy to sight in a new 30-06 scoped rifle. The unfortunate target was a slow moving armadillo, which John hit from over 100 yards.

BREAKING ALL THE RULES

One of our members shared his trailer with a lady friend one trip. He persuaded the very reluctant lady to go with him and set up in the stand nearest to his own. Against all tradition and practice, she presented herself in a white fur coat, bedecked with make-up and reeking of cologne. Everyone knows you wear camo and mask any scents foreign to the woods … right? Well, she was helped into a stand as she was, and her friend headed to the next closest stand.

After an hour or so, a loud gunshot rings out from the direction of the lady's stand. Then, he hears her screaming his name. Racing to the clearing beneath his friend's stand, he comes upon a trophy buck breathing his last. They return to the camp in triumph. The veterans all praise and congratulate the novice hunter, before asking her if she'll be back out tomorrow. Genuinely bored, she says, "What's to do? You climb up in a tree, the deer walks out, and you shoot it." She never went out again. Been there. Done that. Most of the regular hunters spent the entire season without seeing a buck.

A TURKEY FOR FRENCHY

Before the deer season, I joined my fellow club members on a workday, which we spent repairing and building our stands and sowing feed plots. I noticed that there were large flocks of wild turkeys, feeding in the open fields. I commented on how abundant wild turkeys were on our lease to Frenchy, and he begged me to shoot one for him, which presented a problem. There was no season on turkeys until spring.

Well, one morning, I got into my tree stand before dawn. As day broke, turkeys began raining down from a nearby tree, where they had spent the night. Led by three large Toms, the flock paraded past the base of my tree. I didn't want to fire a shot with my .44 magnum lever-action marlin, as the sound would have ruined the morning for deer hunting.

Well, around 11 a.m., the flock returned. I thought again of Frenchy. He so wanted a wild turkey, and he and his wife were great cooks. Succumbing to temptation, I aimed at the head of the lead Tom. A body shot would ruin the meat. A head shot would be nearly impossible to pull off. That target was in constant random motion. I moved my aim point to the bottom of the neck where it joined the chest. This target was moving at a constant speed along a straight line.

When I fired, the big Tom collapsed and flapped around in a circle, scattering leaves. The other two Toms circled their fallen leader curiously before walking away with their flocks. I could have had shots at two more, but I needed to return with Frenchy's bird unseen. I carried the big Tom to the bottom of the hollow and plucked him under the cover of the underbrush. I carried him back to my trailer in my backpack, packed him in ice, and called Frenchy.

He drove over from his camp within the hour. Talk about a happy camper! Frenchy later told me the Tom dressed out at 22½ pounds. He also brought over a large serving of turkey stew for my family, as well as a turkey call, fashioned from one of my Tom's bones. Frenchy was so impressed with the performance of my rifle and scope in bagging the turkey that his attentive wife had me secretly arrange to buy the same rig to surprise Frenchy on his next birthday.

PATTY GOES TO THE CHURCH HILL HUNTING CAMP

I persuaded Patty to go to Church Hill for one weekend, but she refused to hunt a stand. I left her in the trailer and came back around noon. She had spent the day reading and relaxing in the trailer. I did persuade my city girl to take a walk in the pasture behind the farmhouse, pointing to all the natural beauty around us, especially a pecan tree. She just gave me that look she had when she first saw our chickens on Abbot Mountain. When I asked her what was wrong, she said, "There's an awful lot of bugs out here." Well, at least she tried. She caught a ride home with one of the families that left early.

THE 12 OAKS HUNTING CLUB

Next season, I joined a club that was located just over the state line in Mississippi, near Angola, the Louisiana state prison. John and I slept in a bunkhouse and had a common breakfast cooked by the managers of the 12 Oaks Hunting Club. At the morning hunt, beagles were turned out to drive deer through the woods. Hunters were on stands or positions assigned by lot. One morning, a 150-lb buck approached John, and he wounded it with a blast of buckshot from his 10 gauge. He then finished it off with a single shot to the neck with his .44 magnum Ruger revolver. It had an 8.75-inch barrel and was equipped with an extended eye-relief scope.

The very next day, John and I took up positions about 200 yards apart, near the top of the same ridge. After a while, I heard a deer galloping along the ridge and moved to intercept it. It was a beautiful buck, but it passed my position without offering a clear shot. I knew it was headed straight for John's position, so I yelled a warning to him.

Just after the deer disappeared from my view, I heard a blast from John's 10 gauge. I hurried ahead to find John standing on the ridge. "I hit him, Dad," John said. He showed me where the deer was when he fired, and I found bright red blood at that spot.

John indicated that when he fired the deer whirled to his right and headed toward the bottom of the ridge. The deer was nowhere to be seen from the ridge. I told John to just sit down and wait a while, and we would track the deer. If we went after the deer immediately, he might push on a lot further away before expiring. I was convinced from the blood on the ridge that the buck was fatally wounded. The blood trail led me 150 yards diagonally down the slope to the bottom of the hollow, where I spotted our dead buck. He was a beautiful 200-lb specimen with a great set of antlers.

John's 200-lb 10-point buck

The taxidermist I located in our local phone book was located in Chalmette, LA. His name was Ronald Reagan. Another Ronald Reagan occupied the White House at the time. We had venison in our freezer for some months. Much of it we had made into sausage.

AN ACADEMIC MOTIVATION SYSTEM THAT WORKED

By the time John finished high school, he had quite a collection of firearms. I've already mentioned his 30-06 bolt action rifle (scoped), his 10 gauge single-shot shotgun, and his .44 magnum Ruger revolver (scoped). He even obtained a .300 Weatherby magnum bolt-action rifle (scoped).

After John joined the FBI, his firearms background stood him in good stead. When he became interested in competitive pistol shooting, I gave him a customized Colt model 1911 .45 caliber pistol. The guns John acquired over his high school years were related to a monetary awards program I established to motivate him to get good grades. I gave him the option to get a gun he wanted or take the cash after each nine-weeks grading period. Early in his high school years, he usually opted for the latter.

My system for motivating John to do well in high school was based on my years of observing students who did and did not do well. When John was in grammar school, Patty oversaw his schoolwork for the most part. I stepped in if John had a problem with conduct. As long as elementary school students do their assignments and behave in class, they will lay a good foundation for high school success. My mother used to advise, "You don't have to be the smartest kid in school, but you can be clean and behave yourself!" Self-discipline and respect for yourself and your teachers can go a long way.

About the time John was in 7th grade, he succumbed to peer pressure and brought home a bad conduct grade, along with a note from the teacher describing John as a "class clown." I was so upset, I simply sent John to his room to wait for my action. I didn't want to make a decision, while I was so angry. I went to my room and thought about it, and prayed for guidance. I left John to stew in his room for about 30 minutes.

My decision was as hard on me as on John. I burst into his room belt in hand and strapped him across his legs "Misbehave in class, huh? Class clown, huh?" I accompanied these expressions with three or four applications of my belt, and abruptly left John, legs stinging, sitting on his bed.

John finally got the message that I had failed to verbally communicate to him. It was John's first whipping and his last. It so got his attention that he never got less than an A in conduct afterwards. It was a turning point, and I thank God for his guidance as I believe it turned John onto the right path.

No one can be motivated by an award of which he is ignorant. All of the special awards a school presents at their graduation ceremony are listed in the student handbook, but who reads every section of the handbook? The significance of these awards comes home to the graduating seniors, as they watch their peers called to the stage to receive them. You can see the look on their faces that says, "I could have done that." Too late now—you would have had to set those goals four years ago.

I didn't want John to be unaware of these awards, so I had him attend the Rummel graduation with me that immediately preceded his enrollment as a freshman. John watched as some 100 of the 300 graduates had their academic scholarships announced, when they approached the stage to receive their diplomas. He saw the look of pride on their faces and that of their parents. Their names and scholarships were printed in the program as well. Of course, not every parent would think to take their child to a high school graduation prior to beginning high school, but I had the perspective of someone who had attended some two dozen such ceremonies as a faculty member. I thought it could be highly motivating.

There was another step I took to help John do better with his high school experience. I enrolled him in two classes for the summer preceding his freshman year. One of the classes was a class in how to take notes and organize one's schoolwork. The other class was typing, which would not be part of his regular curriculum, but could contribute a lot to his education and work experience.

Another fact I had noted in teaching high schoolers was that many of them had evening and weekend jobs, especially the upper-classmen. It was that time of life when their thoughts turned to dating and driving, two relatively expensive pursuits. Since average parents couldn't support these activities to the satisfaction of their kids, many of them allowed their kids to take after-school jobs. Not only did this work-related opportunity have its own educational value in practical living, it also affected their ability to perform to their maximum in their studies and to participate in the many valuable extracurricular activities offered by their school.

I was determined that John would not have his high school experience diluted by hours spent stocking shelves at some supermarket. Accordingly, I set up a system of monetary rewards for academic effort and results. I explained to John that his job would be to be a student, and I would pay him a minimum salary, plus bonuses based on results. Every evening that was followed by a school day, he was to be in his room by 7 p.m. and study until "lights out" at 10 p.m. No TV. Exceptions were made for extracurricular activities in which he was involved.

My deal was straightforward. John would receive $20 each week just for being in his room. He would also receive bonuses, based on his report card results that were published every six weeks. He would receive $20 for each A and $15 for each B. Since he would receive six grades, he could earn a maximum bonus of $120. For making straight As, however, I would double his earnings to $240. He would receive no bonus for a C or lower grade, since that would indicate that he was just spinning his wheels in his room.

Well, John joined a lot of clubs, served on the student council, and played freshman football and tennis … along with making straight As. I knew I would come out ahead this way, because John's GPA and extracurricular experience would assure him of academic scholarships to several universities. Both John and I would be debt-free, when he graduated from the University of New Orleans. My motivational system worked for both of us.

Near the end of his freshman year, John approached me for advice regarding his coming sophomore year. He had been selected for honors classes and was considering not playing varsity football. He asked me what I thought he should do. "Mom and I enjoy going to the games and will continue to support your playing. But, the decision must be yours. Just remember our "no quit" rule. You do not have to join the varsity but, if you do, it is a three-year commitment."

When John realized I would not offer any opinion he said, "OK, Dad, I've made up my mind. I just want to know what you think." When I gave my reply, John could have been knocked over with a feather. "I think football is a glorious waste of time. You're honored at every pep rally and play under the lights every week during the season, but you spend more time on football than all of your subjects put together." I don't think John expected this reply coming from me, but he was glad to hear it and happily gave up football.

I was well aware, from attending graduations, that about one-in-three graduates received academic college scholarships, while only one-in-100 received athletic scholarships. Football was a crap shoot and could result in as many bad things as good. Spending time practicing and playing was, however, a lot safer than spending that time running the streets in cars.

JEFFERSON AUTO SERVICE

When I returned from Kentucky, I still had my '57 Jaguar XK-150 for my basic transportation. After bringing it to a specialist for a while ("limey bastard" as my WW II friends called his ilk) for repairs on Tchoupitoulas St., I discovered Jefferson Auto

Service, at a much closer location on Schewsbury Rd. They could handle all my needs and for a lot less money.

There's a saying that even late-model Jaguar owners need two such cars, since one of them can be driven, while the other is in the shop. I can vouch for the veracity of that statement. Frank Maone was the second-generation owner of Jefferson Auto Service, and my wife and I became good friends with the rather large Maone family.

Frank had two passions: vehicle mechanics and cooking. The former stood him in good stead for the business he ran. When business took a dive in the recession of 1987, Frank used his talent as a chef to open a restaurant on the property that he owned adjacent to his repair shop. The restaurant was known as the "Garlic House," and workers from the surrounding area came in on their lunch hour to eat. Others called in their orders, and we delivered to their place of business.

I pitched in by both waiting tables and delivering called-in orders. In the off hours, I visited businesses and distributed our bill of fare to owners and employees. The Garlic House could never produce the margin of profit of the vehicle-repair business, but it could tide the Maones over until the recession passed.

The bulk of Jefferson's customers had been individuals from the neighborhood, who, pressed by hard times, began to work on their own cars. Frank assigned me the task of soliciting fleet accounts, since businesses had to keep up their vehicles to deliver their goods and services. Frank had little formal education, but he came up with the brilliant idea of having a salesman represent his single-location, vehicle-repair business to all businesses, large and small, who used vehicles in their operation. While every garage, small or large, had an ad in the yellow pages, only Jefferson had a salesman dedicated to bringing in fleet business. That was me.

I developed a method of using the phone, targeted mailings, personal visits, and follow-ups to lure business vehicles to Jefferson for maintenance and repair. Within a year, Frank's business quadrupled, and he shut down the Garlic House. I was even able to get business from businesses that had their own full-time mechanics and repair facilities. Frank had to build a new bay between Jefferson Auto and the Garlic House property to accommodate the likes of bucket-lift trucks, buses, and motor homes. Subsequently, I went to Frank and told him it was time for me to go. His business had reached the point of diminishing returns, and I was no longer needed. He only had to keep satisfying his clientele. He understood this perfectly, and Patty and I continued to go to the parties he held. We were family.

AAA DETECTIVE AGENCY

As I ended my salesman job for Jefferson Auto, I was invited by O'Neil DeNoux to go to work for the AAA Detective Agency. O'Neil managed the business, which was owned by Chief Keith Casey and his wife. At this time, the agency operated out of

Chief Casey's residence in Kenner. Casey was a reserve captain for the Kenner Police, and O'Neil was a retired homicide detective, formerly with the New Orleans Police Department. O'Neil's dad was head of the crime-scene photography department of the Jefferson Parish Police.

Between Casey and the DeNouxs, we had many invaluable contacts with the three major police departments in our area. In addition, Frenchy had taught crime-scene photography all over Louisiana and knew all the sheriffs. These connections were extremely important, since most of our cases involved stakeouts in vehicles unfamiliar to people in the area and the local police could blow your cover by rolling up on you in response to some citizen calling in a suspicious person report. It was standard practice to call in a description of our vehicle, as well as info on when and where we expected to be on surveillance. Of course, we never revealed the name of our subject.

Private detective agencies usually perform three services: domestic cases; Insurance fraud cases; and servicing of court orders. Our domestic cases involved gathering evidence of a married person cheating on his or her spouse. Our insurance fraud cases entailed gathering evidence of a person falsely claiming to be injured or disabled. Our servicing of court orders was solicited when a court's normal process serving system failed.

Chief Casey charged his clients by the number of hours his detectives spent on a case (in the field, writing reports, and testifying in court) and their expenses (mostly mileage). The most lucrative cases were the domestic ones, because they nearly always involved the deployment of two detectives and two vehicles, and they often went on and on before being resolved.

We had one female client who spent over $35,000, proving her husband was committing adultery. We did it for her on three instances, and each time she would reconcile with her spouse, until he returned to his wayward ways, and she would hire us again. On one occasion, the client called us on short notice to advise that her husband was leaving early Saturday morning with a fishing pal to spend the weekend at a fishing camp, way out in the marshes south of Houma, LA. She suspected that he was up to his old tricks.

Since I was the only detective available, I decided to follow the "other woman." She was picked up at her apartment, well before daybreak, by another woman, and they drove nearly to the Gulf, before pulling into a parking lot across the road from a small store that sat beside a boat dock. I continued a few hundred yards until I was out of sight, before parking my vehicle. I changed my outer coat and hat, and walked back to the store.

While I killed time in the store, the "other woman" came in and actually stood beside me at the register. When she left, I saw our wayward husband and his pal dock their fishing boat. The girls loaded some of their stuff onto the boat, and the two couples shoved off. The men had launched their boat at a marina some five miles up the bayou.

Had anyone followed them they would have just seen two men launch a fishing boat and sail away. Ah, "the best laid plans of mice and men." It would have been much more difficult to have followed the men, and I would have lost them, when they launched their boat without ever observing the rendezvous at the second site. It is to be noted that I did not gather the evidence needed to prove adultery on this excursion into the marshes, but only the information our client wanted to know, viz., that her husband was still seeing the "other woman."

PROVING ADULTERY

To convince a judge that a man and a woman are guilty of adultery, an investigator must observe that they spend several hours alone together, with no other adults present. The identity of the offending spouse's lover must be established, along with the time and location of the adultery. Beyond these basics, there are many other details that can be observed to add credence to an investigator's testimony.

Usually, the lovers would change their clothes after meeting up and go out to dinner at a nice restaurant, before returning to their love nest for most of the night. They often appeared in a different set of clothes when they left, separately, in the early morning. We would observe all the details of their activities, as much as possible, without revealing to our subjects that they were under observation. Our reports would also include photos when they could be taken unnoticed.

Most of the time, when our client's attorney would reveal our reports in discovery, the opposing attorney would concede adultery, and we didn't have to testify in court. The wait for most divorces to be finalized, if they were on common grounds recognized by law, could be a year or more, but divorces on grounds of adultery could be finalized in less than a month. The provision that separates unfaithful spouses quickly probably lowers the murder rate, given that "hell hath no fury like a woman scorned." Or a man.

A SPECIAL CASE

Our clients were, of necessity, persons of means, given the costs of the investigations. Most of them were lawyers and doctors or their spouses. This factor led me to work a few cases "on my own" for friends who could never afford our AAA fees. One of these stands out in my memory.

One of my tennis students confided that she suspected her husband of adultery, and after interviewing her, I had to agree. I told her what was involved, if she wanted proof of adultery for purposes of getting a divorce. She replied that she only wanted "to know." Well, I could satisfy that desire without a second investigator, saving a lot of expense from the get-go. I would also be able to work her case at only one location over one night. In addition, I was willing to work the case gratis, but she would have none of that, and we settled on half the going hourly rate.

It turned out that her husband was banging his secretary in her own house, where she lived alone (a dog doesn't count). After calling my client with what I had observed, I picked her up and drove her to the secretary's house and pointed to her husband's car parked right out front. We sat through the night, until her husband left in the morning.

Now that she knew, she had a change in attitude. She wanted me to conduct a surveillance that would prove her husband's adultery in court. For a second witness, I recruited my son, who was enrolled at UNO at the time. I explained that we would work the case Friday night and would be finished Saturday morning, after our subject departed his love nest. My son said that would work for him, but he had to work a dance at UNO Saturday night. I assured him that we would be done in time for his prior commitment.

Well, as fate would have it, our surveillance dragged on to after 4 p.m. Saturday. The miscreant couple had entered her darkened house shortly before midnight, turned the lights on, then off, and never showed themselves, until she greeted a young man who came to the front door around 1 p.m. They spoke at the door for a few minutes, before he raced off and returned about 20 minutes later with a bag of take-out food. The secretary took the bag at the front door, and the delivery man raced off again.

"Darn!" I thought to myself, "They may be holed up in there all night again." I had to do something to finish the case. My son was going nuts. We had only observed the couple enter the house since the night before, but we had not established that no other adult was present.

I took some flyers that my cousin Donald used to advertise "Hanson Brothers Painting" and gave a few to my son, telling him to wait for me at the sidewalk, while I went to the door. He would be in earshot of any conversation between me and anyone who came to the door. I pinned a half-dozen flyers and five-dollar bills against my left palm under my thumb and knocked.

The secretary came to the door. Glancing toward my son, I explained "My son and I are in the neighborhood, passing out flyers to advertise our business. May I leave one with you?" She couldn't help notice the five-dollar bills, as she glanced at the flyers in my left hand. "Oh, I almost forgot. This is a corner house. We offer everyone in corner houses a chance to win a five-dollar bill." She gave me a very interested look.

"I don't know anything about football but I know the questions and answers we are using. Do you know how many players are on the rosters of each NFL team?" She smiled and said, "40." I was all smiles and congratulations, as I handed her a flyer and a five-dollar bill. Then, I asked if she had any other adults in the house who could try to win five dollars. She practically screamed out a command for her lover to come to the door.

I almost felt sorry for him, as he tried to impress me with his knowledge of football but could not answer my question. I had asked him for the battle cry that quarterback Joe Kapp had used throughout the season to rally his Minnesota Viking teammates to their Super Bowl appearance. It happened to be "40 for 60," and he never came close. When I offered to give anyone else in the house a chance at five dollars, she offered, "We're the only ones in the house, except for the dog." I had everything I needed, and my son made it to the dance. I went to court to testify for my client, but after the attorneys went over my report in a pre-trial conference, I wasn't even called to the stand. The opposing attorney caved.

A CASE OF FRAUDULENT DISABILITY

Once, an insurance company retained AAA to investigate a disability claim of a man in a rural community in Southwest Louisiana. After one of our detectives checked the location of his house and its surroundings, it was decided to use two detectives to work the case. We needed one man to observe what the subject did around the house. This man would have to stay hidden in a fixed and camouflaged position along a fence line about 100 yards behind the house. From there, he could videotape the subject on the two sides and rear of the house. He could also inform his partner, when the subject drove away from his house.

My partner and I rode to our subject's house in one vehicle, and I was dropped off about 200 yards from the fence line, at the rear of our subject's property. My partner drove to a position that our subject would have to drive past, if he left home, and I worked my way to a good hiding spot in the brush along the rear property line. It was still pitch dark. As daybreak came, I noted a driveway along the left side of the house that led to a detached shed. There was also a carport attached to the right rear of the house. The fenced backyard covered about three acres and contained a small pond.

There was one serious threat to reveal my presence. A flock of about a dozen Guinea hens slowly patrolled the fence line. Nearly everyone in the area kept such hens as sentinels. I happened to know that if one of the hens spotted me, the flock would raise holy hell, and our surveillance would be compromised. Each time the flock passed my position, I remained motionless and squinted in order to hide the whites of my eyes. They never spotted me and eventually stopped patrolling.

About 7 a.m., two young boys exited a back door and went up the driveway to the road, where they boarded a school bus. About 10 a.m., our subject exited the same door, and I started videotaping him. He had backed a pickup truck up to the detached shed. He went in and out of sight, as he made trips in and out of the shed. For 20 minutes, he carried large boxes from the shed and manhandled them into the bed of his truck.

When he drove off, I called my partner to watch for him. My partner followed him to another house, where he observed him unloading the pickup. From there, the subject returned back to his house the way he had left. I had been alerted to his return and videotaped him as he drove up his driveway, dismounted, and reentered his house via the carport door. It was now about noon.

Around 3 p.m., the subject's boys were returned by the school bus and went inside. Within a half hour, I saw them fielding and returning baseball grounders. They were in the opening between their house and their neighbor to the right. The source of the grounders was hidden from my view by the subject's house. After about 15 minutes, the source of the grounders swapped places with the boys, and I videotaped our subject expertly fielding grounders and hurling them back. Our subject was about as disabled as a major-league shortstop!

An unusual thing happened, when my partner and I testified in court against our ball player. As a witness, I had to remain in the hallway outside the court room, until I was called to the stand. Contrary to the purpose of this practice, I could hear the testimony and cross-examination of my partner from my chair in the hallway. This situation is not supposed to happen, and this was the only occasion in my career that it did.

I was well-advised of the approach of the opposition attorney and answered his every question to his disadvantage. I enjoyed the looks of dismay on the faces of our subject and his attorney, as I backed up my testimony with my video. Smile! You're on candid camera! We racked up a lot of hours on that court date, given that attendance at the trial courthouse involved about seven hours of travel time alone. Easy money. We earned even more on travel time, when we traveled to the subject's home. Frankly, sitting a couple of hours in an air-conditioned building was a lot easier than spending all day hiding in the bushes.

MIXING IN ADULTERY WITH DISABILITY

Another disability case we worked involved a woman who faked a disabling back injury. It turned out the attorney who represented her was her employer. In the process of proving that her disability was bogus, the facts we gathered also established that she had committed adultery with her attorney. My guardian angel was in on my surveillance, since, for a short while, some kids had left the trailer and fired shots over my "hide." They were unaware of my presence, fortunately, and I was hunkered down safely behind a tree.

The attorney and his client were videotaped clearing brush around a trailer home in a remote location in Mississippi. No disability here. The rub was the facts also showed they had spent the night in the trailer, with no other adults present. Oops! This married attorney might have to face more embarrassment than simply losing his disability case. He would be seen in open court to be an adulterer, and he might have to face his wife in a divorce proceeding. I know for a fact that Chief Casey called this attorney and advised him to have another attorney take his place in court. That was nice of Keith. Professional courtesy.

A DIFFICULT COURT ORDER TO SERVE

Every Monday morning, the AAA detectives met around a large oval table in the agency conference room. Chief Casey chaired our meetings and as always, went through the cases we were working, alphabetically by client name. As each name was called, the detective assigned to the case would give a progress report, and then the floor would be opened to questions and discussion. Chief Casey would end the meeting presenting new cases the agency had accepted and assigning them to us.

One Monday morning, after I had worked about a year at AAA, I found myself with no new case to work, which meant no money to be earned. As a result, I approached Chief Casey privately and asked if I could work a case I knew to be open. It was the serving of a court order on a woman. Her name always evoked smiles all around, because she had avoided service for month after month, and none of our detectives—even Chief Casey and his wife—were able to nail her. I had never tried to serve her or anyone else for that matter. All of my cases had been of the domestic and insurance fraud ilk.

Undoubtedly, this factor probably explains Chief Casey's surprised reaction to my request to take her case. "You? You want this service?" "Yes, Chief," I replied. "I don't have any other work to do." The Chief shook his head, smiled, and said, "OK, you can try." I then asked him, "How is a valid service of a court order executed?" He simply directed me to get the order from the last detective assigned to the case, at which point, he would explain the details to me.

The last detective turned out to be our most senior detective, a laid-back Afro-American named Renard Allen. At brunch at a restaurant on St. Charles Ave. with the other detectives, Renard pointed out the apartment building across the famed avenue. It was a massive, multi-storied brick building that occupied the entire block. Its wings formed a square around an interior courtyard and above a ground-level parking garage. The only ingress and egress were from and to St. Charles Ave., via an entrance guarded 24–7 by a security team.

Renard advised that I simply watch for a woman fitting the subject's description to drive out of the only exit, follow her until she exited her vehicle, and then serve her. This approach had never got the job done before, but Renard and the other detectives were content to sit in their car for a shift, write a report, and be paid for the hours they staked out the entrance. The only variation tried was to have Chief Casey's wife visit a beauty parlor beside the entrance, on the (fat) chance that the mark would show there.

You see, this woman was wanted from Florida to Louisiana for a mail-fraud scheme she used to bilk her victims. She could conduct her scam, without ever leaving her fortress. Because she had no schedule to follow, her comings and goings from her fortress were completely random. Security handled her shipping and receiving right from and to her apartment.

I've always agreed with Einstein's definition of insanity, as continuing to do the same thing over and over and expecting a different result. If our subject would not come out to us, I had to devise a way to go in to her. By 6 p.m. that same Monday, I had come up with a plan. I had no idea if the subject would be home that Monday evening, but because most people don't go out on Monday nights, the odds were she would be.

My first step was to call the office of the apartment building after business hours on the probability that someone in security would answer. A man's voice said simply, "Security." So far, so good. I began to explain the purpose of my call. "My name is John Thomas. I've been employed at Loyola University and a colleague of mine told me about your facility ... how great the security is and how the streetcar runs right in front of the building. My problem is my wife and I need to see the facility this evening, because we are returning first thing in the morning to arrange our move from Tallahassee. I wouldn't expect to be allowed to roam around unescorted. Would it be possible for someone from security to show us around?"

The security man seemed eager to accommodate us, as he answered, "Meet me in the lobby at around 7." Patty and I were in the lobby at the appointed time, and the security man brought us a brochure, with the various floor plans available. As we were following him from the lobby, I casually said to Patty, "You know, Dr. Barfield has a friend who lives here." The guard didn't know it, but my words were intended for his ears, and they had the desired effect. He spun around to face us. "What's their name?" he asked. I said our subject's name. "Oh, I know her real well," the guard offered. Then I buttered him up a little, "You must know everyone in the building." "I know her well. She gets a lot of packages," he explained.

I immediately dropped the subject, and Patty and I focused on three apartments that the guard showed us. I had told Patty we were going to pretend to look at some apartments for a case I was working and for her to just play along. She did a magnificent job of checking out everything, as only a wife could do.

As we left the last apartment, I said to Patty and the guard, "You know, Dr. Barfield asked me to say hello to your friend for him. Do you think that would be possible?" "Sure, I'll take you by her apartment," he offered. As we approached the apartment on the other side of the complex from our last stop, I prayed that she would be home. As I knocked on her door, a small dog began barking excitedly from within, but no human approached the door.

I stalled, on the hope that my subject might return before long. I started by having the guard explain the building's policy regarding pets in great detail. Well, I was able to keep him telling me everything he knew about company policy for a good five minutes. Suddenly, I heard the elevator doors open down the hall. I turned to look, and so did the guard and Patty. I recognized my subject from a mug shot, but the guard excitedly confirmed her identity for me, "There she is, now!" I met my subject several paces from her door and served her the court order that I had tucked under my sweater.

Patty still laughs when we recall the look on her face. Her lower jaw dropped four inches, as she was completely stunned when she realized what had happened. After telling her not to hold it against the guard, since I had deceived him, I said "C'mon, Patty" and headed for the elevator.

The guard spoke with my subject for several minutes, before joining us at the elevator. I didn't know if he would return ready to punch me out or with his tail between his legs, but I wasn't about to move through his building unaccompanied. He returned meekly, with a worried look on his face. Go, guardian angel! On the way to the lobby, I offered him $20 for his trouble and asked to speak with his supervisor. He adamantly refused the money but took me to his supervisor. I explained exactly how I had used his interest in promoting occupancy to deceive him. I gave him my AAA business card and invited him to call me if he had any questions. He never did.

Because our AAA office was only a few blocks away, I took Patty with me to write my report on one of the office computers. All of our detectives had keys to the office and knew the alarm codes. Patty and I were alone as I composed my report, until Chief Casey walked in as I was finishing up. Chief was obviously surprised to see both Patty and me in the office after hours, and asked as he breezed by me, "What are you doing here?" I replied, "I just served that court order, and I'm writing my report."

Chief said, "Oh," and took two more strides before it hit him. He spun around and exclaimed, "You what?!" He couldn't believe that I had accomplished in two hours what he and his detectives had spent many eight-hour shifts failing to do. He was so elated, he paid me for four times the two hours Patty and I had worked. At the next Monday morning staff meeting, Chief extolled my ingenuity and had me tell the story to all the detectives assembled. What a way to execute my first service of a court order!

FAIS-DO-DO

Frank Maone worked in support of some prominent politicians, and I often assisted him at preparing and serving meals in connection with meetings and fundraisers. Every August, a huge birthday party was held at the Hilton Hotel in New Orleans as a fundraiser for the honoree, Sheriff Harry Lee. Tickets were sold at $100 a head. Both ballrooms were filled with round tables that seated 10 guests each.

This party was called Sheriff Lee's *Fais-do-do*, a French name given to some Cajun dance parties. The funds raised supported Sheriff Lee's reelection campaigns and charities. The Sheriff had some 1,500 employees, and their evaluation depended more on their prowess at selling *Fais-do-do* tickets than job performance. Celebrities were brought in to provide music and entertainment, and the Governor led a parade of who's who in Louisiana. Such a gala doesn't just happen. Stephen Segal regularly visited with Sheriff Lee, and Frank Maone has pictures of himself with Mr. Segal displayed in his office.

Every Tuesday, Mike O'Brien, the owner of Avondale Containers, hosted a luncheon for some 35 movers and shakers, who would chow down and then work on the planning of the coming *Fais-do-do*. This scenario went on for months, and I helped Frank Maone with the cooking and serving. I also partook of Frank's excellent fare, but was not involved in the planning activities. Some of the wealthiest men in Jefferson Parish attended these gatherings. I mingled amicably with these big shots, but never became friends of any but Mike O'Brien. Sheriff Lee never attended these gatherings, but his colonels, captains, and lieutenants were spread among the prominent businessmen in attendance.

The two-story wooden building that housed these luncheons was the headquarters of Avondale Containers. It was isolated among acres of shipping containers that carried goods by truck, rail, and ship all over the world. No one traveling the nearest public roads would have a clue that these meetings were happening. Looking out the second-floor kitchen window, I sometimes wondered if an uninvited person might not end up as tiger dung. The window looked down on an enclosure that housed a Bengal tiger. The tiger had plenty of room to roam and a swimming pool in which to cool off and relax. How many people do you know that have a Bengal tiger at their place of business?

JEFFERSON PARISH SHERIFF'S DEPUTY

Working for Frank Maone, I became aware of a job that I would like to try ... serving court orders as a Jefferson Parish Sheriff's Deputy. It was a job usually considered a reward for friends of Sheriff Lee. The Sheriff's process servers delivered the myriad of orders issued by the courts of the Parish. These orders mainly were subpoenas to appear in court, but they also included repossessions of goods, usually automobiles, but occasionally the entire stock of a business.

The deputies assigned to process serving were given an unmarked car, which could be used for personal travel within a 30-mile radius. The sheriff provided insurance, gas, and all upkeep and repairs. This truly represented a monetary value over and above the modest salary paid.

These deputies were not involved in ordinary police work. They didn't patrol a beat or do traffic control. They carried badges and police radios, and were provided windbreakers and caps with identifying patches. All carried their badges, but most wore ordinary clothes on the job. They did not have to go through the Police Academy.

Unlike most jobs, the application process involved being fingerprinted and passing a lie-detector test. It was an easy job and could be worked around any personal business or schedule one had. Many of these deputies were retirees, and all were supporters of the sheriff (in my case, a friend of a supporter). Directly or indirectly, these jobs were rewards for political support of the sheriff.

I wound up working as a deputy sheriff for three-plus years. I worked out of the Second Parish Court House at David Drive and West Metairie Ave. This court served all of Jefferson Parish east of the Mississippi River. All court orders originated from the main court in Gretna, LA on the west bank. Each working day, a courier delivered a pouch to Second Parish Court, which contained all the court orders intended for residents of the east bank. Clerks distributed the orders to the deputies, based on the address of the person to be served.

Because we each had a fixed geographical area to work, the number of orders we received to process varied from day to day. Our first responsibility was to log in the new orders. Then, we attempted to serve them and logged in the results. It was a bit discouraging, once I realized, over time, that promotions up the ranks had nothing to do with job performance. In fact, some of the least effective servers who made the minimal effort to successfully process their orders were the ones receiving promotions. What they did do well was sell tickets to the sheriff's annual *Fais-do-do* fundraiser.

"I'M CALLING THE POLICE"

Once, my lieutenant who knew of my experience with difficult services at AAA Detective Agency ordered me to serve a business man, who had successfully avoided service for a long period of time. Furthermore, a lot of powerful people wanted him in court. The location was outside my area of responsibility, but pressure from the colonel in charge of all service of court orders had been brought to bear on my lieutenant.

When I knocked at the locked front door of the subject's business during business hours, there was no reply. I walked about 200 feet along a truck entrance that ran along the left side of the building and opened into a lot behind the building. I saw an employee near an open delivery entrance, and he led me down a long hall that led to a lobby behind the locked front door.

Behind a sliding glass window to my left, sat a receptionist. She told me that my subject was in a meeting behind a set of closed double doors behind me. In order to give her no chance to buzz the owner, I immediately knocked lightly on the meeting room doors and barged right in.

Straight ahead of me, the owner/subject sat behind a large desk, upon which sat his ornate name plate. A few men sat on chairs to the left and right. They all had a stunned look on their face. Before they could react in any way to my intrusion, I was standing in front of the owner's desk. I addressed him by name and told him I was distributing flyers to local businesses and offered him a Jefferson Auto flyer.

As he accepted it, I said, "I have this for you too," and handed him his court order. I turned and headed out the way I had entered. The enraged owner caught up to me, as I approached the exit to the rear lot. He bellowed, "You're trespassing!" I replied, "No, sir," and pointing to the employee who had escorted me to the lobby, I said, "He let me in."

He then threatened to call the police. "I am the police," I countered, showing him my badge. He probably had some police contacts well above my rank, because he said, "I'm calling them anyway." I asked him if he would like me to wait for their arrival, and his resistance crumbled. He headed back to his office, and I left, after calling my lieutenant. He was pleased and highly amused at the subject's threat to call the police.

AN ENCOUNTER WITH A FREIGHT TRAIN

One night upon returning home, the unmarked Mustang provided me by the sheriff's office was struck by a freight train. Adding to the seriousness of this event, it occurred during a special campaign to decrease the number of accidents between vehicles and trains. Talk about bad timing. At Clay St. and Kenner Ave. in Kenner, LA, there is an ungated train crossing. There are two sets of tracks running east/west, parallel to Kenner Ave. I was heading east on Kenner Ave., intending to turn south (right) and cross the tracks at Clay St. I stopped at Clay and waited for the train heading west on the far tracks to clear Clay St.

As it did, I turned and started to cross the first set of tracks. At that point, I then saw an east-bound train bearing down on my car, whose hood was on the tracks by then. I hadn't seen it until my final check, because its headlight blended in perfectly with a very long stretch of streetlights along Kenner Ave. I put my Mustang in reverse to back up, but the transmission slipped and didn't grip soon enough to get quite all of the hood off the track, before the locomotive crashed into my car near the right front wheel.

From what I had learned in physics about collisions, I quickly estimated how my car would move if it was knocked clear of the tracks. I could brace myself for that, but there was nothing to save me if the train dragged my car a mile down the track. If knocked clear of the track, my car should go into a counterclockwise spin, while moving off the road at about a 45-degree angle. The centrifugal force generated would tend to send me crashing toward the right front door.

I lay over toward the passenger seat to get below window level, while gripping the steering wheel at the 6 o'clock position with my left hand, and pushing against the right front door with my right. I was able to hold onto that position, while my car moved about 40 feet to the northeast, rotated 270 degrees, and stopped on a grassy area beside Kenner Ave. I was now facing west.

The strain on my pectoral muscles resulted in a deep bruise on my chest, but I was otherwise OK. I managed to get my radio loose from its mangled bracket and called in the accident. When I exited my car, I was greeted by a small group of black men, who had been standing on the corner, and had observed the whole incident. I assured them that I was OK, and one of them said unbelievingly, "You're not shaking!" I confirmed his observation by holding out a perfectly motionless right hand.

It took the train's engineer a while to get to the scene, since it took him about a mile to get his train stopped. The police arrived before he did. One of the police arrivals was the colonel who ran my department. He was an unhappy camper. It would bring embarrassment to him as the whole force was in the midst of a train safety campaign. I had already called my wife to assure her that I was fine. I assumed the incident might make the evening news and didn't want her to worry. I'm sure now that my colonel pulled the strings necessary to keep the story under wraps … no TV, radio, or newspaper reports.

AFTERMATH OF TRAIN CRASH

I rode with the wrecker driver to our motor pool on Airline Highway. There, I checked out another vehicle and drove to Ochsner Hospital to be checked out, in accordance with our standard operating procedures. After being cleared to return to work, I drove home to a late supper.

The next morning, I was out serving court orders in my "new" car. After the "buzz" over my wreck subsided, my colonel dropped the hammer. I was suddenly called to report immediately to the colonel's office on the West Bank (Gretna). For a month, I lost all personal use of my department car and had to leave it at the 4th District Station, when not working, which meant that I would be walking a couple of miles between my house and the 4th District every working day, along the same railroad tracks involved in my accident. I was also compelled to complete a safety course for driving offenders.

The teacher of the course was amazed, and I had to tell the story to the entire class. I didn't tell anyone about my guardian angel, who probably called in some of his kindred spirits to assist him on my rescue. A strange thing happened to my totaled Mustang. Before the accident, the passenger door didn't work properly. After the accident, that door was the only thing that worked properly.

HEART FAILURE

Shortly before I left the sheriff's office, I began to feel congested to the point that Patty sent me to see our doctor. It so happened that he wasn't in that day, so I was checked out by a lady doctor who was substituting for him. She did all the usual stuff, including taking an x-ray of my chest. Then, she sent me off with a diagnosis of a post-nasal drip.

That evening, I felt so poorly that I was about to retire early, when I told Patty I thought I was dying. She instinctively called a girlfriend to give us a ride to Oschner's emergency room. With me in the back seat and the girls in the front, we ran all the lights and reached Oschner in record time. It was a good thing, too, because I was dying of congestive heart failure.

One of the emergency-room doctors showed Patty the x-ray taken earlier that day by the substitute. My heart was enlarged to twice its normal size. Patty called the lady doctor and dressed her down but good. She even asked the doctor, "Where did you get your degree? Schwegmann's?"

From the emergency room, I was moved to intensive care for a couple of days, before spending the rest of the week in a private room. Atrial fib was the culprit overworking my heart. My cardiologist tried a series of medicines to no avail. He then applied an electric shock to jolt my heart back into its normal rhythm, advising that the return to normal might not last more than two days. He was right.

He then performed a radio-frequency ablation, which cauterized a connection in my heart that was causing my irregular beat. He advised that though my normal beat was restored, my heart might remain enlarged.

When I asked if I could exercise, I was informed that I could do all the working out that I could stand. Not one to do things halfway, I put myself through the Navy Seal 12-week physical conditioning program. After that, I continued the maintenance program for a year. My cardiologist was pleasantly shocked to see that my heart had been restored to near normal size. Eventually, when an ablation could no longer be done, a Talent pacemaker was implanted in my chest. I often joked that I had a hidden talent. What I really had was a great guardian angel.

A NEW CAREER IN THE MOVING & STORAGE BUSINESS

About the time I quit the sheriff's office, my son John was invited to join the FBI and had to move to the FBI Academy in Quantico, VA. The move was paid for by the Bureau. Because most of John's possessions (but not John) were still in my house at 401 Little Farms, it fell to me to meet with the representative of the moving company that surveyed the move. I took notice as the representative recorded every item to be moved and/or packed. I thought to myself that was a pleasant enough job. You get to visit with new people and a new location on every assignment.

As fate would have it, an ad appeared in the *Times-Picayune* shortly afterwards for just such a job. I interviewed for the job, which was offered by Security Van Lines. Their offices and warehouses were located just west of the Louis Armstrong International Airport, about five miles from my house. I was offered the position and gladly resigned my job as a deputy sheriff to accept it.

I came to learn that Security Van Lines was owned by Mark and Jim Johnson of Denver, CO, two brothers who grew up in the business, part of a lineage of father and grandfather Johnsons. Grandfather had started the business in Denver, just before 1900. The home office was in Denver, but the Johnsons owned some dozen moving and storage businesses in seven states. Each business did intrastate and local moves, but they were agents for United Van Lines on interstate moves. The Johnsons were heavily involved in the creation of United.

TRAINING TO BOOK MOVES

Jim himself took me out and had me observe how the requirements of a move were recorded and how the move was priced. He gave me some forms that described what was to be packed and moved along with the origin and destination, and had me calculate the cost of the moves. He had me go with two other salesmen on moves they were attempting to sell. He was very impressed with my attention to detail and accuracy.

That was it. I was considered trained, and I was given the contact information of potential customers who had requested estimates. My pay would be based on the commissions on my bookings. I reported to work early in the morning and studied the *"Tariff,"* a thick book of federal regulations governing every aspect of interstate moves. I did likewise with the regulations governing intrastate moves and the company regulations on local moves.

When I was given leads that were phoned into the office, I began to book moves at a record pace. One morning about 7 a.m., Mark Johnson walked through the room, where our salesmen had their desks. All the desks were unoccupied except mine. He told me he had never seen a salesman at work so early. I introduced myself, and Mark and I hit it off immediately. I offered to pick him up after work and take him out to eat. I took him to the five-star Windsor Court restaurant. Thankfully, Mark insisted on picking up the tab.

After a couple of months at my new job, I began to be unhappy when things went wrong. The process of moving is very complicated and involves many different people doing their job well to effect a perfect move. This perfection rarely occurs. My moves were going way more smoothly than the average, but I didn't know that.

I was unhappy when one of my customers was unhappy. This situation wore on me (the perfectionist), and I told the Johnsons I was quitting my job. I was told that none of their salesmen had booked as much business as I had in my first months in the last hundred years. They asked to have a face-to-face meeting with me in New Orleans to see what they could do to keep me. I agreed. I've always had a difficult time saying no, especially to friends.

A MEETING AT COMMANDER'S PALACE RESTAURANT

Jim and Mark Johnson flew into New Orleans, where they had arranged to dine with me at Commander's Palace, considered one of the finer restaurants in a city renowned for its cuisine. I had never been to Commanders before, but I could see immediately that its clientele was well-heeled. The prices on their bill of fare confirmed that this was not the Garlic House.

After listening to my misgivings with the moving business, Jim asked me, "If you can't be part of the problem, how about being part of the solution?" Jim then offered me a new salaried position that would have the title, "Director of Recruitment and Training." Fair enough. I accepted.

I would be responsible for recruiting and training the employees of 12 moving and storage companies in seven states, a daunting task for a neophyte in the moving industry. The good news ... my earnings would be predictable year round and better than I had ever made before.

A MAN WITH A PLAN

My first move was to travel to Denver to check out the home-office operation. Evenings, I was wined and dined by Jim, Mark, and one of their vice presidents. I was a guest in Jim's beautiful home and had the use of a company vehicle. On one Denver trip, I stayed at Mark's house and enjoyed his beautiful indoor swimming pool, as well as the company of his St. Bernard, Leo. His was the first house I had ever been in that had a wine cellar (a well-stocked one I might add).

On my first trip, I was able to meet with our general managers in Colorado Springs, Fort Collins, and Cheyenne. It gave me a good idea how they recruited and trained their employees. The most difficult employees to recruit were household-goods drivers. They had so much more to do than just drive some freight from point A to point B. One incentive for them was that they had the potential to make more money, albeit with the assumption of more responsibility and having to deal with stressed-out housewives.

Moving is one of the most stressful things in life, right up there with divorce and death. Add to that, when consultants who have underestimated the weight of the shipment or delays due to accidents and bad weather are considered, a driver has a lot on his plate. Moreover, the book (*tariff*) of federal regulations governing the interstate movement of household goods could choke a horse. Loading, driving, and unloading household goods have challenges and rewards far greater than transporting a trailer of TVs. In reality, some of the general managers for Security Van Lines were better than others, simply because there was no common system they used to recruit or train. It was just a case of the cream coming to the top.

CHANGES WERE A-COMING

I introduced training programs and testing to certify our drivers and made them available to our general managers. I also found and directed them to an ever-growing pool of heavy vehicle drivers. New lists of them were available every day from the military. These were men leaving military service. They needed jobs, and many of them were trained to drive tractor trailers. A manager just had to go on the Internet to get the personal and contact information of potential recruits. I also made improvements to the ads that we were running in local newspapers.

One of the changes I introduced was based on my experience booking moves. I had pretty much been left to my own devices to learn how to book moves. One of the first changes I promoted was to call our booking agents *consultants*, not salesmen. When I went out on a call, I first discussed and addressed the concerns the customer had. I avoided coming across as having something to sell them, but rather as someone advising them, viz., a consultant. I only made my survey of their belongings to be shipped, after listening to and addressing their concerns.

I was very detailed in my survey, and this practice instilled confidence in the customer that I had their best interest at heart. To illustrate my attention to detail, I recall that I once was only 16 pounds off on a shipment of 14,000 pounds. This approach took more time than my competitors were spending with the clients, who often called several moving companies for estimates.

But, the only thing I was selling was my integrity and my competence. I booked many moves where my estimate was the highest offered, which ticked off my competitors. They didn't realize that by being honest with the customer and advising them according to their concerns, I was selling myself, not the move.

Once, I was sent to a large loft apartment on Decatur St., across from the Jax Brewery in New Orleans. The client was a diminutive, elderly lady who had spent her life painting and collecting artwork. I was soon aware that though her body was frail and her hair was grey, she was as sharp as a tack.

She had been wintering in her French Quarter loft for years, while living the rest of the year in her home in Naples, Florida. Now, she had decided it was time to move to Naples and abandon her loft. I might as well have been tasked with planning to move a museum. The loft was packed with paintings, sculptures, carvings, tapestries, and specialty artworks that my client had done and collected from Europe to the Far East.

Undaunted, I carefully measured every item and wrote a careful description of each, as my client led me through every room. When I was finished, I said to her, "Ma'am, I have never moved such fine art before, but my company has specialists skilled in doing so. If you would like, I will arrange for one to come over and plan your move." She looked me in the eye, with her clear blue eyes, and replied, "No, I want you." The move went so well that she tipped our driver $200.

Another point of emphasis I made was the importance of being on time for your appointment with clients. It is a matter of courtesy. It is not acceptable to be even five minutes late, and you should inform your customer of any unavoidable delay you might experience. Many salesman types would waltz up to a customer's house 10, 15, 30 or even 40 minutes late, with not so much as a heads-up phone call. Another thing I emphasized was getting all of your paperwork completed and ready for the client's signature within 24 hours.

Based on my own very successful experience consulting with clients and booking moves, I created a training manual. The pages were perforated for a three-ring binder, so that they could be easily changed and replaced as the tariffs or company policy changed. My thinking was to create consistency in the training of our consultants in their approach to our potential customers by teaching them a common and proven method. Prior to my introduction of a training manual, new consultants were all trained differently. It depended on their general manager. In other words, it was very much a "hit-or-miss" approach … and, too often, a "sink-or-swim" one.

With offices spread over seven states, I did quite a bit of traveling. Once, after spending three weeks in Denver, I was so ready to come home that I accepted a flight that flew to Las Vegas before heading to New Orleans. At the Las Vegas airport, I noticed that the concourses and waiting areas were lined with "one-armed bandits." I put a coin in one and pulled the lever. I didn't win and walked away, but now I could say that I had gambled in Vegas.

Another time, I spent three weeks in Chicago, training a new consultant. Once, I flew to Dallas to train and then rode in a tractor trailer to Denver. The traveling got old. Because I didn't like being away from my family and friends, after a few years, I resigned my position with Johnson Storage & Moving.

I'm confident I left the company better than I found it. I have remained friends with Mark and Jim. We are in regular contact by phone and e-mail. They have given me a standing invitation to be their guest with my family at their ranch in Colorado and their beach house near San Diego.

While making a moving survey for an oil business magnate, I had occasion to meet Norris Songe, a real-estate magnate who owned Prudential of Louisiana. Norris was a houseguest of the oilman at the time. I didn't see much of him subsequently, because he moved to Houston. He also traveled the world, playing high stakes bridge with Omar Sharif. Another circle I didn't move in … at all.

I continued to have breakfast with Norris nearly every Saturday morning for years. We are still fast friends. I was his houseguest several years later, after moving to Bristol, VA. I had come to New Orleans for my brother-in-law's funeral. Norris and his wife Kathleen drove up to Bristol to spend a few vacation days with Patty and me in 2007. On October 25, 2014, Norris flew to Bristol for Patty's funeral. This enduring and close friendship all began with me introducing Norris to the Johnson brothers to form a referring pact between Prudential and Johnson Storage & Moving.

Once, after I was no longer in the employ of the Johnsons, I saw an opportunity for them to turn a monthly expense into a stream of revenue. They were paying to have the grass cut on a large vacant lot fronting their property in Kenner. I called Jim and told him that he could fence it in and rent parking space to owners of house and boat trailers. It would be easy to keep it full as the city of Kenner had just passed an ordinance forbidding parking such trailers in residential driveways. Jim called his general manager in Kenner, and the monthly rental fees began to flow in.

FROM AVIS RENTAL CARS TO BROTHER MARTIN

After retiring from the moving and storage business, I entered a completely different line of work. I began driving an airport shuttle bus for Avis. There were about 10 of us, working three shifts around the clock, 8 a.m. to 4 p.m., 4 p.m. to midnight, and midnight to 8 a.m. Although it was a step down in pay, as well as in stress, there was opportunity to move up the corporate ladder if I chose.

When I went home, I left everything connected with the job behind. Avis had its rental office, vehicles, garage, and fuel station right in the Louis Armstrong International Airport complex, as did Budget, Enterprise, Hertz, and National. I had made friends with all their managers in the course of serving them court orders as a deputy sheriff.

To illustrate the point, once when I needed a comfortable vehicle to accommodate our afflicted backs on a 2,000-mile roundtrip to the FBI Academy, one of these managers made my wife and I a great deal. He provided us with a new Lincoln Town Car for a week for $200. The charge per mile was waived, and we only paid for the gas used. Now, that's a friend! Patty fell in love with the Town Car and yearned to have one. A few years later, I swung a deal and surprised her with one of her own.

After I had driven the Avis shuttle bus for a couple of months, management asked me to work the desk, booking rentals. This undertaking was a much more complicated job, requiring people skills, as well as computer skills. On the other hand, it did pay better and held the promise of promotion. Avis had devised its own training software, so that trainees could complete each module at their own pace.

I was well into the program, when one morning, I was awakened at home by a phone call. It was Sister Lawrence, chair of the math department at Brother Martin. Completely by chance, she had met my sister Ann in the waiting room of her dentist. Sister Lawrence expressed her desperation at having one of her math teachers quit just before school was about to begin. Ann told her she had a brother who was a math teacher and gave her my number. Sister Lawrence begged me to come to her rescue. I still had difficulty saying "no" to someone in need, so I left my budding career with Avis and agreed to teach algebra and geometry to some freshmen and sophomore classes.

A SECOND STINT AT BROTHER MARTIN

I had been out of teaching for a generation, and the kids and parents had changed drastically … for the worst, in my opinion. The administration would not allow me to have "Saturday night" school for failing students. I did everything I could think of to hold the attention of my classes.

For example, I got an innovative idea from a presentation a visiting Sacred Heart Brother made at a faculty meeting. He had a special projector, which he used to project a PowerPoint presentation onto a large screen, in a room with normal lighting. The projector was connected to a laptop computer on which his presentation was saved. The projector would show on a large screen exactly what was on the laptop screen.

The school had no such projector for our use. I had to have one. I purchased a laptop and a projector and began using it in both my algebra and geometry classes. Soon, I was getting requests from administrators and faculty to borrow my projector. Since I was using it five periods a day, it was impractical to lend it out, so pressure built on the school to buy one to add to our supply of audiovisual equipment that could be checked out through our librarian.

This wish came to pass. It also came to pass that one of my students stole my laptop. When I reported the theft to the principal and asked him to call the police, he decided the school would buy me another laptop instead. The school wrote me a check, and I replaced the stolen laptop. There was never a police report.

MY BACK AND PATTY'S HEART ATTACK

During my first year back at Brother Martin, I began having trouble with my lower back. The pain became so great after a night in bed that I could not put my pants on. I got around that by sleeping in my pants. During the day, I would walk the halls at school at every opportunity, since doing so gave me some relief. Finally, with about two months of school left, my neurosurgeon performed a laminectomy near L5 to relieve pressure on my sciatic nerve. It took about two months for the pain to subside enough for me to resume my normal activities. Brother Martin hired a substitute to replace me, but continued to pay my salary and hold my job for the following year. I was very grateful for their generosity and agreed to return in the fall.

In the spring semester of my second year at Brother Martin, my wife had a severe heart attack and nearly died. Brother Martin came through for me again and allowed me time off, which enabled me to stay with my wife around the clock. I slept in whatever room she was placed, and we were only separated when she went to surgery. If I had gone to work, I would not have been any good to my students. I was a mess.

The nurses and staff who worked on the pediatric floor with Patty were a great support. They all loved and respected her. I used the joyful occasion of her discharge to surprise Patty with a Town Car. It was a certified pre-owned vehicle still in warranty. Patty was waiting with her doctor, who had wheeled her down to the parking garage. I had let the doctor in on the surprise, and when Patty didn't see me in the line of cars picking up patients, she asked Patty, "Isn't that your husband in the green car?" "No," Patty replied, "I have a little white car." When I stepped out and opened the passenger door for Patty, she asked me, "Whose car is this?" "It's yours," I replied. It was one of the biggest surprises I ever pulled on Patty.

When Patty returned to work in a couple of months, her head nurse gave her all day shifts and the lightest assignments. This schedule enabled Patty to work long enough to get her full retirement from both Ochsner and Social Security. At that time, all of her friends at Oschner threw a big retirement party for her in the atrium at Oschner.

A few weeks later, I rented the same hall we had our wedding reception in, and we had another party, much like the one we had on our wedding day, complete with great food and drink from Messina's restaurant, a giant cake, and a dance floor, as well as a disc jockey and photographer. About 100 relatives and friends joined in the festivities. Many of these individuals had been with us at our wedding and reception some 35 years earlier. Again, I got a great deal from the owners of Messina's, having made friends with them when I was serving them court orders.

BUSINESS NETWORK INTERNATIONAL (BNI)

After my second stint at Brother Martin, I returned briefly to the employ of the Johnsons. They had secured the right to act as agents for Mayflower, to go along with their long held rights as agents for United. This arrangement basically doubled their chances of booking moves, without purchasing new land, warehouses, and equipment.

Now, in addition to Security Van Lines (a United agent), they opened Audubon Moving (a Mayflower agent). Both moving companies were at the same location, having separate offices for only the two general managers. I was tasked with helping the manager of Audubon get things going.

The manager's father had a long association with Security Van Lines. He asked me and his crew of consultants to each join a different local chapter of Business Network International (BNI). Each chapter's members would meet once a week for breakfast or lunch and provide leads to one another. Naturally, no two members could be selling the same product or service.

My time with BNI was a wonderful experience. The chapter I began with consisted of about a dozen members. We met in a small conference room at the offices of one of our members, who was a financial adviser. We ate take-out. Soon, I had secured the hall at Messina's Restaurant, the scene of my wedding reception. We needed the room, because I had sponsored about two dozen new members on my own.

My chapter was still flourishing there when I had to resign (I was then president) upon leaving the moving business. I had done about as much as I could to get Audubon well under way. Subsequently, I was asked by another good friend to help him with his business.

RAYMOND'S JEWELRY CREATIONS

Greg Raymond, whom I had recruited into our BNI chapter, asked me to work at his store. He was one employee short, and he had to thoroughly vet any applicants before trusting them to work among millions in gold, silver, and precious jewels. Always one who found it difficult to say "no" to a friend, I agreed to fill in, until he could find a suitable and trustworthy person to sell his products in his showroom.

I knew Greg from his attendance at Rummel. Greg had gone on to play football at LSU and was on one of their Orange Bowl teams. He had worked in his dad's jewelry store after school and summers for years. Subsequently, he had become a licensed gemologist and had inherited his dad's business when he retired.

It was Greg who had fashioned the gold mariner's cross and chain that I bought myself, when I retired from teaching in 1986. I'm still wearing it. Since Greg was already representing the jewelry business at my old BNI chapter, he asked me to join another chapter that had no one from the jewelry business. I did, which enabled me to continue to enjoy the benefits of that organization.

I was tempted by all the beautiful jewelry surrounding me every day ... not to steal any of it, but to buy it for Patty. Greg would sell it to me at a great discount. I just loved to surprise Patty with unexpected gifts, and Raymond's was a rich source. I would do this not only on the expected days like her birthday, our anniversary, or Valentine's, but on random days throughout the year. She amassed quite a collection, because I continued to enjoy my discount after Greg found his replacement, and I moved on. After Patty contracted cancer in December, 2010, she passed her collection on to our daughter-in-law, Janine. She wanted to do this personally, while she was still alive. It was an emotional moment for both women.

One of the pieces I had Greg make for Patty was a solid gold pin in letters that read, "Oschner's Finest." Oschner Hospital picked an outstanding employee every quarter and designated them by that title. They were given a choice parking space for their three-month reign and had a plaque placed among past recipients in a hallway to the cafeteria. They were also given the cheapest-looking pin I could imagine.

I wanted Greg to fashion Patty a gold pin that was commensurate with the honor she had earned. She loved the surprise, but she had the good sense not to wear it. She didn't want to "show up" Oschner or perhaps other employees who had won the cheap pin.

BOBBY JINDAL

Patty and I had begun to attend monthly wine tastings at the St. Louis Hotel in 2003. For a modest price, a couple could enjoy the best cuisine offered by the hotel's excellent restaurant, while sampling the finest wines. They also had a bar that served cocktails. Patty's favorites were the fruit-flavored martinis.

On one trip to the St. Louis gathering, Bobby Jindal gave a short talk about why he was running for governor and mingled with the attendees. I introduced myself to Bobby, and we talked about our ideas on education. We hit it off. I could tell from our conversation that he respected my views. I was very impressed with Bobby and lent my support to his campaign, with a modest campaign donation and attendance at all of his rallies in and around New Orleans.

When a rally got a piece of the evening news, I could be seen near Bobby on TV. As I had taught thousands of students in Louisiana, it was a subtle way of endorsing Bobby. Well-heeled supporters of Bobby would host parties similar to the gatherings at the St. Louis Hotel at their mansions.

Patty enjoyed going to these parties. Of course, we were unknown to most of the attendees, but always welcomed warmly by Bobby.

Patty often had me slip homemade pecan pralines to Bobby at outdoor rallies, where food wasn't served. At one of these soirees, Bobby posed for pictures with donors who had donated a certain amount. Patty and I hadn't made the required donation, but Bobby pulled us before the photographer. I still have that picture of Bobby and his wife, Supriya, with Patty and me ... somewhere.

One morning, we attended a breakfast rally at a mansion in Metairie, and a gentleman I knew from playing tennis at the Beach Club walked into the foyer. He was an oil business multimillionaire, and people began to crowd him and press him for his attention. He ignored them, but upon spotting me standing off to the side, he bellowed, "John," and walked up to me to shake my hand. We had a friendly conversation and left those who had pressed upon him wondering who the hell I was. I never saw anyone else there that I knew except Bobby and his wife. Of course, my net worth was but a tiny fraction of theirs, so we were not likely to have met unless it was at a tennis club. I was not the Boston Club type.

It was a festive occasion turned sad when the election returns showed that Bobby's opponent, a woman named Katherine Blanco, narrowly defeated him. I was one of those who offered Bobby my condolences, as he stepped from the stage after acknowledging Blanco the victor and thanking his supporters. Perhaps, it was a foreshadowing of sorts, when the crowd chanted "Bobby for president." Blanco received a lot of negative press before, during, and after hurricane Katrina ravaged New Orleans and much of Louisiana. Bobby was elected governor in 2007 and again in 2011. With Bobby, what you see is what you get. He is totally honest. He is also brilliant. Typically, when politicians make promises on the campaign trail, they are short on how they are going to keep them. Bobby published on his website exactly what steps he would take to achieve his promises.

THE AUDUBON INSTITUTE

The last job I held in New Orleans was as an assistant director of the Audubon Park tennis courts, under the aegis of the Audubon Institute, which maintained the zoo, the golf course, the horse stables, and all the sports fields. I had played on the Audubon courts many times, while part of a men's doubles league, which rotated play between Audubon and the City Park and Stern courts.

This position was an ideal job for me, since I loved teaching and playing tennis, and plenty of that could be squeezed in between my duties. My main duties were dressing the courts before and after they opened each day and renting them out to individuals and groups. Ten rubico courts encircled the office from which I served the players.

The office was air-conditioned and had a desk, chair, couch, and refrigerator. The director stocked the refrigerator, and we sold cold drinks for twice what he paid for them. He kept all of the profits. The director was apt to waltz in well after the courts opened, stay a short while, and drive off. He often crashed on the office couch. On certain days, he had a few wealthy clients come in for lessons. He occasionally set up some kids' clinics for me to run. He gave me some of the proceeds and all of the work.

I got to use a ball machine with a large hopper, when things were slow, and I got to meet and play with some outstanding players. One visitor to the courts was Hamilton Richardson, a former Tulane star, who had won the NCAA championship twice and was ranked in the top 10 multiple times. "Ham" advised me, "Hit the ball to a spot as far away from your opponent as possible."

HURRICANE KATRINA

Life changed for thousands of individuals when Katrina visited New Orleans and the Mississippi Gulf Coast near the end of the summer of 2005. Patty and I had been living at 401 Little Farms Ave. in River Ridge, since 1977. Patty loved the house and could not envision ever moving. I had seen many hurricanes pass over or near New Orleans, but had never suffered any significant personal loss.

During Hurricane Georges in September, 1998, I evacuated my Mom, mother-in-law, and sister-in-law to a safe house in Picayune, MS. It was fully furnished and vacant and was owned by Patty's aunt, Mary Alice Thompson, who owned a cattle ranch in nearby McNeil, MS. Georges was a monster storm, and it was predicted to make a direct hit on the Crescent City. My evacuees were terrified. Patty stayed with other Oschner nurses and employees at the hospital.

But for my concerned relatives, I would have ridden out Georges in my solid raised home on the highest ground in the area. As it turned out, Georges missed New Orleans. People still remembered their unnecessary evacuation for Georges seven years later, when they were warned to evacuate in the face of Katrina. Far too many suffered the terrible and well-documented consequences of not evacuating. I am reminded of the story of the boy who cried "Wolf!" when there was no wolf. When a real wolf came, no one came to his aid.

In May of 1995, our area experienced the worst flooding due to heavy rainfall to occur between Hurricanes Betsy (1965) and Katrina (2005). To illustrate my house's elevation, even the houses on my block that were on slabs were not flooded. Further down the street, the houses on slabs had to pull up and throw out their carpets. Friends, who lived a little further away, had water lines two feet up the walls.

I was confident that if my house, which was built on brick pillars on the highest ground in the area, was ever flooded, the whole of the New Orleans metropolitan area would become part of Lake Ponchartrain. Moreover, my house was covered with the old formula stucco, a compound virtually impregnable to windblown debris. I had metal shutters that could be dropped down over my windows in a matter of minutes. Another preparation I had in place was a full-house natural gas generator that kicked in when the regular electricity went out and kicked off with its return. My only weak spot was my shingled roof. As it turned out, all the houses on all sides of mine had to have their roofs replaced after Katrina, and I didn't lose a shingle! I can only conclude that my guardian angel sheltered us under his wings.

We had an old-fashioned antenna on my chimney, which weathered the storm, like my shingles, and so, we were able to get some info from a Baton Rouge station. I left the house early Monday morning in an eerie darkness. All of the streetlights were off, and I had to use a flashlight to pick my way through branches and fallen power lines.

I had the crazy idea that I could catch the 6 a.m. mass at St. Matthews, but the church and parking lot were totally dark. Imagine that! I walked the half mile back home and waited for Patty to get up. My son in Fredericksburg, VA kept calling us and urging us to come stay with him.

Patty was determined to stay where she was, until a policeman stopped by and informed us that the hospitals were in lockdown, and no pharmacies were open. By Thursday, the authorities had cleared the state road that passed in front of our house and which led to the all-clear major highway to Baton Rouge.

Since we had to have our medicines, we loaded up our Lincoln Town Car and began the long drive to Virginia. We were the only car on the road for most of the way to Baton Rouge. Those who evacuated were long gone. They had poked along that same road, bumper-to-bumper, just a few days ago. We were going a round-about way by heading west, then north, and finally east, but there was absolutely no way to drive or even walk (swim maybe) east through and out of the city. The water was up to the rooftops, and the bridges were destroyed.

152 HAMLIN ST., FREDERICKSBURG, VA

My son and his wife, Janine, and their first daughter, Madeline Michelle (Maddie), were living in a spacious house at 152 Hamlin, when they took us (Patty, Tootsie, and me) in. It had a private bedroom and bath in their basement available for us. Maddie was 33 months old.

On October 13th, Janine gave us our second granddaughter, Lauren Elizabeth. I developed a special bond with Lauren, as I changed her in the morning and fed her her formula. This undertaking by me allowed Mom to get a few extra winks.

That isn't all I did. John's property sat on a half-acre of land, with about a four-acre pond behind his fenced-in backyard. I fixed his gate. I discovered (unknown until then) how Dini his white lab was escaping and blocked his exit. I cut the grass. I painted the living room and installed crown molding. I repaired his dryer and garage door. I got him new tires for his Chevy Tahoe. The boy didn't want me to ever leave.

Of course, we couldn't return home until medical services were restored. It wasn't all work. I fished in the pond, too, and fed the geese with Maddie. Patty, and I visited the historic district of Fredericksburg, just five minutes away. We also visited the Washington, D.C. sights. Amtrac ran a direct line into D.C.

It was during this sojourn in Fredericksburg that Patty decided she never wanted to be involved again with running from a hurricane. Patty began to have me drive her around to look at houses. She had no intention of living in Fredericksburg. She hated the traffic, and the acceptable houses were beyond our means. She just liked to look at houses. Back in our basement apartment, she hit the Internet and researched Virginia towns that were on the road back to New Orleans. She wanted one that was an easy day's drive from Fredericksburg, so that we could visit John, Janine, and the girls on holidays and special occasions, without being available to babysit at the drop of a hat. She sought a small town with light traffic. The town had to have three things: a Catholic church with weekday and Sunday masses; a great medical facility; and a Super Walmart. She found all three in Bristol, VA, the town of her dreams.

HOUSE HUNTING ON OUR RETURN TO NEW ORLEANS

We had been in Fredericksburg for three months, when in early December, we began our drive home. Services had been restored, and we had a lot to do. We had to find a house to buy in Bristol, as well as sell our house in River Ridge. Patty had arranged with a real estate agent to spend a day in Bristol, looking for a suitable house.

We planned to make the 330-mile drive to Bristol the first day and check into a motel. Our appointment with the agent was for the following day. We arrived with plenty of daylight left and decided to check out a couple of houses advertised in a local rag.

One address was on Fairmount Ave, a segmented street paralleling Euclid Ave, a main drag. By pure chance, we saw a "for sale by owner" sign with a pocket of flyers in front of 814 Fairmount. It was a solid two-story brick home with a detached double-garage. It was perfect in my view. It was only a half mile from St. Anne's Catholic Church, five miles from a great medical center, and five miles from a Super Walmart. And, it was affordable. I was ready to deal with the owner right then, but Patty had some reservations, and we spent the whole next day being shown houses by the agent

Patty had contacted. Following our "parade of homes," I made a handshake deal to buy 814 Fairmount, and we continued our return drive home.

A LEAP OF FAITH

Kermit "Ace" Atkins was a retired State Farm top executive. He had taken to "flipping" houses. When he heard our Katrina story and why we were moving to Bristol, his empathy was evident. A mutual trust was born, and we made a verbal deal, putting any paperwork off until later. When Ace said he would hold the house for us, until we could sell ours, Patty asked, "For how long?" "As long as it takes," replied Ace. Neither of us had a legal leg to stand on to enforce our agreement, but we both kept our word. I suppose we both were good judges of character, but I would not advise anyone to do business without a written contract. You had better have a great guardian angel, if you do. I did.

A couple of months after returning home, I sent Ace a written *agreement to purchase*, along with a down payment of $5,000. He hadn't asked for the money, but every month that passed with his property vacant was costing him money. I felt it only fair to cover that loss, while I negotiated the sale of my house. Ace allowed us to move into 814 Fairmount on May 1, 2006, while the sale of our house was still a work in progress. My friend, the real estate magnate Norris Songe, oversaw the transaction and represented Patty and me at the act of sale. He mailed the settlement check to me, and on July 14th, we paid Ace the full purchase price and registered the deed at the courthouse … sans mortgage. My old friends at Johnson Storage & Moving had facilitated our move. We had been living in our new house for two and a half months.

10

BRISTOL, VA: 2006–2014

THE HAPPIEST DAYS OF HER LIFE

Life was good for us in Bristol. Patty loved her house and our neighbors. She especially loved St. Anne's Catholic Church, which was established in 1836. In the beginning, we walked there for daily mass in the attached chapel ... whatever the weather. When our hearts weakened, our cardiologist would not allow these walks if the temperature dropped below 40. Later, we both weakened to the point that we only drove to church. Toward the end, when Patty was ravaged by cancer (2010 to 2014), I put her wheelchair in our car trunk and rolled her into the chapel.

These masses were attended by a core group of about 20 regulars, with whom we became fast friends ... worshipping together for over eight years can have that effect. In addition, many of the group would breakfast together after mass at Hardy's or McDonald's. I also made it a point to introduce Patty and myself to folks we saw only at Sunday mass or other Holy Days of Obligation.

I rejoined the Knights of Columbus, and Patty joined the Catholic Daughters of America, both moves further expanding our circle of friends. I became a member of the Bristol Racquet Club. I became a substitute teacher in the Bristol city school system and covered for absent teachers in the elementary, middle, and high school. I also filled in for a missing physics teacher at Virginia Intermont College for a short time. In addition, I served as the assistant tennis coach for the men and women teams at King University. I still communicate regularly with some of my former players and their parents.

In spite of having to suffer the ravages of multiple myeloma and its treatment for the last four years, Patty told me that her eight plus years in Bristol were the happiest days of her life. As would be expected, the aforementioned associations gave rise to us establishing many friendships in our small community.

For our first four years in Bristol, Patty and I engaged in what, for us, were great recreational activities, which cost little or nothing. As time went on, we did so less and less often as our health deteriorated … with one exception. Patty loved to go to the Golden Corral's buffet. That we did after nearly every Sunday morning mass for eight years … through sickness and in health.

We also enjoyed the scenery of southwest Virginia. Bristol is at an elevation of about 1,700 ft. and is surrounded by the Appalachian and Blue Ridge Mountains. This sightseeing we could and did enjoy, while simply traveling anywhere within a five-mile radius of our home. The sunrises and sunsets delighted us, as did the changing colors of the flora displayed in four distinct seasons.

In our earliest years in Bristol, we took some long rides to the Breaks Interstate Park and had lunch at its restaurant overlooking the "Grand Canyon of the South." Patty particularly enjoyed the Bristol Caverns. She first fell in love with these fascinating underground structures when we took a motor vacation in Tennessee, the summer after our wedding.

In Chattanooga, we had visited Ruby Falls, deep below Lookout Mountain. Patty was simply enthralled. We've always thought that our son was conceived on that trip. We also enjoyed riding our bikes in the nearby Steele Creek Park. We made one overnight trip to Prestonsburg, our old stomping grounds, to take in a marvelous Christmas show at the Mountain Arts Theater. The experience delighted Patty to no end, and she talked about it for years.

Other than the aforementioned, the only nights we spent away from home were those we spent in Fredericksburg, with my son and his family, when we celebrated special holidays or events in the lives of our granddaughters. Of course, the drive back and forth was through some of the most beautiful scenery anywhere. Some folks think you have to spend a lot of money to have a good time. You don't, if you'll just open your eyes and take in the beauty of God's creation that surrounds us … and give gratitude and love to the artist.

PATTY AND COMPUTING

Shortly after moving to Bristol, Patty ordered an Alien computer. She had it custom-built to her specifications. It was so hot, it had to be cooled by a circulating liquid refrigerant. She wore that one out and replaced it with a new one that wasn't custom-built but had all the latest features she required.

Patty did everything one could with a computer, but she especially loved to play games and produce top-level graphics. One fruit of this hobby was the personalized, original Christmas cards she prepared each year. They always featured our current photos, as well as those of our granddaughters. Our friends and relatives watched us age and our granddaughters come to life and grow up through these cards. Patty even designed the envelopes. She never used the same design twice. Patty's sister, Sharon, has kept them all.

MY ACTIVISM IS AWAKENED

It was in Bristol that I became aware of the Fair Tax plan. I loved it. It was all about freedom. It brought us back to our original constitution, which forbade the federal government from taxing our income. That prohibition, along with our freedom, was ended by the 16th Amendment, which was a far bigger mistake than the prohibition amendment.

If passed, the Fair Tax Act would repeal the 16th Amendment, like the mistake of prohibition was repealed. No more IRS. Our nation would be even better supported by a national sales tax, and the poor would be exempt. The economy would boom, and April 15th would just become another spring day.

I wrote letters to the editor and articles for FairTax.org. I was a guest speaker at numerous civic clubs in Bristol, Bluff City, Johnson City, and Abingdon. I was invited to speak at tax-day rallies in Boston, MA, Woodbridge, VA, and my own Bristol, VA. I accepted the Woodbridge and Bristol invitations.

A local billionaire came to the latter and introduced himself to me after my speech. Through his company, he is responsible for a lot of philanthropic work throughout the world, but shuns publicity. He and his wife became friends with Patty and me, and we both have often been guests in each other's homes. He loved to come over and talk gardening with me. He greatly admired the garden in my front yard and always referred to it as my "English garden." We continued to trade e-mails and phone calls several times a week, after I moved to Fredericksburg.

At a convention in Arlington, VA, I helped man a table promoting the Fair Tax. There, I met a gentleman and scholar named Ralph Benko. He was a partner in a consulting firm in downtown D.C. Our conversation resulted in my starting up a website. Ralph made his living in large part doing just that, but he never charged me a penny, as he guided me through the process. Ralph remains a great friend.

I remember how Ralph was so excited, when Leo Linbeck, one of the Texas billionaires who started the Fair Tax movement, joined Zap. I traded some friendly e-mails and calls with Mr. Linbeck, but never met him. The site was named "Zap the IRS." I did two 30-minute local TV shows on the Fair Tax and one appearance on our Bristol noon TV show.

I made a first annual "Profiles in Courage" award to Congressman Steve King of Iowa in his House office. We published a picture of the presentation and an interview with King on our website. We also visited with Congressman Steve Scalese, a Rummel grad. In addition, we presented Zap t-shirts to Governor Hucklebee and his wife on his campaign stop in Bristol and put photos of it on the Zap website.

QUITTING THE ACTIVIST LIFESTYLE

Soon, I ran out of money and energy, and Patty wisely put her foot down. My health was failing. She had been my rock all along and supported me in all my activities, but her good judgment demanded that we shut down Zap and turn over our members to another organization that Zap had inspired. She immediately did so, and thus our excursion into activism ended.

Without the stress associated with that activism, our hearts figured to last a little longer. We could use our "good health days" to enjoy our final years together. We both had our heart problems under control, with the help of our cardiologist. We both had pacemakers, and Patty had some stents, but we still kept up our favorite hobbies and made trips to Fredericksburg.

I had to give up tennis after rotator-cuff surgery, but I continued to work my gardens, in both my front and back yards. My flowers and plants were a great joy to me and Patty, as well as our neighbors and passersby, and I could care for them at Mother Nature's own pace, which is never rushed except for grass growth. The dad of one of my lady tennis students attended to the grass cutting. Patty enjoyed reading and her computer. Little did we know, that cancer would rear its ugly head on December 8th, 2010.

THE YELLOW ROSE BUSH AND THE COMING OF JESUS

The first neighbor on Fairmount St. that we met was Anna Rush, who lived directly across from 814 Fairmount. Patty introduced herself to Anna in early December of 2005, while we were checking out prospective houses on our trip back to New Orleans, following our sojourn in Fredericksburg necessitated by Katrina. Anna was a wonderful neighbor and kept an award-winning garden. She greatly admired a huge old rose bush that grew next door to me. Though unattended and completely neglected by its owner, it produced the largest and most beautiful yellow roses. When I proposed to Anna that we take a cutting from it and reproduce the bush, she advised that a rose-growing expert, who supplied roses to his church, had attempted to do just that and could not succeed. That was a challenge to me.

Soon, I had reproduced a half dozen or so bushes of this beautiful rose. Patty did so also. After I gave the first one to Anna, I received many requests for these beautiful rose bushes. Still finding it difficult to say "no," I honored them all.

About 2008, I saw a life-sized concrete statue of the Sacred Heart of Jesus for sale and contracted with the vendor to have it delivered, painted, and installed amidst my plantings on my front yard. On the day of delivery, I saw Anna and said to her, "Anna, Jesus is coming." "Oh, John," she chided, "I know Jesus is coming." "No, Anna, he's coming this afternoon." She gave me that "I know you're joking, John" look, and we said no more. After the statue was installed, I knocked on Anna's door, and when she stepped out, I said, "Jesus is here," and pointed to the statue across the street. The look on her face was priceless, as she smiled and slowly shook her head.

THE DIAGNOSIS

As we both had the same primary physician, he scheduled our regular checkups at the same time. Since May of 2006, it was the norm for both Patty and me to be together in the exam room, when we saw our PCP or cardiologist. That fateful day in December, when Patty revealed to our PCP how she had been feeling, he ordered some blood tests for Patty. Those tests revealed that Patty was in stage four kidney failure, and our PCP set up the earliest appointment possible with a nephrologist. We had to travel 20 miles to Kingsport to see him, but our PCP would broach no delay. The tests run by the nephrologist in Kingsport confirmed what he suspected. Patty had multiple myeloma.

OUR LIFE-AND-DEATH BATTLE

Patty had the cancer, not me, but after 43 years of marriage, her battle was very much to be mine. We were one, in sickness and in health. On one of the first visits to the oncologist assigned by Bristol Regional Medical Center, Patty asked the doctor for a chest x-ray, as she was experiencing distress in her chest.

He listened with his stethoscope to her lungs, but said that because he already had a recent x-ray of her chest, an x-ray wouldn't be necessary. We were allowed to go home. I had to get Patty back to the emergency room in an ambulance later that afternoon, when she collapsed from the effects of pneumonia. The stethoscope exam should have revealed that, and the x-ray requested would have confirmed it.

Patty was admitted to the hospital for a week. I spent the nights in a lounge chair in her room. That first morning, her oncologist stepped into our room and without so much as a "good morning" asked Patty, "How are you?" Patty replied, "I have pneumonia." "That's not what I asked you," he said, coolly and chidingly. Normally, I got up and greeted doctors, but my urge was to knock his lights out. Biting my tongue, I turned toward the window and said not a word.

When he left the room, I told Patty, "I'll be right back." I went immediately to the nearby oncology office building, and we never saw that oncologist again. Patty was assigned to a brilliant and empathetic oncologist, named Dr. Alton Blow. He would be with us in our struggle to the end.

PATTY'S GIFT TO CANCER PATIENTS

About noon on October 12th, 2014, Patty collapsed in my arms at our home at 814 Fairmount Ave. in Bristol, VA. We made our final of many trips made over the last four years to the Bristol Regional Medical Center. It was the last of several we made by ambulance.

Her cancer had stormed out of remission once more, but this time with a vengeance that could not be addressed. I was to spend the next two nights sleeping on a recliner in her hospital room and the following three nights doing the same in her room at the center's hospice. By Wednesday night, she was too weak to utter a word or open her eyes.

In spite of her suffering, Patty had forced herself over her years battling cancer to complete a guide to help other cancer patients. She drew on her experience, as both a nurse and a cancer patient to give incredible advice and well-researched references for anyone who faced cancer. She was a patient-advocate until the end.

I was alone with her at our Bristol Hospice. All of our visitors had gone home around 11 p.m. that night of October 16th, a Thursday. I lay on a couch beside her bed, listening to her labored breathing. At 4 a.m., she called to me in that wordless method of communication that we had perfected over the years. I moved to a chair beside her bed and grasped her left hand with my right. We spoke to one another without words … as we had done for years. I never let go until 8 a.m. when she, wordlessly, said goodbye and joined my guardian angel. It was the first time in 48 years that I was without my special angel. It was October 17th, 2014.

ADDENDUM

In her guide for cancer patients, Patty reveals only a little about her life. Her focus is on how to help patients fight cancer. Of course, in reading *Farewell to an Angel*, the reader sees the many adventures she shared with me through our 47 years and nine months of marriage. Since she is the "better half" of *Farewell to an Angel*, I wish to hereby give the reader a glimpse into Patty's sweet nature and highlight some of her accomplishments in medicine.

—John Hanson

PATTY HANSON, REGISTERED NURSE EXTRAORDINAIRE

A career nurse, who was a leader in developing progressive-care techniques for dialysis patients and who helped to establish the first intensive care units at Touro Infirmary in New Orleans, Patricia "Patty" Hanson believed laughter was a key component of any healthcare routine.

Patty was invited to study cardiology nursing in a special program run by Dr. Michael Debakey, arguably the most accomplished heart surgeon of the 20th century. While studying under Debakey, Patty served as the private nurse of the Duke of Windsor and the King of Greece.

Writing about her own battle with cancer, Hanson said laughter "is the mighty sword that slays the sleeping snake. I think of cancer as a vicious poisonous snake." Cancer was something she fought for four years, using what she called her arsenal of angels: faith, laughter, hope, meditation, courage, and her friends and family.

"I never prayed to be cured. I left that up to God," she wrote. "I asked for courage and strength." She offered up the intense suffering visited upon her by her multiple myeloma for the souls in purgatory. She was an advocate for these souls and had a special prayer composed by St. Gertrude printed on business cards, which she passed out to get others in on her campaign to get souls out of purgatory. Family and friends said Hanson's laughter and faith were just part of her nature. "She was so ... childlike, in everything," said her son, John Hanson III. "She was a very smart woman, but always expressed this childlike excitement about everything. She would just light up, when she was learning and experiencing new things. She also loved watching movies–particularly scary ones–spending time with family and friends, and playing with her grandchildren."

In addition, she was active for a time in Toastmasters, winning a 1st-place award in 1985 for "Humorous Speech" [Toastmasters International, Area 6 (Louisiana)]. Her speaking skills also served her well when she was invited to give the keynote address to 10,000 nephrologists at their convention at the Superdome in New Orleans. Patty received a standing ovation.

Father and son agreed on one particular point–Hanson's favorite place to go was Disney World. Yet, on every trip the family took, she would persistently point with joy at the new sights and wonders they encountered. She always wanted to learn something new, her son said. And she always had a smile for everyone she met. Those traits made his mother a really sharp nurse, John Hanson III said. "And then, on this other side, this kid," full of joy and wonder.

Hanson, who was born Feb. 9, 1939, entered nursing school at the Touro Infirmary School of Nursing in New Orleans, right out of high school. She grew up in the heart of the Crescent City and took the entrance exam for nursing school, because her friend was doing so. When the school offered her a full-ride scholarship for the three-year, post-high school program, she said she couldn't refuse.

"After about a year as a RN, and going to night school, I knew I would never leave nursing," Hanson wrote in her manuscript about battling cancer. "Over the years, I took many classes and earned certifications in many specialties. It just seemed that I never tired of learning how to give the best care to my patients."

While working as a board-certified enterostomal therapist, Patty created a pouch that enabled her patients to better cope with their condition. A representative from Hollister saw the pouch, and his company patented it. This devise has helped patients around the world. She also devised a diet for her ostomy patients. After she published an article on this diet in a medical journal, she received accolades from doctors as far away as Canada, applauding this diet. The good she did for her own patients is still helping other patients, far beyond her own reach and time.

Hanson spent most of her nursing career working for Ochsner Hospital in New Orleans, retiring in 2002. She earned several awards from the hospital, including an "Ochsner's Finest" honor. During that time, she worked on developing procedures and writing manuals on medical devices for home use by dialysis patients. She introduced the first continuous ambulatory peritoneal dialysis program in Louisiana (at Oschner)–only the third such program in the country.